AI Techniques for Multimedia Data Processing

Ahmed A. Abd El-Latif
Prince Sultan University, Saudi Arabia

Mudasir Ahmad Wani
Prince Sultan University, Saudi Arabia

Mohamed Hammad
Prince Sultan University, Saudi Arabia

Akram Belazi
National Engineering Scool of Tunis, Tunisia

Aceng Sambas
Universiti Sultan Zainal Abidin, Malaysia

IGI Global
Scientific Publishing
Publishing Tomorrow's Research Today

Vice President of Editorial Melissa Wagner
Director of Acquisitions Mikaela Felty
Director of Book Development Jocelynn Hessler
Production Manager Mike Brehm
Cover Design Jose Rosado

Published in the United States of America by
IGI Global Scientific Publishing
701 East Chocolate Avenue
Hershey, PA, 17033, USA
Tel: 717-533-8845
Fax: 717-533-8715
Website: https://www.igi-global.com E-mail: cust@igi-global.com

Library of Congress Cataloging-in-Publication Data

Names: Abd El-Latif, Ahmed A., 1984- editor. | Wani, Mudasir Ahman, 1987- editor. | Hammad, Mohamed, 1990- editor. | Belazi, Akram, 1988- editor. | Sambas, Aceng, 1990- editor.
Title: AI techniques for multimedia data processing / edited by Ahmed Abd El-Latif, Mudasir Wani, Mohamed Hammad, Akram Belazi, Aceng Sambas.
Description: Hershey, PA : Engineering Science Reference, an imprint of IGI Global, [2025] | Includes bibliographical references and index. | Summary: "The book is expected to have a significant impact on the research community by providing a comprehensive and up-to-date resource on AI for multimedia data processing"-- Provided by publisher.
Identifiers: LCCN 2024010206 (print) | LCCN 2024010207 (ebook) | ISBN 9798369329351 (h/c) | ISBN 9798369329368 (ebook)
Subjects: LCSH: Multimedia systems--Data processing. | Artificial intelligence--Data processing.
Classification: LCC QA76.575 .A425 2024 (print) | LCC QA76.575 (ebook) | DDC 006.7--dc23/eng/20240524
LC record available at https://lccn.loc.gov/2024010206
LC ebook record available at https://lccn.loc.gov/2024010207

British Cataloguing in Publication Data
A Cataloguing in Publication record for this book is available from the British Library.

Table of Contents

Detailed Table of Contents

Recent AI and multimedia analysis advances have changed our visual content viewing and interaction. This study evaluates new AI multimedia recognition and segmentation technologies. Multimedia object, scene, action, and emotion recognition is crucial in entertainment, healthcare, security, and education. AI-based recognition systems are studying CNN, RNN, and deep learning architectures. Photo, video, and multimedia segmentation algorithms that correctly detect and extract areas of interest are also explored. AI-driven multimodal data fusion improves detection and segmentation by combining photos, videos, text, and audio. This paper evaluates their progress. Multimedia AI analysis concerns dataset bias, scalability, real-time processing, and ethics. AI multimedia recognition and segmentation are thoroughly studied in this article. This field's successes, limitations, and promise are highlighted. These technologies could change how we perceive and interact with massive amounts of visual data, enabling new applications and advances in many fields.

The chapter offers a comprehensive exploration of the dynamic landscape of social media slang and its integration into Natural Language Processing for data analytics. It delineates key objectives, encompassing an overview of the unique linguistic landscape of social media slang, an investigation into the challenges of processing slang, an exploration of lexical innovations and emerging trends, and a deep dive into sentiment analysis specifically tailored for social media slang. Additionally, it explores strategies for integrating slang into traditional language models and examines multilingual considerations in processing slang globally. The chapter showcases practical applications, including brand monitoring and market research, demonstrating how Natural Language Processing-driven insights enhance marketing strategies and brand perception. Tailored for researchers, linguists, data scientists, and professionals, this chapter serves as a roadmap for unraveling the complexities of social media slang within the evolving field of Natural Language Processing for data analysis.

This paper deals with,a very unique way of implementing the Long Short Term Memory Algorithm (LSTM) in the field of musical melody generation. We have used this LSTM in an advanced way which can be amalgamated with another special deep learning architecture, known as the Restricted Boltzmann Machine (RBM), thus giving rise to a completely new form of LSTM Algorithm for Musical Melody Generation, which we call the Deep Mixed Activated Long Short Term Memory Restricted Boltzmann Recurrent Neural Network Machine (DMA-LSTM-RBRNN). The DMA-LSTM-RBRNN can generate melodies with a corresponding training accuracy of 80.78%, validation accuracy of 81.52% and corresponding training loss of 0.5965, validation loss of 0.5634, and we see that the DMA-LSTM-RBRNN's validation accuracy is leading the training accuracy and the validation loss is lagging the training loss.

Mobile health (m-health) refers to the practice of monitoring health using mobile phones and patient monitoring devices, and it is considered a significant technological breakthrough in the contemporary era. Recently, the integration of artificial intelligence (AI) and big data analytics has been introduced in m-health to enhance the efficiency of healthcare systems. Modern medical research utilizes various types of data, including electronic health records (EHRs), medical images, and complex text, which are diverse, poorly interpreted and extensively unorganized. It conducts a systematic analysis of the application of AI and big data analytics to enhance the m-health system. It discusses various AI-based algorithms and big data frameworks

identification are the two operational modes of biometric systems. When a claimed identity is verified, it is either approved or rejected, whereas when a claimed identity is identified, a description of the claimed identity is given. Like fingerprints, each person's tongue print is distinctive. The tongue was chosen for this case study because it is different from other similar organs. The lips provide protection for the tongue. This prevents the capturing of a tongue print via force. It is a special structure that displays data on physiological texture as well as geometric shape, both of which could be helpful in identification verification. With more explanation, the tongue can be utilized as a new method for identifying a person because even identical twins have varied tongue shape, color, and texture. Some people alter their fingerprints, rendering fingerprint identification software useless. The tongue was utilized as a fingerprint in this case study because accidents can alter the face, which makes it difficult for the system to tell apart facial prints. The exposed part of the tongue carries information that can be used to distinguish between individuals and is therefore useful for identification. The database consists of 2405 tongue images and the images are trained with various deep models such as CNN, VGG16, VGG19, MobileNetV2 and RESNET50. Since the deep models predicts the exact details of the patient it would suggest the specific doctor based on the artificial intelligence. The proposed system is planned to set as an GUI for the hospital to book appointments and for the consultation purpose and treatments.

We embark on a journey to decipher the synergies between AI technologies and the intricate world of multimedia, unravelling their combined potential to reshape the way we perceive, analyse, and interact with diverse forms of digital content. This paper commences with a comprehensive overview of fundamental AI concepts, establishing a solid foundation for readers unfamiliar with the field. Delving into practical applications, the narrative illustrates how AI enhances content understanding, manipulation, and generation across various multimedia domains. Throughout the exploration, emphasis is placed on real-world use cases, shedding light on how AI-driven advancements are influencing industries such as entertainment, healthcare, education, and beyond. Considerations for ethical implications and responsible AI practices are woven into the fabric of the discussion, underscoring the importance of mindful deployment in this rapidly evolving landscape. “Unveiling the Future” serves as a gateway for both novices and seasoned professionals to grasp the profound impact of AI on multimedia data processing. By fostering an understanding of these interconnected technologies, this paper aims to inspire curiosity, spark innovation, and pave the way for a future where AI and multimedia seamlessly converge to redefine the boundaries of human-computer interaction.

Preface

The rapid evolution of Artificial Intelligence (AI) has significantly influenced how multimedia data is processed, interpreted, and applied across a broad spectrum of fields. As multimedia content—ranging from images and audio to textual and biometric data—continues to grow exponentially, the integration of AI techniques offers unprecedented opportunities to harness this complex information for intelligent decision-making, user-centric applications, and enhanced human-computer interaction.

AI Techniques for Multimedia Data Processing presents a comprehensive examination of state-of-the-art methodologies, algorithms, and applications that leverage AI to extract meaningful insights from diverse multimedia sources. This volume is the result of collaborative efforts by distinguished researchers from across the globe, encompassing academic institutions in India, Saudi Arabia, Malaysia, Tunisia, and the United States. It brings together innovative contributions addressing healthcare, social media, biometrics, entertainment, emotion recognition, and more, reflecting the interdisciplinary nature and global impact of AI-driven multimedia technologies.

The book opens with **Chapter 1**, where Tina Babu and colleagues explore the transformative role of AI in multimedia healthcare applications, emphasizing medical imaging, wearable technology, and predictive analytics.

Chapter 2, which delves into multimedia recognition and segmentation, with Saranya G and co-authors analyzing cutting-edge deep learning models and multimodal data fusion techniques.

Chapter 3 shifts the focus to social media, where Kannimuthu Subramanian and team decode the complexities of slang within Natural Language Processing (NLP), presenting its implications for sentiment analysis and brand monitoring.

In **Chapter 4**, Amartya Mukherjee and collaborators introduce a novel hybrid model—DMA-LSTM-RBRNN—for piano melody generation, showcasing innovation at the intersection of AI and music.

Chapter 5 by Bhupinder Singh and Saurabh Chandra examines the convergence of AI, deep learning, and big data analytics in mobile health (m-health), offering insights into smart healthcare systems.

Sudha Senthilkumar, in **Chapter 6**, presents a facial emotion-based music player that customizes music playlists by interpreting human emotions through image processing.

Chapter 7, led by Saba NS and colleagues, explores NLP applications in social media data processing, highlighting its utility in sentiment analysis, misinformation detection, and strategic communication.

Chapter 8 introduces a unique biometric modality—tongue image recognition—by Revathy G and team, expanding the frontiers of biometric security using computational intelligence. Finally,

Chapter 9 by Preeti Rathi serves as a foundational overview, unraveling the synergy between AI and multimedia, while also addressing ethical and societal considerations.

This book serves as a valuable reference for researchers, practitioners, educators, and students in AI, multimedia computing, data science, and related disciplines. It aims to foster understanding, stimulate further research, and promote responsible development and application of AI in multimedia environments.

We express our sincere gratitude to all contributing authors for their rigorous research and thoughtful insights. Their diverse perspectives and expertise have been instrumental in shaping this volume. We also thank our institutions for their continued support and encouragement throughout this endeavor.

Ahmed A. Abd El-Latif

Prince Sultan University, Saudi Arabia

Mudasir Ahmad Wani

Prince Sultan University, Saudi Arabia

Mohamed Hammad

Prince Sultan University, Saudi Arabia

Akram Belazi

National Engineering School of Tunis, Tunisia

Aceng Sambas

Universiti Sultan Zainal Abidin, Malaysia

Acknowledgment

We sincerely thank all those whose contributions made this edited book possible.

Our heartfelt gratitude goes to the authors for their insightful chapters, which have enriched this volume with depth and value. We also thank the reviewers for their thoughtful feedback, which significantly improved the quality and rigor of the work.

Special thanks to the editorial and publishing teams for their professionalism and dedication throughout the process. Your commitment ensured the successful realization of this project.

We are also grateful to our families, friends, and colleagues for their unwavering support during the many hours devoted to this book. Your encouragement has been a constant source of strength.

To our readers—thank you for your interest. We hope the ideas within these pages inspire meaningful dialogue and future innovation.

A personal note from Dr. Mudasir Wani:

I extend special thanks to my son, Zohan, and my 3-month-old daughter, Zenurain, for their patience and love throughout this journey. Zohan, your resilience and joy remind me daily of what truly matters. This book is, in part, a tribute to your quiet support.

To my wife, Kashish—thank you for your unwavering care and for selflessly shouldering responsibilities that allowed me to focus. Your love and support have meant everything.

With deep gratitude,

Mudasir Wani

A Personal Note from Dr. Mohamed Hammad:

I would like to express my deepest gratitude to my sons, Hamza and Yousef, whose understanding and quiet strength have been a constant source of motivation throughout this endeavor. Their patience during my extended hours of work has been invaluable, and their presence a grounding force.

To my wife, Asmaa Maher—your unwavering support, patience, and dedication have made this journey possible. Your willingness to manage countless responsibilities with grace allowed me the focus needed to complete this work. I am sincerely thankful for your steadfast encouragement and belief in my efforts.

With Regards,

Mohamed Hammad

This work was supported by a research grant from the Research, Development, and Innovation Authority (RDIA), Kingdom of Saudi Arabia (Grant No. 13325-PSU-2023-PSNU-R-3-1-EF). The authors extend their sincere gratitude to Prince Sultan University for their continued support.

Additionally, we wholeheartedly acknowledge the unwavering support, patience, and encouragement of our families and children throughout this endeavor. Their unconditional love and understanding have been invaluable to the completion of this work.

Chapter 1
AI for Multimedia Healthcare Applications

Tina Babu
https://orcid.org/0000-0001-7846-3679
Department of Computer Science and Engineering, Alliance School of Advanced Computing, Alliance University, Bengaluru, India

Rekha R. Nair
https://orcid.org/0000-0002-7207-2877
Department of Computer Science and Engineering, Alliance School of Advanced Computing, Alliance University, Bengaluru, India

Kishore S.
Nitte Institute of Professional Education (NIPE), Department of Computer Applications, Nitte University, Mangalore, India

ABSTRACT

This book chapter explores the profound impact of Artificial Intelligence (AI) on multimedia healthcare applications, showcasing its transformative influence on patient care and clinical practices. The narrative unfolds across several key domains, beginning with the revolutionary role of AI in enhancing medical imaging through advanced algorithms and deep learning models. The integration of AI into wearable devices for remote patient monitoring is examined, emphasizing its potential for continuous health assessment and early anomaly detection. The chapter delves into the

DOI: 10.4018/979-8-3693-2935-1.ch001

realm of predictive analytics, highlighting how AI processes vast datasets to predict disease risks, progression, and outcomes, ultimately contributing to disease prevention and early intervention. The chapter serves as a guide for researchers, healthcare professionals, and policymakers navigating the dynamic intersection of AI and multimedia healthcare, offering valuable insights and exploration in this critical field.

INTRODUCTION

It should be noted that nowadays, there is an essential change in the healthcare sector, the main line of which is the use of artificial intelligence. This chapter focuses on analyzing multimedia healthcare applications that are affected by AI in various fields. To do so, we first consider AI in radiology, in which algorithms have improved diagnostic accuracy and speed (Babu et al., 2020. We then shift our focus to AI-based wearable technology that is creating new paths to home monitoring. Such solutions are bringing about preventive health care that entails constant assessment of the patient's health status and potential health complications.

We also talk about how AI is transforming the use of predictive models in the field of health care. With big data and through machine learning techniques, diseases' risks and progression can be therefore predicted, opening new possibilities to enhance patient treatment and prevention plans. The chapter also describes NLP and the manner in which it can be utilized to obtain valuable information from unstructured health information, such as notes and records.

While acknowledging these advancements, we identify several key research gaps:

- Difficulties with the implementation of AI in the current healthcare facilities.
- This latter consideration is the reason why there is a demand for explainable AI models in medical contexts.
- Evolving a code of ethics for using artificial intelligence in the delivery of healthcare services.

- Therefore, designing the artificial intelligence system that is efficient in catering to multiethnic, multicultural, and multimodal patients.
- Investigating the sustainability of the impacts of AI on the outcomes and financial status of healthcare.

We then turn to examine the concerns of the ethical use of AI in health care with more emphasis on the different types of bias experienced by algorithms and patients' data privacy. Thus, to sum up the objectives of the chapter, the author seeks to put the interests of patients and innovation advocates in parallel. Last but not least, we discuss some of the yet unexplored fields such as explainable AI and federated learning, that may hold a promise to reshape future consumer healthcare augmented by artificial intelligence. This present paper provides the audiences with a panoramic view of the use of AI in healthcare and presents AI applications that are relevant to them.

AI IN MEDICAL IMAGING

Being a new dimension in the delivery of healthcare, AI in medical imaging offers a new managing element in diagnostic procedures with reasonable potential for positive changes in patient status. This integration of IT with the field of radiology that substitutes improved imaging techniques by using advanced algorithms and deep learning models as supplements to conventional imaging tools is spectacularly revolutionizing the diagnosis of illnesses. Diagnosis is a concern and is based on Born et al. (2021).

At the very core of this new paradigm, it is the dictum of AI that it can assess complex diagnostic images with levels of accuracy and speed that have hitherto been unimaginable. As modern machine learning algorithms have been trained on a vast number of various medical picture datasets, there is no question that they can distinguish those patterns and peculiarities that a human would not be able to see Krishnan et al. (2023). Enhancing the efficiency of diagnosis might help identify severe diseases at an early stage thus enabling early intervention and individual management plans.

Some of the use of AI in the medical field is illustrated by the use cases shown in Figure 1 below.

Figure 1. AI Use cases in the Medical field. Krishnan et al. (2023).

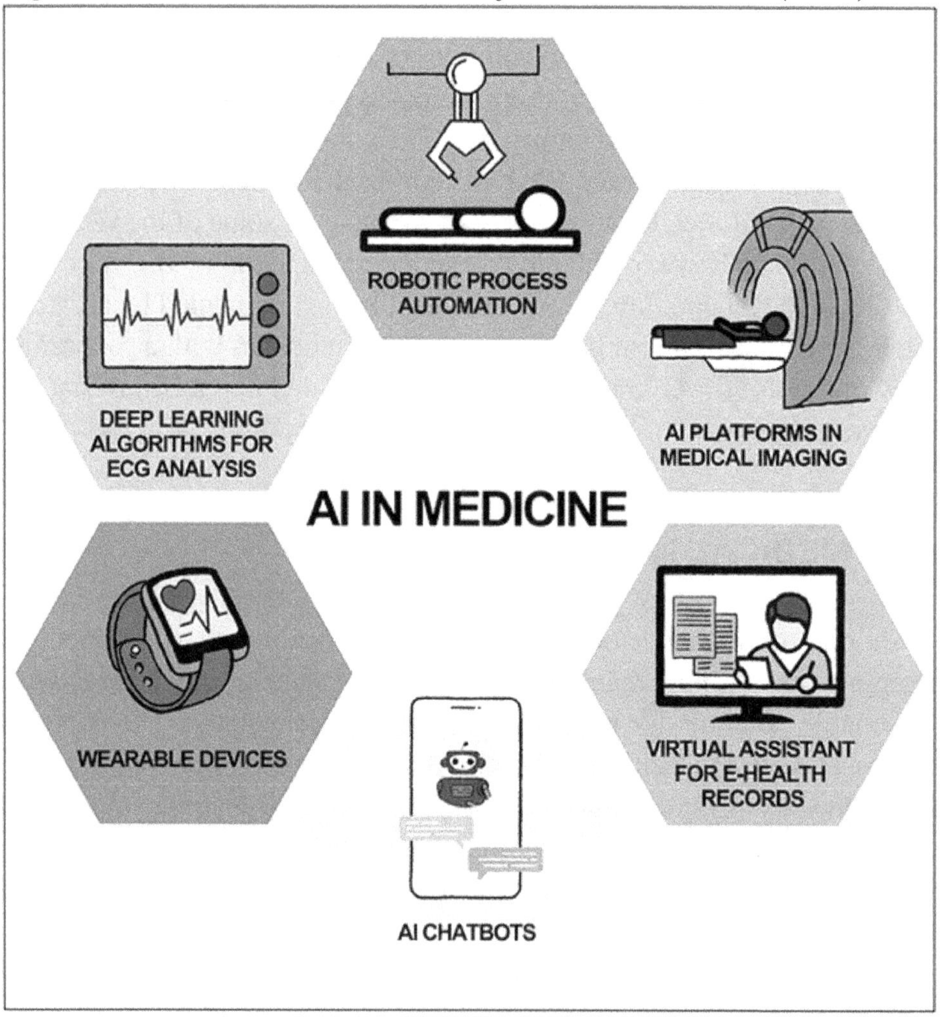

AI-based Medical Imaging Use Cases

AI is significantly changing many facets of medical imaging and improving the diagnostic outcome and speed. Here are some of the prominent use cases with a detailed analysis of how the topic impacts these cases and scholarly articles and books used: Below are some of the use cases that will require the help of AI on medical images as illustrated in Figure 1. The main use cases to be investigated are stated as follows.

1. **Cardiovascular Related:** Concerning the diagnosis of cardiovascular diseases, ordinary methods, and examinations always include taking chest X-rays for purposes of discovering diseases such as cardiomegaly which is commonly understood as an enlarged heart.
    a. Diagnosis and Automation: Previous palpation methods of cardio assessments included radiography for signs of cardiomegaly, which is an enlarged heart. These processes are enriched with the support of AI for analysis of the aortic valve, detection of the carina angle, and measurement of the pulmonary artery's diameter. Such automation results in accurate and faster identification of things such as left atrial enlargement which is a sign of heart issues.
    b. Impact on Diagnosis: Greater accuracy and speed in cardiovascular diagnosis results from the application of highly complex algorithms in medical imaging. Xiong et al. In a research published in the Journal of the American College of Cardiology, investigated the use of AI-assisted ECG interpretation that was found to identify left ventricular systolic dysfunction with an AUC of 0. 93 and was much better than the true traditional criteria of ECG. This implies improved diagnosis and early stages of the disease, hence early treatments and healthier patients.
    c. Precision Medicine Applications: AI is not just a diagnostic tool in cardiovascular imaging but it performs a lot more functions. Petersen et al. (2019) of Nature Review Cardiology also found out that, the commonly used machine learning approaches such as image recognition can be used to analyze Cardiac MRI images in a bid to determine patient-specific disease progression and response to certain treatments. Hindering generalizations of therapeutic approaches can therefore prevent pursuits of generalized approaches to specific patients, which may or may not benefit a patient's health.

2. **Neurological abnormalities:** While diagnosing neurological issues is rather challenging, AI has proven to be efficient in extracting relevant information from scans of the brain.
    a. Data Extraction from Brain Scans: As the nature of the task, diagnosing neurological disorders is a very difficult task. For instance, the use of AI in advertisements to extract information from brain scans is efficient. For instance, Mount Sinai Health Systems is using AI models to identify the root causes of Alzheimer's disease, revealing how AI can analyze detailed neurological information comprehensibly.
    b. Speed and Accuracy: AI solutions help in faster diagnosis of diseases like amyotrophic lateral sclerosis (ALS) wherein important aspects for long-term management are determined. Research that has made a great impact is the paper by Wen et al (2020) where the authors used deep learning to identify ALS from MRI images with 84 percent accuracy and were able to indicate how far the ALS had progressed. These statistics could potentially change the way that patient treatment and clinical trials associated with ALS are developed.
    c. Multi-Modal Integration: The techniques in AI have progressed to the point that it is not only possible to merge information from past imagery with new diagnoses received from different imaging modalities (MRI, PET, and CT scans). Shen et al. showed in Frontiers in Neuroscience that a multimodal deep learning system is capable of diagnosing Alzheimer's disease with 86% accuracy, which is more effective compared to the results of using singular-modality. Thus, this new paradigm of neurological imaging analysis offers the opportunity to improve the diagnostic capacity of a wide range of intricate neurological diseases.
3. **Cancer screening**: It is an immensely important part of early diagnosis and intervention and has registered high growth with the use of AI in medical imaging. In breast cancer, the main problem is to differentiate benign and malignant tissue microcalcifications Babu et al. (2021) as illustrated in Figure 2. AI takes advantage of quantitative imaging that proves helpful in increasing the precision of microcalcifications' detection.

a. Early Detection and Treatment: Cancer screening especially breast cancer has been enhanced by the use of AI in medical imaging. The first one comprises the detection of malignant tissue from benign microcalcifications.
b. Quantitative Imaging: The utilization of AI algorithms as discussed by Babu et al. (2021) improves the specificity and sensitivity will detect microcalcifications. This advancement decreases the false positive which reduces treatment that is not necessary and at the same time increases on early detection of malignancies which is very important for positive medical results.
c. Radiomics and Precision Oncology: Besides diagnosis, AI is advancing the radionics that go beyond the analysis of images and their detection. In the framework of integrating AI in healthcare, Chaddad et al. (2019) in Medical Image Analysis, provided a review to demonstrate that radiomics derived from imaging features could capture cancer genetics, treatment response, and prognosis. For instance, in lung cancer, the radiomic features computed using AI from the CT scans could establish the EGFR mutation status with an AUC of 0. 69, which may help direct therapy choices without the often destructive biopsies.
d. Screening Efficiency: AI increases not only the assessment accuracy but also the effectiveness of the screening process. McKinney et al. (2020) also conducted a big study in Nature that showed that AI could decrease the workload of second readers in breast cancer screening by up to 88% and presented a rather equivalent efficacy. This could significantly IF the number of women that could be screened within the same resources.

Figure 2. Breast Cancer Screening McKinney et al. (2020)

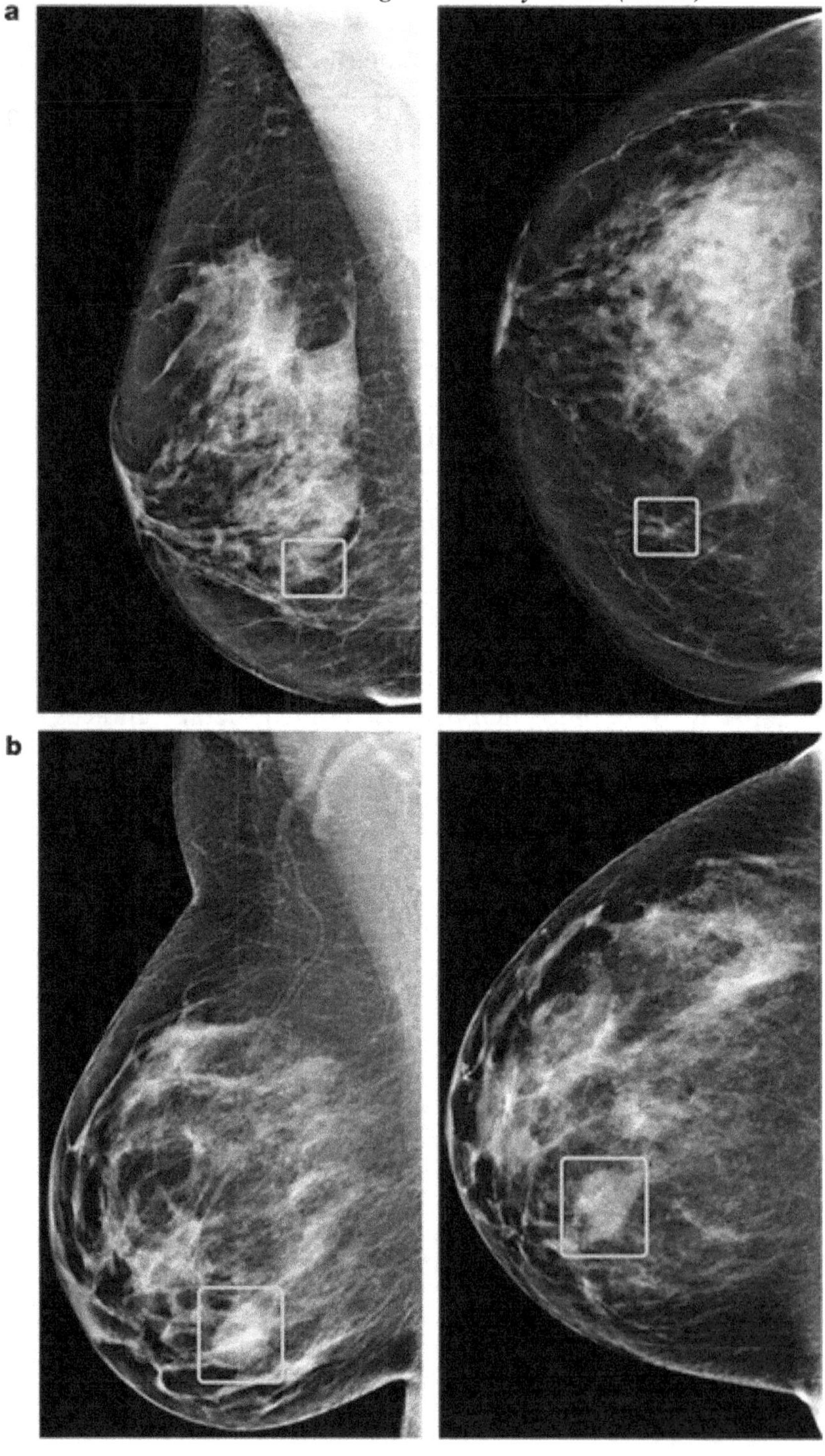

4. **Brain Tumors**: Even the identification of the brain tumors was able to be reduced from 40 minutes to an effective classification function which is another indication of the impact of AI.
    a. Classification Efficiency: AI can completely cut the time needed to classify the cases of brain tumors which previously took about 40 minutes with the help of MRI images and machine learning algorithms.
    b. Accuracy and Non-Invasive Methods: Information presented by S et al. (2023) shows that present AI models can effectively and accurately detect pulmonary embolism with a rate of 98. An example is in the detection of tumors by classifying them into benign or malignant, with an accuracy of 56%. This noninvasive approach is optimal for patients of all ages, especially pediatric ones as it increases diagnostic accuracy in certain clinical settings.
    c. Tumor Segmentation and Treatment Planning: Apart from this, AI has the most definite advantage in the accurate segmentation of the tumor for planning the diagnosis and treatment. A study by Kickingereder et al (2019), published in Lancet Oncology, defined that segmentation of gliomas using non-interventional MRI through an AI system theoretically predicted OS with a discriminative accuracy of 0. 70, outperforming human experts. Such accuracy can be useful for neurosurgeons who want to remove the tumor while causing as little harm as possible to the rest of the brain.
    d. Radiotherapy Optimization: There are also algorithms in AI that are being used in determining the best radiotherapy plan for brain tumors. In the journal Medical Physics, Fan et al. (2019) showed that with machine learning, radiotherapy treatment plans for glioblastoma patients could be produced that have better dosimetry characteristics than those produced by a human, arguably improving the patient's treatment prospects, shortening the time required for planning from a few hours to a few minutes.
5. **Fractures and musculoskeletal injuries**:
    a. Detection in Older Adults: In particular, it is vital to mention that fractures and musculoskeletal injuries are quite typical for elderly people and cause chronic pain and decreased physical activity. For

fractures or dislocations that cannot easily be seen by X-ray, CT scan, or MRI, the use of AI technology is highly useful.

b. Early Detection and Improved Care: In their study, Patel et al. (2023) show that non-prejudiced learning algorithms can pick up on nuances on time and enhance trauma treatment and, consequently, the patient's survival possibilities.
c. Comprehensive Fracture Analysis: Thus, it is possible to state that the application of AI will not be limited solely by the data acquisition on the nature of fractures. Using mobile chest radiography, Olczak et al. (2017) in Acta Orthopaedica found that AI could not only detect fractures with 83% accuracy, but the authors also noted that AI could classify fractures according to AO/OTA classification with 70% accuracy, which is on par with human experts. Such a comprehensive analysis can help with the decisions on the treatment of the patients and the prospects of their healing.
d. Osteoporosis Screening: It is also widely embraced in osteoporosis screening as well. Cheng et al. in Nature Communications in the year 2020 showed that an artificial intelligence model can estimate the fracture risk of osteoporosis for patients scanned with CT, even if it was not for bone density examination alone. This opportunistic screening could significantly increase early detection of osteoporosis without additional radiation exposure or cost.

All the varied uses of AI in medical imaging signify its significant role in improving the delivery of care within various subfields of medicine. Promising to revolutionize medical diagnostics as well as treatment, AI is claimed to have the potential to diagnose more accurately, implement efficient processes, and offer target-like treatment plans. In line with Tang (2019), the present contributions to integrating AI in medical imaging are not going to augment the present practices but are presenting new horizons in healthcare facilities in addition to the increased precision medicines.

Benefits of AI-powered Medical Imaging

This is because there are so many benefits of incorporating the use of AI in medical imaging, some of which are; FPGAs for improved patient care, recognizable workflow, and enhanced diagnosable accuracy. Here are a few main benefits: Here are a few main benefits:

1. **Increased Efficiency**: Many medical images can be processed by AI algorithms in a faster manner than by a human being. Due to the ability to reduce the time required for picture interpretation, this rapid evaluation accelerates diagnostic activities. Obtaining quicker results assists in the execution of required treatments and activities on time Khan M et.al (2024).
2. **Enhanced Diagnostic Accuracy**: Applying AI in medical imaging means that the possibility of correct diagnosis is significantly raised. Using machine learning algorithms in medical photos, it is possible to see certain patterns and compare them with regular ones or notice certain irregularities that a human observer would not be able to see. Because of the increase in the precision in the Testing segment, diseases can be identified more accurately and early.
3. **Early Detection and Intervention**: Such software is helpful in the early detection of irregularities and diseases; through such ways, medical personnel can intervene as soon as it is possible. It is here especially that timely diagnosis becomes critical, especially for diseases such as cancer whereby patient prognosis and treatment probabilities are likely to be favorably altered.
4. **Personalized Medicine**: By applying the technique of medical imaging through the use of artificial intelligence, the differentiation of treatment becomes possible. AI algorithms can assist in developing individual approaches to treatment since such factors as the patient's genes and previous condition can be assessed by the algorithm. This makes it possible for therapy tactics to be optimized in a bid to get the best result or outcome.
5. **Quantitative Analysis**: Many times, analyses of medical images are qualitative and descriptive; however, with the help of AI, the analysis is quantitative with measurements that can be considered precise and

standardized. It is really helpful in such cases as long-term diseases, assessing the effects of the therapies, and the progress of the ailments. Quantitative data generated by AI improves the decision-making capacity among physicians.

6. **Access to Expertise**: In a way, through providing access to such diagnostic skills those with access to AI can get expert-level diagnostic service while in areas with fewer specialized physicians and other practitioners that can perform such operations, the AI bridges the inequality gap in healthcare. On the international level, this democratization of expertise or dissemination of knowledge results in cheaper and more readily available universal healthcare services.
7. **Research and Innovation**: These intensive volumes of data for medical imaging with AI processing support distinct continuing studies and advancements. New biomarkers, therapies as well as diagnostic methods may be discovered with the help of AI analysis and contribute to the expanded knowledge in the field of diseases.
8. **Continuous Learning and Improvement**: AI systems always evolve through the process of learning new information and experiences that take place frequently. Intelligence medical imaging systems are assured to remain some of the leading innovations and will always get better in diagnosing diseases because they can learn from past experiences.

Thus, AI Medical Imaging is likely to provide one of the most significant technological advances to the healthcare sector in the future aiding in change, accuracy, efficiency, and personalized medicine making healthcare better in results and stronger in infrastructure.

There are certain obstacles to the broad use of AI in medical imaging, though. An ethical and careful integration of these technologies into clinical practices is necessary because of data privacy issues, algorithmic bias mitigation, and ethical considerations. The collaborative efforts between AI and medical imaging show potential for redefining care standards as the area develops, providing a window into a future where personalized medicine and diagnostic precision will come together to improve global healthcare.

WEARABLE DEVICES AND REMOTE MONITORING

Smart devices, which are future sensors and AI-integrated devices, have transformed the healthcare system and expanded its outreach beyond hospitals Flores-Martın et al. (2021). This chapter examines the interaction between wearable technology and AI-based applications showing how innovations in remote patient monitoring are evolving. This chapter focuses on the concept of continuous health checkups and early anomaly detection by throwing light on the ability of AI algorithms to analyze data coming from the wearables. It also focuses on how the information sourced from the wearable AI could be integrated into procedures of decision-making in specialties, leaving the accent on the preventive and patient-centered approaches to healthcare.

Smartwatches and other wearable technologies have revolutionized healthcare by shifting from an episodal paradigm toward continuous real-time monitoring. These devices which include a smart band, fitness tracker, and smartwatch, have several sensors incorporated into them and they include; Accelerometers, Heart rate sensors, and Electrocardiograms (ECG). In combination with AI-based technologies, these wearables can convert the so often discussed unstructured data into knowledge that creates new opportunities for the delivery of care. Figure 3 by Shaik et al. (2023) illustrates the patient's wearable device monitoring that is detailed by the authors.

Figure 3. Patient Analyzing. Shaik et al. (2023).

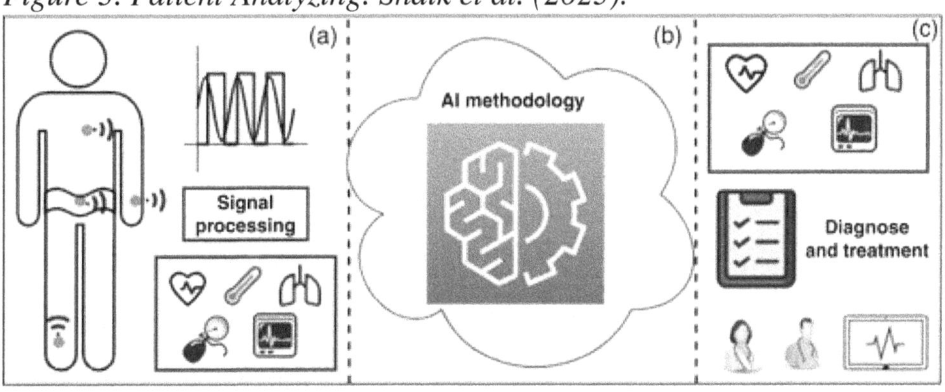

To make sense of the vast amounts of data that wearables' sensors are continuously generating, AI is necessary. For instance, through AI, it would be possible to determine from continued monitoring of the heart rates that these are abnormal or likely to result in cardiovascular complications. It becomes easy to diagnose at an early stage besides the existence of a treatment plan based on the individual's health status. The greatest advantage of wearable technology is that it can give a picture of a person's health status outside a hospital. This is better done by AI because it comes up with a detailed health profile by exploring patterns and differences overtime on the user's health data. Healthcare is becoming more proactive because of this ongoing observation, which is enhanced by AI insights and provides a dynamic and individualized picture of a patient's well-being Rohmetra et al. (2021).

In addition, smart devices with AI-devoted apps can allow citizens to assume the leading role in managing their health. With regards to specific advice and immediate intervention, positive choices toward lifestyles that are beneficial to the health of a person can be made effectively as depicted in Figure 4 by Shaik et al. (2023). Such changes in focus from sickness management to the promotion of prescribed healthy living are an expansion of the broad wellness promotion perspectives. About the concepts of wearable technology and artificial intelligence in the sphere of healthcare, it is critical to discuss the ethical matters concerning data protection and confidentiality. This is as personal health data continue to digitize strong security measures and ethical standards observance are crucial. This means that usage of data, issues to do with consent, as well as utilization of encryption technology, have to be a fully-disclosed process in cases where the responsible deployment is well-deserving.

Figure 4. IoT Devices Patient Monitoring. Shaik et al. (2023).

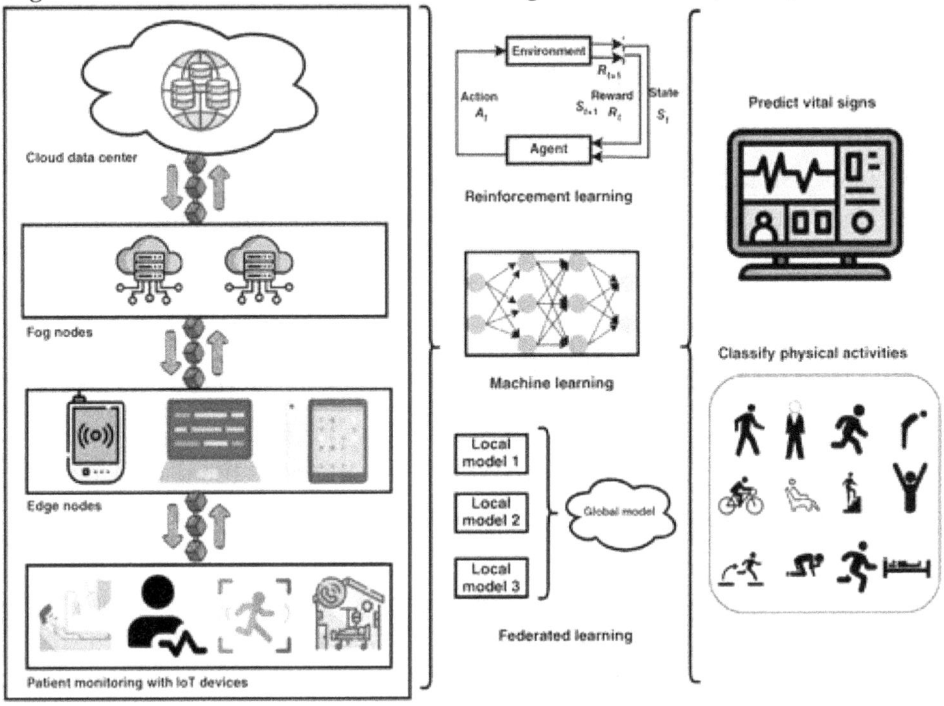

Smart clothing and accessory devices with AI integration become vital tools in the treatment and monitoring of chronic illnesses. Conditions that require long-term care include diabetes, hypertension, and respiratory illnesses. AI could include algorithms to look at data, find instances where patients are deviating from the normal expected range, and trigger alerts or actions. This prevents exacerbation and lessens the demand for emergency medical services. Preventive care is also incorporating mainly AI and wearables besides the other notable advanced technologies. AI can assess an individual's entire health life cycle with the help of vital signs, sleep, and physical activity data. Advocacy for timely healthcare can be supported by the use of prediction models which will possibly analyze possible health problems and recommend avoidance.

In conclusion, it can be noted that a new age in the delivery of healthcare solutions has been birthed by the synergy between wearable devices and AI-supportive applications. Smart textiles and AI analysis make it possible to keep the watches on and do not make changes to the existing treatment courses but turn healthcare from episodic and reactive to continuous. Wearable data becomes valuable especially when added to clinical prescriptive analyses that are applied by artificial intelligence, thus providing medical personnel with a holistic outlook on patient status. Wearable devices in connection with AI can significantly change such aspects of a patient-physician relationship as extubation experience, individual control over one's health, and the advent of preventive, patient-centric medicine in the future.

PREDICTIVE ANALYTICS AND DISEASE PREVENTION

As shown in Figure 5, predictive analytics involves the use of machine learning and statistical algorithms to analyze past data and come up with trends that can be used in predicting occurrences in the future. Predictive analytics is essential in the healthcare industry for spotting possible health hazards and anticipating illness outbreaks Dhasarathan et al. (2023). Predictive analytics is the ability to recognize early warning indicators and suggest preventive actions by evaluating massive datasets, including genetic information, electronic health records, and lifestyle data Ibrahim and Saber (2023). Many Artificial Intelligence-based applications are carried out by researchers such as Nair et al. (2023); Nair and Singh (2022); Nair et al. (2022, 2021); and Manjushree et al. (2022).

Figure 5. Predictive Analytics with healthcare data. Petrova (2023).

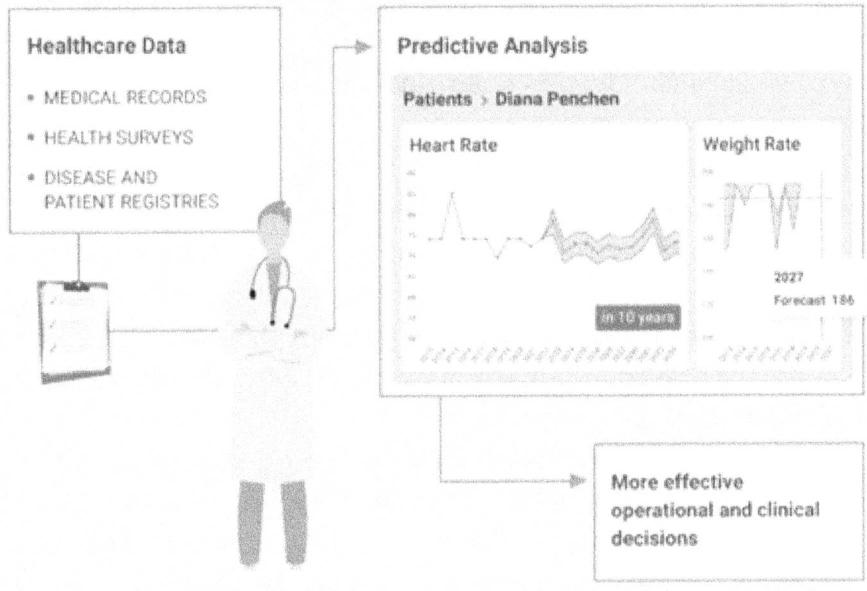

Moreover, multimedia healthcare applications 'enhanced' by AI for applications in healthcare raise the bar for predictive analytics because AI 'understands', and processes complex sources of data. Multimedia data is also well understood by AI algorithms where despite being in the form of images, videos, and audio files, patients' medical histories are of immense value. For instance, the application of AI in the interpretation of medical imaging will quickly pinpoint the early signs of illness such as cancer making it easier to address Nair et al. (2023).

The advantage of predictive analysis is that it helps in:

1. **Overall Higher Quality of Medical Attention:** Predictive analytics' ability to access a wide range of data, including comorbidities, demographics, and medical history, is its most significant contribution to the healthcare sector. Physicians and other healthcare professionals can make informed judgments thanks to the wealth of data available to them. Overall patient care is better when decisions are made more intelligently and using data Suh et al. (2023).

Predictive analytics, for instance, is applied to enhance patient outcomes. Machine learning algorithms can be trained to provide insights into treatment strategies that are most effective for individual patients by analyzing data and outcomes from older individuals.

2. **Individualized Care:** Medicine has always operated on a one-size-fits-all basis. Instead of focusing on individual patients, data from a large population have been used to suggest treatments and medications based on scant information. However, as medical practitioners become more adept at diagnosing patients, they will also be able to choose the best course of action based on each patient's particular set of circumstances.
3. **Management of Population Health:** There are applications for predictive analytics beyond the individual level. It can also be used by healthcare organizations to control population health. Analytics can be used to identify similar patients within a population cohort when they have information about the illnesses, treatments, and personal histories of the patients. Identifying cohorts exposed to a potential disease epidemic can also be aided by it. Healthcare providers can begin considering treatments right once in such a situation, increasing the likelihood that patients will survive.
4. **Determine Patients at Risk**: In order to prevent deeper issues, predictive analytics in healthcare can identify patients who are more likely to experience problems and initiate early innervations. For example, based on age-coexisting chronic conditions and medication adherence, it can identify patients with cardiovascular disease who have the highest probability of being admitted to the hospital. Rather than waiting for at-risk patients to schedule routine checkups, physicians and healthcare organizations can proactively give care with the use of predictions on the possibility of disease and chronic illness.

In addition to individuals with chronic illnesses, additional populations at risk include the elderly and patients just released from the hospital following invasive procedures.

5. **Management of Chronic Diseases:** In addition to being the primary cause of mortality and disability in the US, chronic diseases account for $3.5 trillion of the nation's yearly health expenditures. Seventy-five percent of healthcare costs are related to five chronic diseases: diabetes, obesity, renal disease, cancer, and cardiovascular disease.

The management of chronic diseases is contingent upon the capacity of healthcare practitioners to both avert and mitigate their onset. However, managing and preventing chronic illnesses is a difficult undertaking. In order to treat patients more effectively and at a lower cost, predictive analytics can enable healthcare providers to make prompt, well-informed decisions.

6. **Digitalization and Tracking of Healthcare:** The relationship between patients and healthcare providers is entirely changed by the digitalization of health services. These days, we may use our mobile phones to track our body performance and health at any time by attaching gadgets to our bodies. For instance, diabetics don't need to prick their fingers to track their blood sugar rise.
7. **Avoid Human Mistakes:** Negligence from the side of the human part in the healthcare system is capable of being fatal. Fortunately, it may be used to find potential mistakes and exclude fatal mistakes by providing practical, accurate, and timely information to orient the actions of medical staff.
8. **Lowers Total Medical Expenses:** Another benefit, that can bring predictive analytics, is the reduction of costs linked to healthcare. It can be consequently used to cut unnecessary care and hospital admissions when they are not required, control hospital costs for meds and supplies, and estimate staff demands Suh et al. (2023).

Important elements of AI-based disease prevention and predictive analytics are:

1. **Processing and Integration of Data:**
    - Combination of various kinds of data which include multimedia, gene data, or health records.

    - Cleaning and transforming the data in order to make it suitable for analysis.
2. **Models for Machine Learning:**
    - Deriving models that use the algorithms of machine learning that can detect patterns and trends.
    - Continual learning of the model and changing that particular model to suit new data fed into the system.
3. **Analysis of Multimedia:**
    - AI-powered examination of audio, video, and medical picture data to detect diseases early.
    - Multimedia data integration with additional health information to enable thorough analysis.

Predictive analytics and AI for disease prevention benefits are:

- Early Detection and Intervention: Timely intervention and preventative actions are made possible by the early detection of health hazards and prospective diseases.
- Customizing treatment plans according to each patient's unique traits and risk factors is known as personalized healthcare.
- Resource optimization is the effective distribution of healthcare resources with a concentration on populations at high risk.
- Better Patient Outcomes: Improving patient outcomes through illness prevention and proactive management.

NATURAL LANGUAGE PROCESSING IN HEALTHCARE DATA

NLP offers unconventional techniques for processing, understanding, and coming up with conclusions out of the high volumes of unstructured textual information from EHRs, published research articles, and other healthcare records. The implementation of NLP in analyzing various healthcare data has significant benefits in improving patient satisfaction and care, clinical decision-making concerning an individual's health, and the productivity of the healthcare system as a whole Shastry and Shastry (2023).

Figure 6. Clinical documentation using NLP. Reddy (2019)

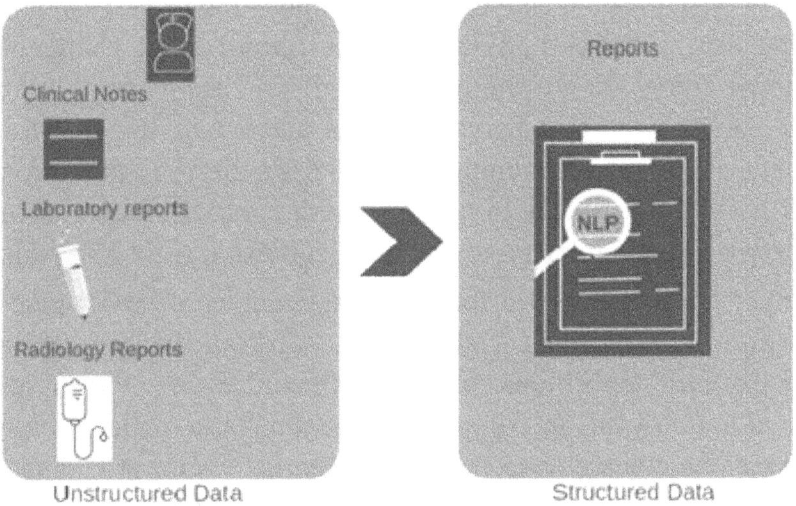

To use an example, as illustrated in Figure 6, one of the areas in which NLP is widely applied in the healthcare sector is information mining from clinical text, including reports and free text. NLP algorithms can transform unstructured text into organized, useful data by analyzing and extracting pertinent information about symptoms, diagnoses, and treatment plans.

Among the duties that NLP is capable of are:

- Providing an overview of long, unstructured clinical notes
- Converting unstructured data into structured data in electronic health records (EHR) that is valuable
- Transforming data into natural language from machine-readable formats for reporting and teaching
- Text query response via natural language interface
- Transform the photos into insightful analyses and reports.

Furthermore, plans that enable population health management are also supported by NLP. Bigger studies of patient records with the use of natural language processing (NLP) assist healthcare organizations in recognizing patterns, and possible problem in public health. Consequently, the integration of NLP in healthcare data holds a range of advantages, though, at the same time, it has certain disadvantages. Some of the challenges that need to be addressed are the patients' privacy, dealing with numerous kinds of language used in medical records, and reconciling the variations in documentation systems employed by these healthcare practitioners. It means that while dealing with such difficulties, the necessary information must be precise and relevant to the given context in solid NLP solutions.

Further advancements in the NLP applications in health care could reveal even more utilities in the future. All have the general positive impact that NLP algorithms can help with clinical decision support and information Retrieval, and support further changes to patient-centric and data-driven healthcare as technology progresses. Natural language processing is threatening to disrupt the analysis of healthcare data by holding the prospect of extracting never-before-seen knowledge from unstructured text. NLP is revolutionizing the interface that healthcare stakeholders have with information and enables; enhancing population health, and improving health research among others. It also enhances the operational efficiency of health facilities and clinical judgment. More specifically, the application of natural language processing to healthcare data is likely to have a significant positive impact on patients and healthcare organizations over the course of the field's growth.

AI MODELS AND ARCHITECTURES IN HEALTHCARE: A COMPARATIVE ANALYSIS

Healthcare AI could be defined as the variety of methods calculated to model human thought processes. In healthcare, AI can be categorized based on the techniques used – 1) Machine learning 2) deep learning, and 3) NLP.

Comparison of AI Models in Medical Imaging

Convolutional Neural Network (CNN)

CNNs are quite capable of handling structured grid data and this makes it easy for them to be applied in image analysis applications. They have been found to be very useful in learning features from the visual input and can determine multiple structures at different scales in the image. This is the ability that sets CNNs apart because they are able to learn spatial hierarchies. More so, it may take a lot of computation to train and run CNNs, this may require the use of specific hardware. However, CNNs have not disappointed and have been widely applied in medical imaging. They are often employed in such activities as predicting x-ray images and determining tumors in MRI scans. These use cases demonstrate how CNNs can be helpful in helping with key procedures and may even help enhance the value of patients' lives. The human application of AI in healthcare is a revolutionary change that encompasses the field of diagnosis and treatment.

Recurrent Neural Networks (RNNs)

Basically, RNNs are good at analyzing sequential data which is important for time-based medical data. These networks can accommodate sequences of different lengths and are quite good when identifying time-related structures. They also apply it in predicting patient trajectories of treatment in Intensive Care Settings by analyzing the changing trends of the patient's physiological parameters and laboratory measures. Nevertheless, RNNs are not without their demerits. They can find it difficult to model long-term dependencies because of the vanishing gradient problem in which updates from the earlier state are minimally weighed as the sequence goes on. Moreover, teaching these networks might take a lot of time depending on the nature of the medical data. Nevertheless, RNNs are still a valuable tool in medical data processing, which creates temporal patterns that are not easily detected by other models and are perfect for time-series data processing.

Generative adversarial networks (GANs)

GANs employ a pair of competing neural networks: It is important to differentiate between the two as one produces artificial data and the other checks its credibility. The given architectural design facilitates the creation of very convincing artificial content. Therefore in medical imaging great benefits of using GANs are as follows. This can create realistic medical images to supplement scarce data, improving the robustness of diagnostic models' training. Moreover, GANs are useful in image-enhancing tasks as well as in other related tasks.

Thus, GANs have certain disadvantages Nevertheless, Despite the above-listed advantages, GANs have certain disadvantages. However, the following are the challenges that have been observed while working on GANs: Nonetheless, GANs have their practical implication in health care. It is especially effective in generating new realistic medical images for enhancing the training data and optimizing the quality of the medical images overall. Thus, with the development of new technologies, GANs remain applicable to different medical imaging situations.

The comparison of the various models is shown in Table 1.

Table 1. AI Model Comparison for Medical Imaging

Model	Pros	Cons	Use cases
CNNs	Excellent feature extraction learns spatial hierarchies	Requires large labeled datasets, computationally intensive	X-ray classification, tumor detection
RNNs	Handles variable-length sequences, captures temporal dependencies	Vanishing gradient problem, slow training	ECG analysis, patient trajectory prediction
GANs	Generates synthetic data, useful for data augmentation	Unstable training, potential for unrealistic artifacts	Synthetic image generation, image enhancement

AI Architectures for Predictive Analytics

The various models for predictive analytics include the following and the comparison is shown in Table 2.

Random Forest

For random forests, the ability to produce many decision trees makes the final predictive model very strong. This type of technique usually provides an improved outcome rather than the trees in isolation. its attributes are suitability for elaboration of complicated, non-linear interactions between the variables, and freedom from overtraining. The method also performs well even when we have partial measures data. Nevertheless, it takes a lot of time to train and can become highly resource-consuming if the dataset is large; besides, the decision-making process in such an algorithm is not as obvious as in the case of more simple methods. However, it should be noted that even with the mentioned disadvantages, random forests can be seen as rather beneficial in the healthcare context: they can help predict readmissions and assess the risk of diseases, for instance. This approach is flexible and combines here exactness and staleness which has made it to be used for various prediction issues.

Support Vector Machines

This is a classification algorithm that finds the best decision boundary for categorizing information in multiple data spaces. The method has however been useful in the medical disciplines where it is used to classify various types of cancer and or predict how the patient would likely respond to treatment. Because of its efficiency in handling complex data sets, it is relevant in these essential health areas, in which proper categorization goes a long way to shape patient's treatment plans. However, despite these drawbacks, it is still considered one of the significant tools in Machine Learning due to its flexibility and efficiency in solving high-dimensionality problems.

Gradient Boosting Machines

This method joins several simple models, often decision trees into stages to form a highly effect model. Thus, the performance is gradually increasing with each new model, which is corrected based on the mistakes of the previous one. The technique stands out for its precision and applicability to virtually any kind of data, which is crucial for intricate issues. However, it may sometimes over-fit the training data, hence it has limitations as a tool for generalizing new cases. However, the above process can be rather time and resource-consuming from the view of computing power. It has been applied in the healthcare context to predict patients' statuses and evaluate potential costs of treatment. Due to its efficiency in managing the vast information and yielding the correct prediction, it is significant in the medical field and the formulation of financial strategies.

Table 2. Comparison of Performance Metrics

Model	Accuracy	Interpretability	Scalability	Applications
Random Forests	High	Moderate	Good	Disease risk assessment, hospital readmissions
SVM	High in high-dimensional spaces	Low	Moderate	Cancer classification, drug response prediction
Gradient Boosting	Very High	Low to Moderate	Moderate	Patient outcome prediction, healthcare cost estimation

DISCUSSION

Summary of Key Findings

Since the subject of this manuscript is multimedia, its contribution is articulated in utilizing artificial intelligence in disseminating information within the healthcare sector. It explains how AI is transforming radiology by using state-of-the-art algorithms and deep learning techniques to improve diagnostic accuracy and efficiency. Further, the proposed integration of AI in wearable and how it can assist in constant and early monitoring of the patient's health in the context of the distinct categories of remote patient care are detailed. The book covers the exciting area of AI predictive analytics, which is able to forecast risk probabilities and diseses outcomes. This function could substantially augment preventive healthcare tools and timely interventions. The manuscript also looks at the use of NLP in medical domain, underscoring its ability to transform unstructured datasets (eg clinical notes and EHRs) into structured information with interpretable nature.

This is an important document that looks at AI in healthcare, particularly addressing the ethical considerations and challenges of using it. This has implications in terms of data privacy, concerns about possible algorithmic bias and the need for audits on AI systems. These concerns clearly underline why the development and deployment of AI technology in healthcare should be done responsibly. These diverse topics contribute to the significance of this manuscript that gives a full picture about how AI can be used now and in the future for transforming healthcare delivery and outcomes. It highlights the technology as well as ethics that might need to managed side by side when AI is increasingly being incorporated in health systems globally.

Implications of AI in Healthcare

Potential benefits and improvements in patient care

Changes in medical technology are happening so fast and with tools that keep advancing the care of patients. New diagnostic approaches can detect patterns in health data that are similar to those found using more traditional methods, only much earlier. This might result in more timely and accurate diagnosis. Treatment strategies are adapted to each individual's unique situation. By analyzing patient information, the treatment team can develop a treatment plan that minimizes disruption while maximizing effectiveness.

This allows for regular monitoring and encourages moving to a more preventative level of maintenance when necessary. Healthcare services are optimized to reduce administrative burden. This allows doctors to spend more time on patient interactions and important emotional tasks. Forecasting capabilities have improved in healthcare. By identifying factors and risks, health outcomes can be more easily predicted, and resources can be allocated effectively. This approach supports better prevention and treatment planning. The goal of these advances is to increase the overall effectiveness and efficiency of treatment, leading to better patient outcomes.

Challenges in implementation and adoption

This reluctance stems from concerns about job security and doubts about the true potential of medical expertise. Implementing AI solutions often requires significant changes to existing IT solutions; This is an expensive and time-consuming process. The rapid development of artificial intelligence technologies often outpaces the development of control systems. The industry is creating uncertainty about the adoption and use of new AI tools in healthcare. In addition, the use of artificial intelligence in healthcare often involves the processing of sensitive patient information, raising concerns about data protection and patient privacy.

First, investment is required, as the high cost of using AI technology can be prohibitive, especially for healthcare providers with limited resources. This financial impact can slow or hinder the implementation of AI solutions in many healthcare settings. Together, these challenges create a challenging environment for integrating AI into healthcare that requires careful thought and planning to overcome. A transformative paradigm shift. This integrated advancement utilizes the most advanced systems and machine learning technologies and offers the potential to revolutionize healthcare.

ETHICAL CONSIDERATIONS AND CHALLENGES IN AI HEALTHCARE

Artificial intelligence is revolutionizing healthcare by bringing new possibilities in data analysis, clinical decision-making, and providing personalized treatment options. As artificial intelligence advances in medicine, ethical considerations also prevail. Issues such as data privacy and security, the bias of AI algorithms, the protection of patient identity and consent, the necessary changes in the work of health professionals, and the creation of policies and guidelines to clarify the use of artificial intelligence in healthcare will be central. The role of artificial intelligence in analyzing patient-specific information to create personalized treatment plans is particularly important to the advancement of the medical industry. Using AI in predictive analytics to predict patient outcomes and disease progression to improve long-term management and identify patients at risk will be a huge payoff.

AI has shaped the healthcare landscape and impacted healthcare organizations in areas such as diagnosis, electronic medical records (EMR), diagnostic testing, treatment strategies, physician skill development, new drug discovery, vaccine distribution and drug testing, and comprehensive analysis of biological data., process acceleration, and easy data storage and access. Despite this progress, the field still faces many ethical and legal challenges. Although there has been significant progress in using community intelligence to improve health systems, access remains a challenge for many communities.

Listed below are some of the challenges that are faced by healthcare in the field of AI

1. **Privacy and Data Security**: Many ethical issues arise when collecting and managing patient data in artificial intelligence-supported health services. In order to protect people from harm that may arise from information leakage and unauthorized access, the confidentiality and security of patient information should be ensured. In addition, patients should be informed about the use of their data in artificial intelligence applications; Patients should be informed and given options to choose from.
2. **Addressing algorithmic bias**: Bias poses a significant challenge for AI algorithms used in healthcare. When these algorithms are influenced by biased data, they can worsen racial and health disparities that already exist in the healthcare system. Training skewed data can contribute to the problem of conflict in healthcare by creating algorithms to recommend different treatments based on a patient's affiliation with certain groups. Therefore, some groups will receive special treatment, leading to differences in health, while other groups will experience negative consequences.
3. **Cognitive decision-making**: Enabling patient autonomy and consent in AI-enabled healthcare requires solving many challenges. First, achieving consensus on AI systems requires transparent communication and an understanding of AI's intended use and potential impact. Patients may

not understand how AI applications use their data, raising concerns about data privacy.

4. **Ethics for healthcare providers**: Doctors using AI tools have many responsibilities that will evolve as AI advances. Doctors must ensure that medical decisions guided by AI tools are in the best interest of patients. Human oversight of AI tools used in healthcare should be regulated, and doctors should evaluate recommendations from AI tools to ensure they follow treatment guidelines.
5. **Ethical frameworks**: The Health Insurance Portability and Protection Act (HIPAA) exists to establish privacy and security standards for patients' medical information. Additionally, the US Food and Drug Administration (FDA) has its regulatory framework for software such as artificial intelligence used in healthcare. The European Union has the General Data Protection Regulation (GDPR) which sets the rules for the processing of patient data used in AI.
6. **Patient Autonomy and Involvement:** The use of intelligence should complement, not replace, the roles of doctors and patients in decision-making. It is important to ensure that patients participate in the decision-making process and receive understandable information.
7. **Resource Allocation and Access:** Deploying AI systems may require significant funding. Determining how to allocate these resources while taking social benefits into account is difficult to justify. Ensuring that AI technology is accessible to all citizens, regardless of socioeconomic status, is critical to preventing the current healthcare system from becoming more serious.
8. **Job Displacement and Economic Impact:** The integration of AI into healthcare may lead to changes in some businesses, raising concerns about the financial impact on healthcare providers and support staff.
9. **Finding the right balance**: It is important to balance the advancement of medical knowledge with the ethics of using technology in business. The solution is to ensure that AI-powered technology benefits patients without compromising their rights or health.
10. **Medical Consultation, Empathy, and Sympathy**: The integration of artificial intelligence (AI) into all aspects of healthcare poses great challenges and seems an elusive goal. The rapid change in human behavior suggests that people and medical facilities will not change

simultaneously shortly. The ability for doctors and other medical professionals to find colleagues or provide consultation in autonomous (robotic) systems does not yet exist. On the contrary, there seems to be a question of whether patients will accept a "machine-human" medical communication rather than a "human-human" relationship. Doctors and nurses need to provide treatment in an atmosphere of understanding and compassion, which is important to influence the healing process. This level of care is unlikely to be possible with doctors and nurses.

11. **Social Gaps and Justice**: Another challenge that humans face after the development of intelligence is the problem of inequality. With every advance, discovery, and invention around the world, the gap between rich and poor widens and social justice is eroded. Despite AI's increasing access to science, technology, global affairs, climate change, and political information, social networks continue to spread to countries around the world. Guidance and innovation with the ability to transform the business.

FUTURE DIRECTIONS AND INNOVATIONS IN AI HEALTHCARE

The continued development and integration of AI technology with healthcare will lead to revolutionary changes, providing opportunities for better diagnosis, personalized treatment, and better healthcare. As these innovations advance, careful consideration of ethical and regulatory issues is critical to ensuring accountability and equity in healthcare, and some of the main focuses include:

1. **Precision Medicine**: Artificial intelligence will play a key role in making medicine more accurate by analyzing big data to determine personalized treatment based on a person's genetic makeup, activity community, and environment.
2. **Drug Discovery and Development**: AI-driven approaches will accelerate drug discovery by analyzing biological data, predicting drug interactions, and determining the treatment of drug candidates.

3. **Remote Patient Monitoring**: Artificial intelligence will improve remote patient care by analyzing health information in real time, allowing doctors to intervene promptly and create personalized treatment plans for patients outside clinical settings.
4. **Early Disease Detection**: Artificial intelligence algorithms will continue to evolve to detect diseases early by analyzing various biomarkers, medical images, and patient data, thus making intervention more effective and efficient.
5. **Natural Language Processing (NLP) in Healthcare Conversations:** Advances in NLP will make the interaction between artificial intelligence systems and doctors or patients increasingly accurate, facilitating communication and information exchange.
6. **Integrative Analysis:** In its vision, Francis Collins' Precision Medicine Initiative 109 envisions the next generation of scientists developing new ways to analyze, measure, and analyze a variety of biomedical data. This includes molecular, genomic, cellular, clinical, behavioral, physical, and environmental factors. Integration of data from multiple variables provides the opportunity to explain health problems from multiple perspectives. By exploring the integration of this heterogeneous knowledge, a better understanding and understanding of health can be achieved.
7. **Predictive Analytics and Preventive Care**: AI will focus on predictive analytics to predict disease outbreaks, identify high-risk groups, and support preventive care, ultimately reducing the health burden.
8. **Blockchain for Health Data Security** Blockchain technology will be introduced to healthcare to improve the security and integrity of patient information, privacy, and lack of consent.
9. **AI Ethics and Regulatory Frameworks**: The establishment of good practice guidelines and regulatory frameworks will be a fundamental change in addressing AI ethics in healthcare, ensuring accountability and responsible use.

CONCLUSION

The establishment of good practice guidelines and regulatory frameworks will be a fundamental change in addressing AI ethics in healthcare, ensuring accountability and responsible use. The emergence of machines has received significant attention in recent years, driven by significant advances in modern technology, especially artificial intelligence (AI) and machine learning (ML). The use of wearables and smartphones for health monitoring, machine learning for disease diagnosis, and the development of services such as social robots for use in assisted living environments. This section highlights some of the major impacts of AI in Healthcare. Further, the chapter discusses AI in medical imaging, Natural Language processing in healthcare data, Predictive Analytics and Disease Prevention, and Future considerations and innovations. Several potential avenues for future research are suggested to enhance the current healthcare system further. While it may be impractical to entirely replace the medical system with technology, introducing innovative architectures has the potential to alleviate the workload of medical experts. The feasibility of developing assistive systems lies in collaborative efforts between medical professionals and researchers working together on a common platform.

REFERENCES

Azzi, S., Gagnon, S., Ramirez, A., & Richards, G. (2020). Healthcare applications of artificial intelligence and analytics: A review and proposed framework. *Applied Sciences (Basel, Switzerland)*, *10*(18), 6553. DOI: 10.3390/app10186553

Babu, T., Gupta, D., Singh, T., Hameed, S., Zakariah, M., & Alotaibi, Y. (2021). Robust magnification independent colon biopsy grading system over multiple data sources. *Computers, Materials & Continua*, *69*(1), 99–128. DOI: 10.32604/cmc.2021.016341

Babu, T., Singh, T., & Gupta, D. (2020). Colon cancer prediction using 2dreca segmentation and hybrid features on histopathology images. *IET Image Processing*, *14*(16), 4144–4157. DOI: 10.1049/iet-ipr.2019.1717

Born, J., Beymer, D., Rajan, D., Coy, A., Mukherjee, V. V., Manica, M., Prasanna, P., Ballah, D., Guindy, M., Shaham, D., Shah, P. L., Karteris, E., Robertus, J. L., Gabrani, M., & Rosen-Zvi, M. (2021). On the role of artificial intelligence in medical imaging of covid-19. *Patterns (New York, N.Y.)*, *2*(6), 100269. DOI: 10.1016/j.patter.2021.100269 PMID: 33969323

Dhasarathan, C., Hasan, M. K., Islam, S., Abdullah, S., Mokhtar, U. A., Javed, A. R., & Goundar, S. (2023). Covid-19 health data analysis and personal data preserving: A homomorphic privacy enforcement approach. *Computer Communications*, *199*, 87–97. DOI: 10.1016/j.comcom.2022.12.004 PMID: 36531214

Flores-Martin, D., Rojo, J., Moguel, E., Berrocal, J., & Murillo, J. M. (2021). Smart Nursing Homes: Self-Management Architecture Based on IoT and Machine Learning for Rural Areas. *Wireless Communications and Mobile Computing*, *2021*(1), 8874988.

Hossain, M. S., Cucchiara, R., Muhammad, G., Tob́on, D. P., and Saddik, A. E. (2022). Special section on ai-empowered multimedia data analytics for smart healthcare.

Ibrahim, M. S., & Saber, S. (2023). Machine learning and predictive analytics: Advancing disease prevention in healthcare. *Journal of Contemporary Healthcare Analytics*, *7*(1), 53–71.

Kamruzzaman, M. (2020). *Architecture of smart health care system using artificial intelligence. In 2020 IEEE international conference on multimedia & expo workshops (ICMEW)*. IEEE.

Khan, M., Shiwlani, A., Qayyum, M. U., Sherani, A. M. K., & Hussain, H. K. (2024). AI-powered healthcare revolution: An extensive examination of innovative methods in cancer treatment. *BULLET: Jurnal Multidisiplin Ilmu*, *3*(1), 87–98.

Kishore, S., Nair, R. R., Mehra, V., & Babu, T. (2023). A generalized framework for brain tumor and pneumonia detection using streamlite application. In 2023 4th International Conference for Emerging Technology (INCET) (pp. 1-6). IEEE.

Krishnan, G., Singh, S., Pathania, M., Gosavi, S., Abhishek, S., Parchani, A., & Dhar, M. (2023). Artificial intelligence in clinical medicine: Catalyzing a sustainable global healthcare paradigm. *Frontiers in Artificial Intelligence*, *6*, 6. DOI: 10.3389/frai.2023.1227091 PMID: 37705603

Manjushree, R., Bhoomika, D., Nair, R. R., & Babu, T. (2022). Automated detection of diabetic retinopathy using deep learning in retinal fundus images: Analysis. In 2022 3rd International Conference on Communication, Computing and Industry 4.0 (C2I4), pages 1–6. IEEE.

McKinney, S. M., Sieniek, M., Godbole, V., Godwin, J., Antropova, N., Ashrafian, H., Back, T., Chesus, M., Corrado, G. S., Darzi, A., Etemadi, M., Garcia-Vicente, F., Gilbert, F. J., Halling-Brown, M., Hassabis, D., Jansen, S., Karthikesalingam, A., Kelly, C. J., King, D., & Shetty, S. (2020). International evaluation of an ai system for breast cancer screening. *Nature*, *577*(7788), 89–94. DOI: 10.1038/s41586-019-1799-6 PMID: 31894144

Nair, R. R., Babu, T., & Kishore, S. (2023a). Recent and emerging technologies in industrial iot. Opportunities and Challenges of Industrial IoT in 5G and 6G Networks, pages 50–72. DOI: 10.4018/978-1-7998-9266-3.ch003

Nair, R. R., Babu, T., & Singh, T. (2023b). Multiresolution approach on medical image fusion by modified local energy. *Signal, Image and Video Processing*, *17*(8), 1–8. DOI: 10.1007/s11760-023-02636-6

Nair, R. R., & Singh, T. (2022). Optimal wavelet-based multi-modal medical image fusion with quantitative analysis for colour images using different colour models. *International Journal of Biomedical Engineering and Technology*, *40*(3), 262–288. DOI: 10.1504/IJBET.2022.126496

Nair, R. R., Singh, T., Basavapattana, A., & Pawar, M. M. (2022). Multi-layer, multi-modal medical image intelligent fusion. *Multimedia Tools and Applications*, *81*(29), 42821–42847. DOI: 10.1007/s11042-022-13482-y

Nair, R. R., Singh, T., Sankar, R., & Gunndu, K. (2021). Multi-modal medical image fusion using lmf-gan-a maximum parameter infusion technique. *Journal of Intelligent & Fuzzy Systems*, *41*(5), 5375–5386. DOI: 10.3233/JIFS-189860

Nasr, M., Islam, M. M., Shehata, S., Karray, F., & Quintana, Y. (2021). Smart healthcare in the age of ai: Recent advances, challenges, and future prospects. *IEEE Access : Practical Innovations, Open Solutions*, *9*, 145248–145270. DOI: 10.1109/ACCESS.2021.3118960

Patel, P., Babu, T., & Nair, R. (2023). *Breast cancer detection framework using evolutionary search and svm classifier*. DOI: 10.1109/ICoAC59537.2023.10249874

Petrova, B. (2023). *Predictive Analytics in healthcare. Ponnusamy, V., Vasuki, A., Clement, J. C., and Eswaran, P. (2022). Ai-driven information and communication technologies, services, and applications for next-generation healthcare system*. Smart Systems for Industrial Applications.

Rakesh, S., Jeyageetha, K., Nishant, S., Nageswari, D., Prakash, R. B. R., & Mary, S. S. C. (2023, June). Machine learning and internet of things-based driver safety and support system. In 2023 8th International Conference on Communication and Electronics Systems (ICCES) (pp. 955-960). IEEE.

Reddy, V. (2019). Natural Language Processing in healthcare.

Rohmetra, H., Raghunath, N., Narang, P., Chamola, V., Guizani, M., & Lakkaniga, N. R. (2023). AI-enabled remote monitoring of vital signs for COVID-19: Methods, prospects and challenges. *Computing*, •••, 1–27.

Shaik, T., Tao, X., Higgins, N., Li, L., Gururajan, R., Zhou, X., & Acharya, U. R. (2023). Remote patient monitoring using artificial intelligence: Current state, applications, and challenges. *Wiley Interdisciplinary Reviews. Data Mining and Knowledge Discovery*, *13*(2), e1485. DOI: 10.1002/widm.1485

Sharma, M., Savage, C., Nair, M., Larsson, I., Svedberg, P., & Nygren, J. M. (2022). Artificial intelligence applications in health care practice: Scoping review. *Journal of Medical Internet Research*, *24*(10), e40238. DOI: 10.2196/40238 PMID: 36197712

Shastry, K. A., & Shastry, A. (2023). An integrated deep learning and natural language processing approach for continuous remote monitoring in digital health. *Decision Analytics Journal*, *8*, 100301. DOI: 10.1016/j.dajour.2023.100301

Suh, I., McKinney, T., & Siu, K.-C. (2023). Current perspective of metaverse application in medical education, research and patient care. In *Virtual Worlds* (Vol. 2, pp. 115–128). MDPI.

Tang, X. (2019). The role of artificial intelligence in medical imaging research. *BJR Open*, *2*(1), 20190031. DOI: 10.1259/bjro.20190031 PMID: 33178962

Yin, J., Ngiam, K. Y., & Teo, H. H. (2021). Role of artificial intelligence applications in real-life clinical practice: Systematic review. *Journal of Medical Internet Research*, *23*(4), e25759. DOI: 10.2196/25759 PMID: 33885365

Chapter 2
AI for Multimedia Recognition and Segmentation

G. Saranya
SRM Institute of Science and Technology, India

N. Krishnaraj
SRM Institute of Science and Technology, India

Priyanga Subbiah
https://orcid.org/0000-0002-2395-7492
SRM Institute of Science and Technology, India

Kiran Bellam
Prairie View A&M University, USA

ABSTRACT

Recent AI and multimedia analysis advances have changed our visual content viewing and interaction. This study evaluates new AI multimedia recognition and segmentation technologies. Multimedia object, scene, action, and emotion recognition is crucial in entertainment, healthcare, security, and education. AI-based recognition systems are studying CNN, RNN, and deep learning architectures. Photo, video, and multimedia seg-

DOI: 10.4018/979-8-3693-2935-1.ch002

mentation algorithms that correctly detect and extract areas of interest are also explored. AI-driven multimodal data fusion improves detection and segmentation by combining photos, videos, text, and audio. This paper evaluates their progress. Multimedia AI analysis concerns dataset bias, scalability, real-time processing, and ethics. AI multimedia recognition and segmentation are thoroughly studied in this article. This field's successes, limitations, and promise are highlighted. These technologies could change how we perceive and interact with massive amounts of visual data, enabling new applications and advances in many fields.

1. INTRODUCTION

Recent significant developments in artificial intelligence (AI) and multimedia analysis have drastically changed how humans perceive and interact with visual material. Focusing on the abilities of these technologies to identify and distinguish between a broad variety of multimedia components, such as objects, scenes, actions, and emotions, this study examines the most recent instances of artificial intelligence (Zhu et al., 2021). Education, healthcare, law enforcement, and the entertainment business are just a few areas where this is absolutely essential. We will examine the deep learning methods used by AI systems for recognition and talk about the technical aspects. A few examples of these methods include RNNs and CNNs, which stand for recurrent neural networks. We will also take into account algorithms that may identify and emphasise specific areas in multimedia files for potential future research. The fact that AI is merging text, audio, video, and picture data to improve its classification and recognition abilities is one of the most intriguing parts of the technology. An extensive examination of the advancements made in AI multimedia analysis is conducted in this study. Dataset bias, scalability, real-time processing, and potential ethical concerns are among the listed difficulties. The goal of this essay is to survey the state of the art and future prospects of AI-powered multimedia identification and segmentation in order to supply a thorough overview (Belov & Ulaeva, 2019). There is an emphasis on the transformative potential of these technologies, which implies a paradigm change in how humans perceive and handle massive volumes of visual data. Many different industries will be able to take use of these new possibilities for development and innovation.

2. EXPLORING AI ARCHITECTURES

Now, let's delve a little farther into the AI architectures! Just for a second, consider this: your computer is actively working to decipher visual media; this goes much beyond the ability to view still photos and moving films. Artificial intelligence (AI) functions as a smart assistant in this case, able to identify objects in images or videos. These days, when people speak about AI architectures, they're actually referring to the complex frameworks that enable this. Imagine them as the complex patterns housed in your computer superhero's brain (Batra et al., 2022). One example is the function that Convolutional Neural Networks (CNNs) do, which is similar to a computer's eyes. With their pattern and feature recognition abilities, they can aid in object recognition. Because they function more like your memory, Recurrent Neural Networks (RNNs) allow computers to recognise and understand a chain of events. This is due to the fact that RNNs mimic the way human memory operates. Things take an interesting turn when these AI systems start to cooperate instead of operating alone. What we have here is analogous to a detective who, in addition to searching for physical evidence, also listens for noises and reads documents in an effort to solve a crime. By combining these distinct skills, the system's overall capabilities, including picture and video recognition, are enhanced. Our investigation is like taking the top off your computer and looking at it closer; we want to know how these AI systems bring a whole new level of intelligence to our gadgets. Teaching our computers to understand the complete story told by the images is more important than teaching them to only identify objects. On top of that, the exponential growth in AI is unleashing a plethora of exciting new possibilities, elevating our electronic devices from mere tools to sentient beings with extraordinary sensory abilities.

3. MULTIMEDIA SEGMENTATION ALGORITHMS

When it comes to evaluating and organising visual content, multimedia segmentation algorithms provide a sophisticated solution. Modern advancements in multimedia and artificial intelligence have put these algorithms in the front. This article delves further into these algorithms, which provide the technical backbone for accurately identifying and extracting targeted areas of interest in multimedia (Seibold et al., 2022). This has far-reaching consequences for how we perceive and use data. Recognising and distinguishing objects, scenes, activities, and even attitudes within the complex domain of multimedia—which includes images, movies, and other visual data—requires diverse segmentation techniques. Elements are recognised and separated in this domain. Because of their transferability to fields as diverse as education, healthcare, entertainment management, and more, these skills have far-reaching consequences. In the healthcare industry, for instance, these algorithms could be useful for medical image analysis and diagnosis. Their potential to improve monitoring and threat detection also suggests they may be useful in the security sector.

Complex models like as recurrent neural networks (RNNs), convolutional neural networks (CNNs), and others form the basis of deep learning, and this study delves into their inner workings. These frameworks allow identification systems based on artificial intelligence to better spot patterns and qualities in visual data, which in turn improves the accuracy of segmentation. The segmentation algorithms are the centre of attention because of the crucial role they play in decomposing intricate visual situations. This facilitates the sophisticated interpretation of multimedia content (Zhang et al., 2016). The potential for synergy in the integration of AI-driven multimodal data is one of the main foci of this study. These algorithms provide a more complete view of the visual material by integrating data from several sources, including text, audio, video, and images. This enhances their capability to precisely localise areas of interest. Using a multimodal approach enhances the analysis and mimics the intricate way people see and understand visual data. Though it does recognise the advancements in multimodal AI analysis, the study also raises serious issues related to segmentation algorithms. Ethical considerations, limitations on real-time processing, issues with scalability, and dataset bias are all thoroughly examined. This emphasises the need of addressing these challenges to guarantee the efficient and responsible implementation of these technologies. This research delves deeply into the pros, cons, and potential applications of algorithms for multimedia segmentation. It explains how these algorithms will change the game for humans when it comes to dealing with massive volumes of visual data. Not only are these algorithms finding usage in a wide range of contexts now, but they also hold great promise for the future of discovery and advancement across many different industries.

4. IMPORTANCE OF MULTIMEDIA RECOGNITION AND SEGMENTATION

In the context of modern AI and multimedia analysis, the importance of multimedia recognition and segmentation cannot be overstated (Cheng et al., 2017). This is owing to the fact that these innovations usher in game-changing uses across several domains and radically alter our interactions with visual content.

- An enormous boon to the entertainment industry's bottom line has been the use of technologies that can identify and categorise various forms of multimedia material. You may think about the idea of getting personalised content suggestions based on the user's tastes and the emotions expressed through multimedia material.
- The healthcare industry greatly benefits from these technologies' ability to precisely separate medical pictures. The ability to get a detailed knowledge of specific picture regions of interest is a boon to medical research, treatment planning, and diagnosis.
- When it comes to security-related applications, multimedia recognition and segmentation are two crucial functionalities. Accurately identifying objects, situations, and activities in recordings has the ability to enhance monitoring systems. This makes it easier to both avoid security issues and fix them quickly when they do arise.
- These technological advancements have the potential to radically alter the educational landscape. Envision an educational system

where AI-powered interactive resources can identify and emphasise key points, making it easier for students to engage and understand the subject.

- Emotion detection in multimedia is a distinctive feature in relation to emotional intelligence research. Aside from the entertainment industry, fields like therapy and mental health symptom monitoring might benefit from the capacity to understand the emotions conveyed in visual media.
- To get a better understanding of the neural networks that drive these innovations, studies focusing on CNNs, RNNs, and deep learning architectures in the context of multimedia recognition systems are highly beneficial. A knowledge of the architecture of multimedia files is necessary for optimising and refining their analysis. Precise Segmentation for Gaining Focused Understanding: Research into picture, video, and multimedia segmentation algorithms is essential for the accurate detection and extraction of visual content's regions of interest. As the basis for generating tailored insights, this capacity is useful for many different applications.
- Using multimodal data fusion, we can gain a more complete picture by: Artificial intelligence-driven multimodal data fusion is novel since it integrates visuals, audio, and text. This all-encompassing approach improves detection and segmentation accuracy by simulating human perception and providing a thorough grasp of multimedia information.
- The study's focus on scalability, bias in datasets, real-time processing, and ethics shows a commitment to developing and deploying multimedia recognition and segmentation algorithms ethically. The fact that the research addresses problems and ethical concerns demonstrates this level of commitment. In order to guarantee objective and fair results, it is critical to act on these problems.
- All things considered, the ability to recognise and split multimedia documents is crucial because it might revolutionise how we interact with visual data in many different contexts. These innovations might pave the way for further possibilities and technological advancements in the future, which can change the way we view and engage with visual material. The entertainment business is only one

of several that potentially benefit from these innovations. Others include healthcare, education, and security.

5. TECHNOLOGICAL ADVANCES IN OBJECT, SCENE, ACTION, AND EMOTION RECOGNITION

- Through the use of object and scene recognition technology, students may access immersive learning environments, which has the ability to completely transform the educational system. To help students better understand and participate in class, picture an AI system that could instantly recognise and describe geographical landmarks or historical artefacts.
- Healthcare Evaluation and Course of Treatment Development: The discipline of medical imaging greatly benefits from object identification, which plays a vital role in the overall success of the profession. Algorithms powered by artificial intelligence can accurately spot abnormalities in medical images, which can help in early disease identification. Furthermore, scene recognition might be helpful in developing treatment strategies by studying intricate healthcare settings.
- Enhanced video content moderation places an emphasis on action recognition, which is an essential part of online platform content moderation. Because AI algorithms can now detect inappropriate content in films, the internet is a safer place for everyone. When it comes to websites and social media that facilitate video sharing, this is crucial.
- The entertainment business is going through a transition as a consequence of emotion detection technology, which is leading to the development of more personalised entertainment experiences. Streaming services may utilise AI to assess the audience's emotional reactions to content, allowing for more personalised recommendations. Because of this, being entertained is an incredibly engaging and engrossing experience.
- Human-Robot Collaboration in Industry Technologies that can identify objects and behaviours are crucial for fostering safe and

successful human-robot collaboration in industrial environments. Worker safety and output are both improved by robots' capacity to detect and react to human actions.

- When it comes to accessibility, these identification technologies help a lot. For instance, those who are blind or have low vision can benefit from object recognition apps for smartphones since these apps can help them recognise and describe items in their environment.
- Assist with Navigation in the Real World People with navigational challenges in the real world may benefit from scene recognition. Navigation applications get context from artificial intelligence algorithms that can identify landscapes and landmarks. People with vision impairments or who are blind would benefit greatly from this.
- Opinion Evaluation for Market Research Purposes: Sentiment analysis has several possible uses in market research, one of which is emotion identification. Companies may learn how their consumers respond to ads and goods, which allows them to tailor their marketing to consumers' wants and requirements and enhance their offerings.
- Smart environments tailored to people's unique tastes and requirements are becoming more feasible with the help of these identification technologies. One day, we may be able to install AI systems in our homes and offices with the ability to understand and react to human emotions and behaviours. Living spaces would become more intuitive and flexible as a result of this.
- Technological advancements in object, scene, action, and emotion recognition have broadened their applications well beyond their original intent. These developments influence a wide range of industries and have far-reaching consequences for human interaction with nature and one another. Along with increased accuracy and productivity, these developments open the door to novel uses that may enhance many parts of our daily lives.

6. MULTIMODAL DATA FUSION IN AI-DRIVEN ANALYSIS

Multimodal data fusion is a big deal in AI-driven analysis since it opens up a lot of new possibilities for systems that can identify and divide up multimedia. By combining data from several sources, including text, audio, video, and images, this novel method has the potential to provide a deeper comprehension of visual material (Kwan et al., 2021). The use of multimodal data fusion gives AI systems a fighting chance of approaching human visual comprehension. The system may integrate many sorts of data to provide a complete picture of the world. Since this is the case, the system is able to discern not just physical elements but also the nuanced expressions conveyed by photographs and videos. The accuracy of recognition processes is greatly enhanced when many modalities are used together. For instance, improving the identification and classification of multimedia items may be achieved by combining picture data with text descriptions or voice commentary, which can offer a wealth of additional contextual information.

Visual information can be better understood in context when a number of different modalities are used. More immersive and tailored entertainment concepts that incorporate related textual or audio signals with visual components may emerge from this. This approach changes the way people engage with computers, which enhances the human-computer interface. Envision an environment-based system that can interpret not just spoken commands but also nonverbal cues like facial emotions and context. With this whole picture in hand, it's possible to engage in more organic and intuitive interactions with AI-powered apps. In the healthcare industry, multimodal fusion plays a crucial role in providing thorough diagnosis. A more complete picture of a patient's health can be achieved by combining medical photographs with textual descriptions, patient data, and potentially even audio notes. This information can greatly enhance the accuracy of diagnoses and the planning of treatments. Offering the Ability to Reach Decisions Rapidly In situations when quick decisions are required, multimodal data integration is crucial. Integrating audio and textual data with video footage greatly enhances the responsiveness of surveillance systems. In turn, this aids security programmes in making more precise and rapid threat detections.

A resolution to the issue of recognition ambiguity problems of uncertainty in recognition can be resolved by multimodal fusion. In cases where visual content alone would not give enough context, textual explanations or auditory indications might be helpful. The result is that AI systems can reason their way to more reliable and fair conclusions. Although multimodal data fusion is a very effective method, it is not without its difficulties. The smooth integration and synchronisation of data from different modalities (Sood & Sharma, 2016), the development of algorithms that can efficiently use combined data, and the management of any conflicts must all be carefully considered. Fusion and its ethical onsiderations importantly, multimodal data fusion also takes into account ethical considerations. To guarantee that people's rights and society's values are not compromised while emerging technologies are utilised, it is necessary to appropriately manage concerns about privacy, consent, and the ethical use of combined data sources. A great deal of innovation in many different domains might be spurred by the combining of multimodal data. Investigating novel approaches to effectively integrate and use data from many modalities may pave the way for advancements in AI-driven analysis. New possibilities for use and development would emerge as a result of this. Opportunities for more ethical, contextually aware, and complex interactions with visual data have arisen thanks to multimodal data fusion, which is basically a game-changing phenomena in AI-driven multimedia analysis. While resolving issues with unimodal analysis, this approach advances the field into new frontiers of innovation and practicality.

7. EVALUATION OF AI MULTIMEDIA RECOGNITION AND SEGMENTATION TECHNOLOGIES

The accuracy and precision of these methods in detecting and segmenting multimedia components is tested. To assess how well AI systems can consistently identify objects, scenarios, actions, and emotions, several metrics are used, such as recall, accuracy, and F1 score. A crucial component of any evaluation is its relevance to actual, practical settings (Ramadevi et al., 2010). What kind of results can we expect from these technologies when applied to real-world scenarios and businesses? Their real-world impact may be better understood by analysing how well they perform in contexts like medical diagnostics, security monitoring, and educational software. These two measures should be taken with utmost seriousness when dealing with entertainment-related apps. An important step in assessing the worth of AI-driven multimedia identification in the entertainment sector is finding out how much it improves user engagement, customisation, and overall happiness. An important factor to consider when assessing AI systems is their scalability. How well can these segmentation and recognition algorithms handle large amounts of visual data? In addition, we need to test their speed and accuracy in processing massive datasets if we want to know how useful they are. Besides considering technical achievements, the examination also takes ethical factors into consideration. The criticality of knowing how well these technologies handle issues of consent, privacy, and bias cannot be overstated. Making ensuring that AI used for multimedia analysis doesn't go against societal values and standards is the job of ethical evaluations.

8. FUTURE OUTLOOK AND POTENTIAL INNOVATIONS

Upcoming advancements in AI multimedia analysis will most likely centre on making things easier to understand and explain. Building confidence and enabling expanding adoption across many industries will need the development of technologies that allow these systems to clearly explain their decision-making processes. More enhancements are expected to lead to even more smooth integration of multimodal data (Foulkes & Booth, 1997). Anticipated advancements in the integration of text, audio, video, and photo data will equip AI systems with more contextual information, allowing for better classification and identification. Soon, AI systems that can tailor their services to each user will be developed in the healthcare and education industries, according to predictions. It is possible that these systems can adapt to the preferred method of learning for each user, or that they may customise medical diagnoses and treatment plans based on each person's unique traits and medical background. Given the exponential rise of visual data, it is probable that future developments will centre upon addressing scalability issues. For AI multimedia analysis to remain scalable and effective, advancements in distributed computing, edge computing, and efficient parallel processing will be crucial. In the creative sectors, which encompass design and content creation, the use of artificial intelligence is among the most anticipated advancements. One day, AI-powered tools that use recognition and segmentation technologies to increase efficiency and inspiration could be able to help artists with their multimedia projects. As AI keeps making strides in multimedia analysis, we could expect to see more complex decision support systems created. In particular, these technologies may prove useful to those working in healthcare and security by allowing them to access insightful multimedia analysis (Zhang, 2022). There will always be ethical questions with AI, no matter how far the technology gets. Responsible deployment, the elimination of algorithm biases, and the settlement of ethical concerns are all necessary to keep multimedia analysis up to future expectations.

9. CHALLENGES AND CONSIDERATIONS IN MULTIMEDIA AI ANALYSIS

- The existence of dataset bias is a major obstacle for multimodal AI analysis. It is critical to guarantee that training datasets reflect a diverse range of populations, cultures, and situations. Artificial intelligence systems are limited in their utility due to the risk of biassed segmentation and recognition results caused by biassed datasets.
- A major obstacle for AI in multimedia analysis is scalability, which has emerged as a result of the exponential rise of visual data. Developing algorithms and infrastructures that can efficiently handle massive datasets without sacrificing processing speed or accuracy is crucial for putting these technologies to good use.
- Complex algorithms can have high computing needs, making real-time processing challenging to accomplish in the field of artificial intelligence analysis for multimedia. Accuracy and quick decision-making are of the highest significance in security monitoring applications, where efficiency and speed are constantly being improved.
- The investigation of multimodal AI raises a number of challenging ethical concerns. Because these systems automatically analyse vi-

sual data, which can include sensitive information, privacy issues have been raised. Striking a balance between the quest of intelligent knowledge and the preservation of personal privacy is an ongoing debate that need careful consideration.

- The interpretability of AI models is a key factor in user confidence and adoption of those models. The process by which these more sophisticated algorithms reach specific recognition or segmentation decisions is becoming opaquer and challenging to understand and defend. Achieving better acceptability will need the development of methodologies that offer clear explanations of the outcomes produced by AI.
- The challenge increases when emotional recognition is added to AI analysis of multimedia. It is feasible to gather and decipher human emotions from visual data by making use of tiny signals that differ greatly. When dealing with circumstances where emotions are subjective, it becomes much more difficult to design algorithms that can correctly identify complicated displays of emotion.
- While multimodal data fusion adds nuance to AI research, it does come with its fair share of difficulties. We need algorithms with a lot of processing power to combine data from several sources including text, audio, video, and images. These algorithms need to work in tandem and draw from a range of modalities without losing efficiency or generating competing interpretations; this is crucial.
- Machine learning systems must be able to learn and adapt on the fly to keep up with the ever-evolving visual material and user interactions. A long-standing problem with systems that deal with changing user behaviour or environment is finding ways to include continuous learning without sacrificing acceleration.
- Anticipating and addressing unanticipated consequences is crucial since artificial intelligence (AI) technologies are being more and more incorporated into daily life. For example, there's a chance that biassed opinions may spread, or that some user groups may be unwittingly negatively affected. The successful use of AI requires proactive steps to detect and lessen the impact of such consequences.
- It is difficult to achieve substantial cross-domain generalisation in the area of artificial intelligence analysis for multimedia. Problems

with object, scene, or emotion detection in novel or complex environments may arise from training models on specific datasets. Constant study is being carried out to guarantee that AI systems can generalise across various domains.

10. EVALUATION OF PROGRESS

Recent innovations in AI and multimedia analysis have led to considerable improvements in the accuracy of identification across a range of modalities, including object, scene, action, and emotion recognition (Neskovic & Cooper, 2001). As state-of-the-art models, deep learning architectures, CNNs, and RNNs are incredibly good at understanding and making sense of visual material. Thanks to developments in segmentation algorithms, regions of interest in multimedia information like images, movies, and more may now be identified and extracted with greater accuracy and robustness. Medical imaging, security monitoring, and content development are just a few of the many businesses that can benefit from these breakthroughs in segmentation accuracy.

It is a giant leap forward to use AI to combine data from different sources. For a more complete comprehension of multimedia content, it is possible to blend data from images, videos, text, and audio in a smooth way to boost analytical depth.Cases where a holistic view is paramount lend themselves well to this innovation. Applications requiring quick decisions, such security and live event analysis, are driving the need for real-time processing capabilities. Rapid insights and actions grounded on visual material are made possible by artificial intelligence's more responsive analysis of multimedia content, made possible by faster processing speeds. Research into multimodal AI raises a number of ethical questions, which are being more recognised. Researchers and industry professionals are beginning to include ethical considerations into AI development and implementation processes in an effort to resolve privacy, bias, and proper AI use across several industries challenges. Numerous applications, including security monitoring, entertainment customisation, and healthcare diagnostics, have shown the diverse and influential usage of artificial intelligence to multimedia analysis. The results and the user experience have been greatly enhanced by AI models that have been personalised for certain use cases.

11. EVALUATION OF LIMITATIONS

Even though we have come a long way, these issues are still there. Unfortunately, AI models might not be able to generalise well, and biassed training data could provide biassed findings. Dealing with underrepresented groups or exceptional circumstances makes it much more difficult to maintain varied and representative databases. Because the volume of visual data is always growing, scalability remains an issue (Maag et al., 2021). In order to expand AI models while maintaining the requirement for human analysis, especially in cases involving massive datasets, this issue must be carefully considered before broad deployment can occur. The term "black box" describes some complex AI models that are notoriously difficult to understand. Especially in cases where information and responsibility are paramount, these models must be able to succinctly explain their results to inspire trust.

Although a lot of work has gone into this, it is still difficult to accurately extract the nuanced human emotions from visual data. Emotions are complicated and culturally specific, making it harder to develop algorithms that reliably understand them everywhere. Multimodal data fusion poses difficulties in synchronisation, harmonisation, and maximising the capabilities of each modality when integrating information from many sources. If you want a solution that can deal with problems without sacrificing effectiveness, you have to make changes all the time. On situations with limited resources, it could be challenging to run complicated AI models due to their resource and energy demands. For applications with limited computational resources, finding a happy medium between energy efficiency and model complexity is crucial for a sustainable deployment.

12. IMPACTS AND PROMISE OF MULTIMEDIA AI TECHNOLOGIES

With the advent of ubiquitous AI and multimedia analysis, the way we engage with visual content has been truly transformed. A new age of immersive and customised user experiences has dawned, brought about by technologies such as innovative healthcare diagnostics and personalised entertainment recommendations. With the rise of multimodal AI technology, the entertainment industry is poised for a revolutionary shift. Suggestions for personalised content are based on the user's viewing habits, emotions, and interests. Engagement is increased as a result. More realistic and engaging virtual worlds and narratives may be made possible with the help of deep learning architectures such as convolutional neural networks (CNNs) and recurrent neural networks (RNNs). The medical profession is greatly impacted by multimodal AI technology. Together, emotion detection in healthcare and precise object and scene recognition in medical imaging pave the way for more precise diagnoses and individualised treatment plans.The goal is to enhance both the therapy process and the results for the patients.

The potential for enhanced security and surveillance is clearly demonstrated by the use of multimodal AI analysis. Security measures may be made more effective by using advanced identification systems that can detect abnormalities, behaviours, and events in real time. Potentially safer settings might emerge from implementing this technology. One step towards individualised instruction is the use of AI in the classroom. Recognition technology can adapt instructional materials to different learning styles, allowing for more individualised approaches to instruction; scene and emotion recognition help to provide a more nuanced view of student engagement.

13. CONCLUSION

We may soon be able to understand and interact with visual data in whole new ways, thanks to advancements in artificial intelligence and multimedia analysis. A new age defined by creativity and involvement is about to begin, heralded by the predicted breakthroughs in targeted information distribution, human-machine cooperation, and immersive virtual experiences. In the future, we may see more personalised and compassionate interactions made possible by AI that is emotionally sophisticated enough to recognise and react to human emotions. Ensuring appropriate behaviours utilising AI, correcting prejudices, and encouraging diversity are all areas where ethical concerns are likely to play a key role. The seamless integration of multimedia analysis powered by artificial intelligence into everyday life is seen in many ways, including smart homes and personal assistants. In the future, this will be a sign that technology is both accessible and essential to our daily lives. It seems like a revolution is coming to education in the future, where students may have personalised learning experiences aided by AI and where learning materials can be adjusted to suit their unique interests. A better understanding of the potential societal impact of artificial intelligence (AI) may be gained from looking at its use in smart city projects, better urban planning, and the advocacy for sustainable environments. Future years may see much more study and development in the exciting fields of AI and multimedia analysis. As a result of these technologies' revolutionary potential, not only do existing applications undergo radical changes, but new avenues of possibility become accessible. This boosts creativity and expedites progress in many different areas. One bright spot for the future is the potential for visual data to become a powerful tool for ongoing development and transformation, as technology and human experience come together in perfect harmony.

REFERENCES

Batra, A., Gowda, S. N., Sevilla-Lara, L., & Keller, F. (2022). A closer look at temporal ordering in the segmentation of instructional videos. arXiv. https://doi.org//arXiv.2209.15501DOI: 10.48550

. Belov, A. V., & Ulaeva, E. S. (2019). The neural network simulation of instance-aware semantic image segmentation system. https://doi.org/ (Note: Incomplete DOI—please verify)DOI: 10.1109/IT

Cheng, J., Liu, S., Tsai, Y.-H., Hung, W.-C., De Mello, S., Gu, J., Kautz, J., Wang, S., & Yang, M.-H. (2017). Learning to segment instances in videos with spatial propagation network. arXiv: Computer Vision and Pattern Recognition. https://arxiv.org/abs/ (DOI/URL incomplete—please verify)

Foulkes, S. B., & Booth, D. M. (1997). Improved object segmentation using Markov random fields, artificial neural networks, and parallel processing techniques. DOI: 10.1117/12.280826

Kwan, A. C., Salto, G., Cheng, S., & Ouyang, D. (2021). Artificial intelligence in computer vision: Cardiac MRI and multimodality imaging segmentation. *Current Cardiovascular Risk Reports*, *15*(9), 18. Advance online publication. DOI: 10.1007/s12170-021-00678-4 PMID: 35693045

Maag, K., Rottmann, M., Varghese, S., Hüger, F., Schlicht, P., & Gottschalk, H. (2021). Improving video instance segmentation by light-weight temporal uncertainty estimates. DOI: 10.1109/IJCNN52387.2021.9534407

Neskovic, P., & Cooper, L. N. (2001). Object segmentation using an array of interconnected neural networks with local receptive fields. DOI: 10.1109/IJCNN.2001.938468

Ramadevi, Y., Sridevi, T., Poornima, B., & Kalyani, B. (2010). Segmentation and object recognition using edge detection techniques. International Journal of Computer Science and Information Technology, 2(6), [page range not provided]. DOI: 10.5121/ijcsit.2010.2614

Seibold, C., Künzel, J., Hilsmann, A., & Eisert, P. (2022). From explanations to segmentation: Using explainable AI for image segmentation. DOI: 10.5220/0010893600003124

Sood, A., & Sharma, S. (2016). Image segmentation and object recognition using machine learning. In Proceedings of Advances in Intelligent Systems and Computing (pp. [page range not provided]). DOI: 10.1007/978-981-10-3433-6_25

Zhang, J., Gao, Y., Feng, S., Yuan, Y., & Lee, C.-H. (2016). Automatic image region annotation through segmentation based visual semantic analysis and discriminative classification. DOI: 10.1109/ICASSP.2016.7472018

Zhang, X. (2022). Application of artificial intelligence recognition technology in digital image processing. *Wireless Communications and Mobile Computing*, *2022*, 1–10. Advance online publication. DOI: 10.1155/2022/7442639

Zhu, X., Xia, W., Bao, Z., Zhong, Y., Fang, Y., Yang, F., Gu, X., Ye, J., & Huang, W. (2021). Artificial intelligence segmented dynamic video images for continuity analysis in the detection of severe cardiovascular disease. *Frontiers in Neuroscience*, *14*, 618481. Advance online publication. DOI: 10.3389/fnins.2020.618481 PMID: 33642970

Chapter 3
Deciphering the Lexicon:
Social Media Slang in Natural Language Processing for Data Analysis

Kannimuthu Subramanian
https://orcid.org/0000-0002-8606-7278
Karpagam College of Engineering, India

Aishwarya Sundaram
https://orcid.org/0000-0002-5263-5804
Universiti Malaya, Malaysia

Sreeja Balachandran Nair Premakumari
https://orcid.org/0000-0002-6319-766X
Karpagam College of Engineering, India

ABSTRACT

The chapter offers a comprehensive exploration of the dynamic landscape of social media slang and its integration into Natural Language Processing for data analytics. It delineates key objectives, encompassing an overview of the unique linguistic landscape of social media slang, an investigation into the challenges of processing slang, an exploration of

DOI: 10.4018/979-8-3693-2935-1.ch003

lexical innovations and emerging trends, and a deep dive into sentiment analysis specifically tailored for social media slang. Additionally, it explores strategies for integrating slang into traditional language models and examines multilingual considerations in processing slang globally. The chapter showcases practical applications, including brand monitoring and market research, demonstrating how Natural Language Processing-driven insights enhance marketing strategies and brand perception. Tailored for researchers, linguists, data scientists, and professionals, this chapter serves as a roadmap for unraveling the complexities of social media slang within the evolving field of Natural Language Processing for data analysis.

INTRODUCTION

Social media plays a pivotal role in contemporary society, serving as a multifaceted platform for communication, information dissemination, and community building. Its vast user base engages in diverse activities, generating an immense volume of data (Gupta & Hewett, 2020) that holds profound significance for various sectors. The data gleaned from social media platforms is a treasure trove for businesses, marketers, and researchers, offering insights into consumer behavior, market trends, and public sentiment. This wealth of information enables targeted advertising, informed decision-making, and the development of strategies that align with the preferences and needs of the audience (Assiri et al., 2016).

Amidst this data-rich environment, the importance of social media slang becomes evident in the realm of data analytics. Slang, often reflective of cultural nuances (Maskat & Munarko, 2019) and linguistic evolution, adds layers of complexity and context to the data. Understanding and analyzing social media slang allows for a more nuanced interpretation of user interactions, sentiment, and emerging trends (Divyapushpalakshmi & Ramalakshmi, 2021). It enhances sentiment analysis by capturing the informal and expressive nature of online conversations, contributing to a more accurate understanding of public opinion. Moreover, the dynamic nature of social media slang serves as an early indicator of cultural shifts and linguistic innovations, providing invaluable foresight for businesses and researchers.

In essence, the significance of social media lies not only in its vast user engagement but also in the data it generates, and the inclusion of slang in data analytics is instrumental in unraveling the intricate tapestry of digital communication, offering insights that go beyond the surface of conventional language analysis. Platforms like Facebook, X, Instagram, and others have metamorphosed into dynamic spaces fostering real-time conversations, opinion expression, and diverse online community participation (Dmitrichenkova et al., 2020). Within this expansive digital realm, the emergence of social media slang becomes a defining linguistic feature. Characterized by informality, creativity, and context-dependence, slang serves as a succinct vehicle for users to align with evolving cultural expressions, presenting both challenges and opportunities in comprehending user behavior and the dynamics of online discourse (Tan et al., 2016). Indispensable in extracting insights from the vast textual data generated on social media, Natural Language Processing (NLP) models utilize advanced algorithms to decipher language nuances (Kurera et al., 2022). This chapter embarks on an exploration of the vibrant world of social media slang within the broader NLP framework, acknowledging its role in both mirroring digital culture and presenting exciting challenges for data analysts.

The chapter's objectives encompass a thorough survey of social media slang, an investigation into the challenges it poses for NLP applications, and an exploration of innovative methodologies for tracking emerging trends within this linguistic domain. The nuanced task of sentiment analysis tailored to social media slang is also addressed, alongside strategies for integrating these expressions into traditional language models.

Recognizing the multilingual dimension of social media slang, the chapter emphasizes the necessity for NLP models to adapt to diverse linguistic expressions across various cultures and languages. Practical applications, such as brand monitoring and market research, underscore the tangible benefits of incorporating slang analysis into NLP frameworks. Tailored for researchers, linguists, data scientists, and professionals navigating the evolving landscape of online language, this chapter serves as a comprehensive guide. By addressing challenges, exploring innovative methodologies, and highlighting practical applications, it provides a roadmap for unraveling the complexities of social media slang within the context of data analysis.

THE LANDSCAPE OF SOCIAL MEDIA SLANG

Social media platforms have ushered in a distinctive linguistic landscape marked by the pervasive use of slang, shaping the way individuals communicate in the digital realm. This linguistic phenomenon is characterized by its informality, creativity, and rapid evolution. The use of slang on social media is not merely an assortment of colloquial expressions but represents a dynamic and evolving lexicon that plays a pivotal role in contemporary online communication.

Characteristics of Social Media Slang

Figure 1.

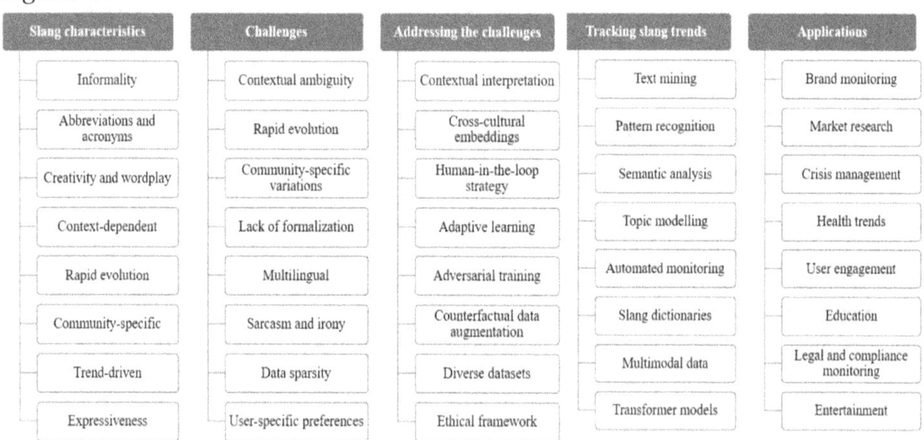

Social media slang is characterized by several distinctive features that set it apart from formal or traditional language. These characteristics contribute to its informality, creativity, and adaptability within the dynamic online communication landscape. Here are some key characteristics of social media slang:

Informality

Social media slang is inherently informal, often deviating from standard grammar and linguistic conventions (Li et al., 2019). It mirrors the casual and conversational tone prevalent in online interactions.

Abbreviations and Acronyms

Slang on social media frequently involves the use of abbreviations and acronyms to convey messages concisely (Kolajo et al., 2020). Users create and adopt shorthand expressions for common phrases or sentiments.

Creativity and Wordplay

Social media slang showcases a high degree of creativity and wordplay. Users coin new terms, blend words, or repurpose existing language to create expressions that resonate within specific communities (Seki & Liu, 2022).

Context-Dependent

The meaning of social media slang often depends on the context in which it is used. Words or phrases may have different interpretations based on the conversation or the community employing them (Kolajo et al., 2020).

Rapid Evolution

Social media slang evolves rapidly. New terms emerge, gain popularity, and may fall out of use quickly. This dynamism is influenced by internet culture, memes, and the ever-changing nature of online communication (Park et al., 2021).

Community-Specific

Slang is often community-specific, created and adopted by particular groups or subcultures within social media platforms (Tan et al., 2016). Different online communities may have their unique slang terms. It often fosters a sense of inclusivity and community among users who understand and use the same expressions. It creates a shared language that strengthens bonds within online communities.

Trend-Driven

Social media slang is heavily influenced by trends, memes, and popular culture. Terms may gain popularity due to their association with a viral trend or a widely shared piece of content (Permatasari & Karjo, 2023).

Expressiveness

Social media slang allows users to express themselves in a more expressive and personalized manner (Sun et al., 2019). It adds layers of meaning and emotion to messages, contributing to a sense of identity and individuality.

Understanding these characteristics is crucial for researchers, linguists, and data analysts aiming to navigate the unique linguistic landscape of social media slang and harness the insights embedded in it.

Evolution of Social Media Slang

The evolution of social media slang is a dynamic journey intertwined with the rapid expansion of online communication platforms. Originating from the early days of chatrooms and forums, social media slang gained momentum with the prevalence of text messaging and SMS culture, fostering brevity and abbreviation. The emergence of platforms like Facebook, X, and Instagram introduced new communication features, paving the way for the integration of slang into status updates, comments, and hashtags (Lin & Wu, 2022). Meme culture on platforms such as Reddit contributed to the viral dissemination of slang, often accompanied by catchphrases and expressions. Social media slang is heavily influenced by popular culture, reflecting trends from movies, TV shows, music, and celebrity influences. Online communities and subcultures have further contributed to the evolution, fostering their unique slang as a form of identity (Ghounane, 2020) and cohesion. The integration of emoticons and emojis added a visual dimension to slang, enriching expressions with emotional context. Characterized by rapid linguistic evolution, social media slang's popularity can soar or diminish swiftly, often fueled by viral trends or influential users. Cross-platform interactions and technological advances, such as speech-to-text features, contribute to the ongoing adaptability and widespread adoption of social media slang, making it a vibrant and ever-changing facet of contemporary online communication.

Significance in Capturing Nuances

The significance of social media slang in capturing nuances lies in its capacity to infuse online communication with expressiveness, cultural relevance, and conciseness. Beyond conveying emotions through emojis and emoticons, slang serves as a dynamic tool for users to express their identity within specific cultural contexts, fostering community building and a sense of belonging. The brevity and creativity inherent in slang allow for the succinct communication of complex ideas, humor, and irony, capturing nuanced tones that may be challenging to convey through formal language (Li et al., 2019). Its adaptability and constant evolution ensure that users stay attuned to cultural shifts and linguistic innovations, reflecting the dynamic nature of online communication and contributing to ongoing linguistic creativity.

In essence, social media slang represents a rich and dynamic linguistic resource that goes beyond the surface of informal expressions. Its characteristics, evolution, and significance are crucial components for researchers and practitioners seeking to decipher the intricacies of online communication within the context of NLP for data analysis.

CHALLENGES IN SLANG PROCESSING

Slang processing poses several challenges due to its dynamic, context-dependent, and ever-evolving nature. These challenges present obstacles for NLP systems aiming to accurately interpret and analyze social media slang. Here are some key challenges in slang processing:

Contextual Ambiguity

Slang terms often carry multiple meanings, and the intended interpretation heavily relies on the context in which they are used. The same slang expression might have different connotations in various conversations (Karatsareas, 2021), making it challenging for NLP systems to discern the intended sense accurately.

Rapid Evolution

Social media slang evolves swiftly, with new terms emerging and falling out of use rapidly. Keeping up with the constant evolution of slang presents a challenge for NLP models that need to adapt quickly to understand and interpret the latest expressions.

Community-Specific Variations

Slang is often community-specific, with different online communities or subcultures developing their unique expressions. Understanding and interpreting slang require domain-specific knowledge (Park et al., 2021), making it challenging for NLP systems to generalize across diverse online spaces.

Lack of Formalization

Slang often lacks formalized grammar and structure, deviating from standard language rules. It often involves informal spelling, abbreviations, and out-of-vocabulary words (Liu & Seki, 2021), making it challenging for NLP models to consistently recognize and interpret these non-standard linguistic forms.

Multilingual Challenges

Social media slang exists in multiple languages, each with its linguistic nuances. Processing slang across various languages and understanding the cultural contexts introduces additional complexity for multilingual NLP models (Nabiha et al., 2021).

Sarcasm and Irony

Slang is frequently used to convey sarcasm, irony, or humor. Identifying the intended tone behind slang expressions is challenging for NLP systems, as it requires a nuanced understanding of linguistic subtleties and contextual cues.

Data Sparsity

Some slang terms might have limited occurrences in the available training data for NLP models. Data sparsity can hinder the model's ability to accurately learn and generalize the meanings of less common or emerging slang expressions.

User-Specific Preferences

Understanding user-specific preferences and variations in the use of slang for specific groups (de Mendonca et al., 2020) is crucial. Users may have individualized ways of employing slang, and tailoring NLP models to individual linguistic patterns poses an additional challenge.

Addressing these challenges requires advanced NLP techniques that can adapt to the dynamic and context-dependent nature of social media slang, incorporating contextual understanding, cultural sensitivity, and the ability to learn from evolving linguistic landscapes.

STRATEGIES FOR OVERCOMING CHALLENGES

To overcome the challenges in processing social media slang, several strategies can be employed, leveraging advanced NLP techniques and considering the unique characteristics of slang. Utilize contextual embeddings and word embeddings to capture the contextual nuances of slang terms (Arora et al., 2020). These techniques enable NLP models to consider the surrounding words and context when interpreting the meaning of a slang expression. Implement adaptive learning models that can quickly adapt to the rapid evolution of slang. Techniques such as online learning or transfer learning can help NLP systems stay up-to-date with the latest slang expressions. Develop community-specific lexicons or dictionaries (Liu & Xia, 2019) that include slang terms used within specific online communities. Tailoring lexicons to different domains or subcultures enhances the accuracy of slang interpretation. Employ dynamic multilingual models that can process slang across various languages and adapt to cultural variations. Multilingual embeddings and models trained on diverse datasets contribute to a more comprehensive understanding of slang in different linguistic contexts. Develop specialized modules for sarcasm and irony detection within NLP systems (Wilson et al., 2020) to analyze linguistic cues, sentiment patterns, and contextual information to identify the intended tone behind slang expressions. Incorporate models that recognize and adapt to informal spelling patterns, abbreviations, and variations commonly used in slang which involves training NLP systems to recognize non-standard linguistic forms and understand their intended meanings. Augment training data with a diverse set of slang expressions, including less common or emerging terms. Data augmentation and synthesis techniques can help address data sparsity issues, ensuring that NLP models learn from a more comprehensive range of slang expressions. Implement user-adaptive models that learn from individual user preferences and linguistic patterns. Personalized NLP systems can better understand and interpret slang based on the specific ways in which users employ these expressions. Establish mechanisms for continuous monitoring and feedback to keep NLP models updated on evolving slang expressions.

Monitoring social media trends and user-generated content can provide valuable insights into emerging slang terms.

By integrating these strategies, NLP systems can better navigate the challenges posed by social media slang, ensuring more accurate interpretation and analysis of the dynamic and context-dependent nature of online language.

LEXICAL INNOVATIONS AND EMERGING TRENDS

The dynamic nature of social media slang necessitates innovative approaches within NLP to identify, analyze, and track lexical innovations and emerging trends. This section explores how NLP techniques can be leveraged for these purposes, emphasizing the importance of staying ahead of linguistic shifts and incorporating real-time updates into data analysis frameworks.

Identifying Lexical Innovations

Text Mining and Pattern Recognition

NLP can employ text mining (Aly & van der Haar, 2020) and pattern recognition algorithms to sift through large volumes of social media data and identify novel linguistic patterns. This involves detecting new words, phrases, or combinations thereof that deviate from established language norms. Unsupervised learning techniques, such as clustering and topic modeling, can assist in identifying lexical innovations.

Named Entity Recognition

NER techniques can be applied to recognize and categorize entities within social media slang, aiding in the identification of new terms and expressions (J. X. Liu et al., 2022). By extracting entities related to emerging trends, NLP models can highlight lexical innovations and track their usage over time.

Analyzing Emerging Trends

Sentiment Analysis and Emotion Detection

Sentiment analysis and emotion detection algorithms (Annadurai et al., 2023) can be applied to social media slang to discern evolving attitudes and sentiments. Monitoring shifts in sentiment associated with specific terms provides insights into emerging trends and helps contextualize the emotional impact of lexical innovations.

Topic Modeling and Latent Semantic Analysis

Employing topic modeling and latent semantic analysis (Han et al., 2020) can reveal the underlying themes and semantic structures within social media slang. By identifying clusters of related terms and topics, NLP models can discern emerging trends and associations, providing a deeper understanding of evolving linguistic dynamics.

Staying Ahead of Linguistic Shifts

To stay ahead of linguistic shifts, NLP models should undergo continuous training using updated datasets that reflect the latest social media slang. Techniques such as transfer learning and fine-tuning recent data ensure that models remain adaptive to evolving language patterns (Sun et al., 2019).

Incorporating Real-time Updates into Data Analysis

API Integration and Web Scraping

NLP systems can leverage social media APIs (Bhargavi et al., 2022) and web scraping techniques (Mancosu & Vegetti, 2020) to collect real-time data from platforms where slang is prevalent. Integrating these sources into the analysis pipeline enables the incorporation of the latest linguistic innovations into the data analysis process.

Automated slang evolution monitoring

Implementing automated models based on predefined linguistic criteria (Keidar et al., 2022) allows researchers and analysts to capture the evolution of when specific lexical innovations or emerging trends are detected. This proactive approach ensures that relevant updates are promptly incorporated into the ongoing data analysis.

The integration of NLP techniques for identifying lexical innovations and emerging trends in social media slang requires a combination of advanced methods such as text mining, sentiment analysis, and continuous model training. Staying ahead of linguistic shifts involves proactive strategies, including real-time data streaming and automated alert systems, to ensure that data analysis frameworks remain dynamic and reflective of the evolving lexicon of online communication.

SENTIMENT ANALYSIS OF SLANG EXPRESSIONS

In the realm of NLP, sentiment analysis serves as a crucial tool for understanding the emotional tone and attitudes expressed in textual data. This section focuses on the intricacies of performing sentiment analysis specifically tailored for social media slang, delving into how the unique expressions and tone of slang impact sentiment classification. Furthermore, methodologies for accurate sentiment attribution within this context are showcased.

Impact of Unique Expressions and Tone

Social media slang often employs unconventional expressions and tone, contributing to a nuanced representation of emotions. The brevity and informality inherent in slang may convey sentiments that traditional sentiment analysis models struggle to capture. Understanding the subtleties of expressions becomes pivotal for accurate sentiment classification. Slang expressions are deeply embedded in cultural (Karkaeva, 2018) and contextual nuances, with meanings varying across online communities. Sentiment analysis models must account for this variability and adapt to the specific cultural and contextual references present in social media slang to ensure precise sentiment attribution.

Methodologies for Accurate Sentiment Attribution

Contextual Embeddings and Deep Learning

Leveraging contextual embeddings, such as those obtained through deep learning models like BERT (Koroteev, 2021), allows sentiment analysis models to capture the context surrounding slang expressions. This enables a more nuanced understanding of sentiment by considering the broader linguistic context in which the slang is used.

Emotion Lexicons and Slang Dictionaries

Integrating emotion lexicons and slang dictionaries (Gupta et al., 2019) specific to social media expressions enhances sentiment analysis accuracy. These resources provide sentiment polarity scores for individual words, including slang terms, facilitating a more fine-grained analysis of sentiment within the unique linguistic landscape of social media.

User-Generated Training Data

Collecting and incorporating user-generated training data that includes labeled examples of sentiment within social media slang is essential (Seki & Liu, 2022). This allows sentiment analysis models to learn from the diverse ways in which users express emotions using slang, adapting to the constantly evolving lexicon of online communication.

Thus, sentiment analysis tailored for social media slang demands a specialized approach that considers the impact of unique expressions and tone on sentiment classification. By leveraging contextual embeddings, emotion lexicons, and user-generated training data, NLP models can accurately attribute sentiment within the evolving and dynamic lexicon of social media slang. Addressing challenges such as irony detection and multilingual considerations ensures a comprehensive and nuanced understanding of sentiment within the context of online communication.

Benefits of Incorporating Slang

Incorporating slang into social media analytics offers multifaceted benefits, enhancing the authenticity and depth of online communication analysis. By capturing the genuine language expressions used by users within various online communities, the inclusion of slang enriches sentiment analysis, providing a more nuanced understanding of user emotions (Park et al., 2021). Additionally, slang analysis facilitates the identification of cultural and subcultural trends, enabling businesses to stay culturally relevant and engage with target audiences more effectively (Tan et al., 2016). This linguistic approach enhances user engagement strategies by allowing brands to connect authentically with their audience, ultimately strengthening the effectiveness of marketing campaigns (Liu et al., 2022). Moreover, the dynamic nature of slang makes it a valuable resource for trend prediction, helping businesses anticipate and capitalize on emerging expressions before they become mainstream. The incorporation of slang into social media analytics thus not only contributes to a more accurate understanding of user behavior but also strengthens the overall capabilities of NLP models.

MULTILINGUAL CONSIDERATIONS

The exploration of social media slang within the context of NLP necessitates an examination of its multilingual aspects. This section delves into how NLP models can adapt to diverse linguistic expressions across different cultures and languages, discussing both the challenges and opportunities in processing slang in a global context.

Opportunities for Multilingual Slang Processing

Multilingual slang processing offers a multitude of opportunities across diverse domains (Lo et al., 2017). In the global market, businesses can gain valuable insights into consumer sentiments and trends, adapting marketing strategies for international audiences. Improved cross-cultural communication is facilitated by accurately interpreting and translating slang expressions, fostering understanding in diverse settings. Social listening tools employing multilingual slang processing enable real-time monitoring of global conversations, aiding organizations in crisis management on a worldwide scale. Enhanced international brand engagement (Manh et al., 2021) is achievable by tailoring communication strategies to regional slang, ensuring a culturally resonant connection. Customer support systems benefit from better understanding and responding to user queries in various languages, contributing to efficient global support services. Content creators, especially in entertainment and media, can leverage multilingual slang processing for culturally sensitive content creation. Multilingual conversational services of chatbots are facilitated by overcoming linguistic barriers, and the identification of global trends is streamlined through the analysis of slang expressions, offering a comprehensive approach to inclusive and culturally aware interactions on a global scale (Adeniyi et al., 2022).

Challenges in Multilingual Slang Processing

The technical implementation of multilingual slang processing in social media data encounters novel challenges arising from the dynamic and evolving nature of online communication. Some emerging challenges include the widespread use of emojis (Kongyoung et al., 2021) and emoticons in social media communication, adding a layer of complexity to multilingual slang processing. Understanding the nuanced meaning conveyed by these visual elements, especially when combined with slang, requires innovative techniques. With the increasing prevalence of multimedia content on social media, integrating slang with images, videos, and audio presents a novel challenge. Developing models that can effectively process and analyze the synergy between multilingual slang and various forms of media is essential for comprehensive understanding.

Ensuring consistency in processing multilingual slang across different social media platforms poses a challenge (Hagen & de Zeeuw, 2023) due to variations in user demographics, linguistic norms, and the evolution of slang trends on each platform. Developing adaptable models that account for these differences is critical. The rise of deepfake technology and the generation of synthetic content introduce challenges in distinguishing authentic multilingual slang from artificially generated text. Developing algorithms that can discern between genuine and manipulated language expressions is imperative for maintaining accuracy.

Users frequently coin new words and expressions on social media, leading to the emergence of neologisms (Seki & Liu, 2022). Processing these user-generated terms, especially in a multilingual context, requires models that can adapt to evolving linguistic landscapes. Recognizing and adapting to inclusive language, including gender-neutral expressions and terms that respect diverse identities, is an evolving challenge. Implementing models that can navigate and understand the nuances of inclusive language within multilingual slang is a novel technical consideration.

Addressing the challenges in multilingual slang

Addressing the challenges in multilingual slang processing involves employing a combination of linguistic insights, advanced machine-learning techniques, and a nuanced understanding of cultural variations. Utilizing libraries such as spaCy or Natural Language Toolkit for tokenization and integrating pre-trained models like BERT (Yenduri et al., 2021) would enhance the model's capability to interpret multilingual slang, including the nuanced meanings conveyed by emojis. Deploy deep learning frameworks such as TensorFlow or PyTorch to create models that effectively process both textual and visual data concurrently. Adapt models, such as vision transformers (ViTs) (Elbedwehy et al., 2022) and multimodal transformers, to seamlessly integrate slang with images, videos, and audio. Develop adaptable models by incorporating platform-specific training data. Employ techniques like domain adaptation to ensure the model adeptly adjusts to linguistic norms and slang trends across diverse social media platforms.

Implement deepfake detection algorithms using frameworks like OpenCV and TensorFlow for enhancing accuracy. Regularly update the model to adapt to the ever-evolving landscape of deepfake techniques. Identify and cluster new words and expressions through unsupervised learning techniques, combined with algorithms like word embeddings (Word2Vec, GloVe), to capture semantic relationships between terms (Ghosal & Jain, 2023). Regularly update the model with new user-generated content to enable adaptation to continuously evolving linguistic landscapes. Train models to recognize and adapt to inclusive language by incorporating diverse datasets that encompass gender-neutral expressions and terms respecting diverse identities. Implement attention mechanisms to capture language nuances, coupled with regular updates, to ensure the model remains attuned to evolving inclusive language trends.

By integrating these strategies, it becomes possible to develop robust and culturally aware models for multilingual slang processing. These approaches contribute to a more accurate understanding of slang expressions across diverse languages and facilitate effective communication in a global, multilingual context.

GLOBAL CONSIDERATIONS AND ETHICAL DIMENSIONS

In the rapidly evolving landscape of social media slang and NLP, global considerations and ethical dimensions play a crucial role in shaping the direction and impact of data analysis. As we delve into deciphering the lexicon of social media, it becomes imperative to address the broader implications and responsibilities associated with this powerful tool.

Cultural Sensitivity in NLP

Processing social media slang in a global context requires an awareness of and respect for cultural sensitivities. Language models must be designed to avoid reinforcing stereotypes or biases, ensuring that the processing of slang aligns with ethical standards and cultural norms. The technical solution to address cultural sensitivity involves training models on diverse datasets, implementing cross-cultural embeddings, enhancing contextual understanding with transformer-based models, incorporating human-in-the-loop approaches (Wu et al., 2022) for nuanced interpretation, and employing adaptive learning mechanisms to stay attuned to evolving linguistic trends. These measures collectively aim to mitigate biases, improve accuracy, and ensure that NLP analyses of social media slang are culturally sensitive and inclusive

User-Generated Content Moderation

In multilingual environments, user-generated content moderation becomes crucial. NLP models should include mechanisms to filter out offensive or inappropriate slang expressions across different languages, promoting a safe and respectful online environment (de Freitas et al., 2019).

Collaborative Frameworks for Ethical NLP

In the pursuit of global ethical standards, collaboration emerges as a key theme. Collaborative frameworks involving researchers, industry experts, and regulatory bodies foster an international dialogue on best practices and ethical guidelines. By sharing insights and experiences, the NLP community can collectively address challenges, learn from diverse perspectives, and contribute to the establishment of a global ethical framework for social media slang analysis

Privacy, Consent, and Global Standards

Respecting user privacy and obtaining informed consent in the context of NLP for social media slang analysis requires adherence to robust ethical standards. Beyond complying with established regulations such as the General Data Protection Regulation (GDPR) (Torre et al., 2021), ethical practices should involve implementing granular consent mechanisms, allowing users to specify data usage preferences and purposes. Platforms should maintain user-friendly privacy policies that are easily accessible and comprehensible, detailing the NLP analysis process and data utilization. Employing strong data anonymization and pseudonymization techniques is paramount to safeguarding user identities, and a commitment to data minimization ensures only essential information is collected. Regular privacy impact assessments (PIAs) (Fernández & Sindre, 2020) should be conducted to evaluate and address potential risks, and secure data storage practices, including encryption and access controls, must be maintained. User education initiatives should be established to enhance awareness of privacy considerations, empowering users to make informed decisions about their data contribution. Incorporating these ethical standards ensures transparency, user autonomy, and the responsible use of data in NLP analyses, fostering trust and aligning practices with evolving global ethical norms.

Adapting NLP models to diverse linguistic expressions requires a combination of cross-cultural adaptation, context-aware translation, and domain adaptation. By addressing these challenges and leveraging opportunities, NLP can navigate the rich tapestry of multilingual global social media slang, contributing to a more inclusive analysis of online communication.

APPLICATIONS

Social media slang analysis has evolved into a powerful tool with diverse applications, particularly in areas such as brand monitoring and market research. This section showcases practical applications and discusses how insights derived from NLP-driven analysis of slang usage can inform marketing strategies and enhance brand perception.

Brand Monitoring

Sentiment Analysis for Brand Perception

Social media slang analysis, coupled with sentiment analysis, allows businesses to monitor how their brand is perceived online (Liu et al., 2022). NLP models can discern sentiment-laden slang expressions, providing real-time insights into the emotional tone associated with the brand. Positive or negative sentiments in slang can be indicative of overall brand sentiment, aiding in proactive brand management.

Identifying Brand Advocacy and Criticism

By analyzing social media slang, businesses can identify instances of brand advocacy or criticism within online communities. NLP models can sift through the vast amount of user-generated content to pinpoint instances where slang terms are used to express support or discontent. This information is valuable for understanding brand sentiment dynamics and engaging with customers in a targeted manner.

Market Research

Product Perception and Feature Analysis

Social media slang analysis can be applied to understand how users express opinions about products and features. NLP models can identify slang terms associated with specific product attributes or features, providing insights into user preferences and expectations. This information informs product development strategies and allows businesses to align offerings with consumer desires.

Trend Identification and Forecasting

Analyzing slang usage enables businesses to identify emerging trends and forecast market shifts. NLP models can recognize linguistic innovations and evolving expressions, helping businesses stay ahead of the curve in terms of product development, marketing campaigns, advertising, and overall market positioning (Liu et al., 2019).

Crisis Management

Analyzing social media slang during crises or emergencies provides organizations with real-time insights into public reactions. This can aid in crisis management by understanding the evolving sentiment, identifying misinformation, and responding appropriately to concerns expressed through slang (Ghounane, 2020).

Healthcare and Public Health

Social media slang analytics can contribute to public health research by monitoring discussions related to health and well-being (Guo et al., 2022). Tracking slang terms associated with health conditions, lifestyle choices, or mental health can provide valuable insights for healthcare professionals, policymakers, and researchers.

Educational Research and Student Engagement

In the education sector, analyzing social media slang can offer insights into student engagement, preferences, and challenges. Educational institutions can adapt their communication strategies and curricula to better connect with students, fostering a more engaging learning environment.

Legal and Compliance Monitoring

Social media slang analytics can assist in monitoring legal and compliance-related discussions (Raju & Subbaraj, 2020). Organizations can track online conversations for potential legal risks, compliance violations, or discussions related to industry regulations, helping them stay informed and mitigate risks.

Tourism and Destination Management

Analyzing social media slang can provide valuable information for the tourism industry (Ghosal & Jain, 2023). Understanding how travelers express preferences, share experiences, and discuss destinations using slang terms helps tourism boards and businesses tailor their services and marketing efforts.

Entertainment Industry Insights

Monitoring social media slang within the entertainment industry provides insights into audience reactions, preferences, and trends related to movies (Ho et al., 2022), TV shows, music, and celebrities. This information helps entertainment companies tailor their content and marketing strategies.

The applications of social media slang analytics extend into vital areas of brand monitoring and market research, providing actionable insights for informed decision-making. NLP-driven understanding of slang usage enables businesses to enhance brand perception, tailor marketing strategies, and engage authentically with their target audience in the dynamic landscape of online communication.

CONCLUSION

This chapter serves as a comprehensive exploration of the intersection of traditional NLP approaches and the dynamic world of social media slang. This chapter has endeavored to provide valuable insights into the challenges, methodologies, and practical applications associated with incorporating social media slang into NLP frameworks. The chapter recognizes the evolving nature of online communication and the integral role social media slang plays in shaping linguistic landscapes. Acknowledging this, the aim is to bridge the gap between conventional NLP methodologies and social media slang's expressive, ever-changing lexicon. In doing so, researchers and practitioners are empowered to navigate the intricacies of this vibrant linguistic realm.

The challenges posed by social media slang, including ambiguity, context dependency, and the rapid emergence of new terms, are highlighted and discussed in-depth. Strategies for overcoming these challenges, ranging from contextual embeddings to continuous model training, are presented as essential tools for enhancing the effectiveness of NLP applications in processing slang. The chapter delves into innovative methodologies such as sentiment analysis tailored for social media slang, lexical innovations tracking, and integration with traditional language models. These methodologies leverage advancements in NLP to capture the nuances of slang expressions, enabling a more profound understanding of online language dynamics.

Practical applications in brand monitoring, market research, and marketing strategy development demonstrate the tangible benefits of social media slang analysis. By deciphering sentiment, identifying emerging trends, and adapting to diverse linguistic expressions, NLP-driven insights inform strategic decision-making and contribute to a more authentic engagement with online communities. In essence, this chapter serves as a roadmap for researchers, linguists, data scientists, and professionals interested in the intersection of social media slang and NLP. Navigating the challenges, exploring innovative methodologies, and showcasing practical applications, equips readers with the tools and knowledge needed to unravel the complexities of slang within the realm of data analysis.

As social media slang continues to evolve, and online communication landscapes shift, the roadmap provided in this chapter encourages a forward-looking perspective. Continuous adaptation, ethical considerations, and a commitment to understanding linguistic diversity are essential aspects for future research and practical implementation in the ever-expanding field of social media slang analysis within NLP frameworks. In conclusion, "Deciphering the Lexicon: Social Media Slang in Natural Language Processing for Data Analysis" chapter contributes to the ongoing discourse on the transformative role of social media slang in linguistic analysis, providing a foundation for future explorations and advancements in the field of Natural Language Processing.

REFERENCES

Adeniyi, A. E., Olagunju, M., Awotunde, J. B., Abiodun, M. K., Awokola, J., & Lawrence, M. O. (2022). Augmented Intelligence Multilingual Conversational Service for Smart Enterprise Management Software. *Computational Science and Its Applications - Iccsa 2022 Workshops, Part V, 13381*, 476-488. https://doi.org/DOI: 10.1007/978-3-031-10548-7_35

Aly, E. S., & van der Haar, D. T. (2020). Slang-Based Text Sentiment Analysis in Instagram. *Fourth International Congress on Information and Communication Technology,* Vol 2, *1027*, 321-329. https://doi.org/DOI: 10.1007/978-981-32-9343-4_25

Annadurai, S., Arock, M., & Vadivel, A. (2023). Real and fake emotion detection using enhanced boosted support vector machine algorithm. *Multimedia Tools and Applications*, *82*(1), 1333–1353. DOI: 10.1007/s11042-022-13210-6

Arora, S., May, A., Zhang, J., & Ré, C., & Assoc Computat, L. (2020). Contextual Embeddings: When Are They Worth It? *58th Annual Meeting of the Association for Computational Linguistics (Acl 2020)*, 2650-2663. DOI: 10.18653/v1/2020.acl-main.236

Assiri, A., Emam, A., & Al-dossari, H. (2016). Real-Time Sentiment Analysis of Saudi Dialect Tweets Using SPARK. *2016 ieee international conference on big data (big data)*, 3947-3950.

Bhargavi, K., Mashankar, P., Sreevarsh, P. V., Bilolikar, R., & Ranganathan, P. (2022). Machine Learning-Based Sentiment Analysis Towards Indian Ministry. *Computational Vision and Bio-Inspired Computing (Iccvbic 2021), 1420*, 381-391. https://doi.org/DOI: 10.1007/978-981-16-9573-5_28

de Freitas, P. V. A., dos Santos, G. N. P., Busson, A. J. G., Guedes, A. L. V., & Colcher, S., & Assoc Comp, M. (2019). A Baseline for NSFW Video Detection in E-Learning Environments. *Webmedia 2019:Proceedings of the 25th Brazillian Symposium on Multimedia and the Web*, 357-360. https://doi.org/DOI: 10.1145/3323503.3360625 de Mendonca, R. R., de Brito, D. F., Rosa, F. D., dos Reis, J. C., & Bonacin, R. (2020). A Framework for Detecting Intentions of Criminal Acts in Social Media: A Case Study on Twitter. *Information (Basel), 11*(3), 154. Advance online publication. DOI: 10.3390/info11030154

Divyapushpalakshmi, M., & Ramalakshmi, R. (2021). An efficient sentimental analysis using hybrid deep learning and optimization technique for Twitter using parts of speech (POS) tagging. *International Journal of Speech Technology, 24*(2), 329–339. DOI: 10.1007/s10772-021-09801-7

Dmitrichenkova, S. V., Dolzhich, E. A., & Pozuelo, Y. S. (2020, Apr 24-25). YOUTH SLANG IN SOCIAL NETS (A CASE STUDY OF SPANISH LANGUAGE).*European Proceedings of Social and Behavioural Sciences.* 9th International Research and Practical Conference on Topical Issues of Linguistics and Teaching Methods in Business and Professional Communication (TILTM), Peoples Friendship Univ Russia, RUSSIA.

Elbedwehy, S., Medhat, T., Hamza, T., & Alrahmawy, M. F. (2022). Efficient Image Captioning Based on Vision Transformer Models. *Cmc-Computers Materials & Continua, 73*(1), 1483–1500. DOI: 10.32604/cmc.2022.029313

Fernández, A. P., & Sindre, G. (2020). Software Assisted Privacy Impact Assessment in Interactive Ubiquitous Computing Systems. *Digital Transformation for a Sustainable Society in the 21st Century, 573*, 60-71. https://doi.org/DOI: 10.1007/978-3-030-39634-3_6

Ghosal, S., & Jain, A. (2023). Weighted aspect based sentiment analysis using extended OWA operators and Word2Vec for tourism. *Multimedia Tools and Applications, 82*(12), 18353–18380. DOI: 10.1007/s11042-022-13800-4

Ghounane, N. (2020). A Thorough Examination of Teens Drug Slang in Algeria. *Arab World English Journal, 11*(1), 419–431. DOI: 10.24093/awej/vol11no1.28

Guo, J. W., Kimmel, J., & Linder, L. A. (2022). Text Analysis of Suicide Risk in Adolescents and Young Adults. *Journal of the American Psychiatric Nurses Association. Article, 10783903221077292.* Advance online publication. DOI: 10.1177/10783903221077292 PMID: 35130778

Gupta, A., Taneja, S., Malik, G., Vij, S., Tayal, D., & Jain, A. (2019). fSLANGZY: A fuzzy logic-based algorithm for English slang meaning selection [Article]. *Progress in Artificial Intelligence*, *8*(1), 111–121. DOI: 10.1007/s13748-018-0159-3

Gupta, V., & Hewett, R. (2020). Real-Time Tweet Analytics Using Hybrid Hashtags on Twitter Big Data Streams. *Information (Basel)*, *11*(7), 341. Advance online publication. DOI: 10.3390/info11070341

Hagen, S., & de Zeeuw, D. (2023). Based and confused: Tracing the political connotations of a memetic phrase across the web. *Big Data & Society*, *10*(1), 20539517231163175. Advance online publication. DOI: 10.1177/20539517231163175

Han, K. X., Chien, W., Chiu, C. C., & Cheng, Y. T. (2020). Application of Support Vector Machine (SVM) in the Sentiment Analysis of Twitter DataSet. *Applied Sciences (Basel, Switzerland)*, *10*(3), 1125. Advance online publication. DOI: 10.3390/app10031125

Ho, I. H. J., Goh, H. N., & Tan, Y. F. (2022). Inducing a Malay Lexicon from an Unlabelled Dataset Using Word Embeddings. *Lecture Notes in Computer Science*, *13343*, 382–394. DOI: 10.1007/978-3-031-08530-7_32

Karatsareas, P. (2021). From village talk to slang: The re-enregisterment of a non-standardised variety in an urban diaspora. *Journal of Multilingual and Multicultural Development*, *42*(9), 827–839. DOI: 10.1080/01434632.2020.1767115

Karkaeva, M. A. (2018). A socio-cultural phenomenon of youth slang in the cyberspace. *Filologicheskie Nauki-Nauchnye Doklady Vysshei Shkoly-Philological Sciences-Scientific Essays of Higher Education*, (3), 45–49. DOI: 10.20339/PhS.3-18.045

Keidar, D., Opedal, A., Jin, Z., Sachan, M., & Assoc Computat, L. (2022). Slangvolution: A Causal Analysis of Semantic Change and Frequency Dynamics in Slang. *Proceedings of the 60th Annual Meeting of the Association for Computational Linguistics (Acl 2022), Vol 1: (Long Papers)*, 1422-1442.

Kolajo, T., Daramola, O., Adebiyi, A., & Seth, A. (2020). A framework for pre-processing of social media feeds based on integrated local knowledge base. *Information Processing & Management, 57*(6), 102348. Advance online publication. DOI: 10.1016/j.ipm.2020.102348

Kongyoung, S., Trakultaweekoon, K., & Rugchatjaroen, A. (2021). Thai Language Tweet Emotion Prediction based on Use of Emojis. *16th International Joint Symposium on Artificial Intelligence and Natural Language Processing (Isai-Nlp 2021)*. https://doi.org/DOI: 10.1109/iSAI-NLP54397.2021.9678160

Koroteev, M. (2021). *BERT: A Review of Applications in Natural Language Processing and Understanding*. https://doi.org//arXiv.2103.11943DOI: 10.48550

Kurera, W. S. A., Rajapaksha, R. K., Rupasinghe, H. A. P., Liyanage, K., Kasthuriarachchi, S., & Rajapakshe, S. & Ieee. (2022, Nov 30-Dec 01). Building NLP Tools to Process Sinhala Text Data Written using English Letters.*International Conference on Advances in ICT for Emerging Regions*, Univ Colombo Sch Comp, Colombo, SRI LANKA.

Li, D., Rzepka, R., Ptaszynski, M., & Araki, K. (2019). *A Novel Machine Learning-based Sentiment Analysis Method for Chinese Social Media Considering Chinese Slang Lexicon and Emoticons.*

Lin, M. F., & Wu, D. D. (2022). Rapport building by Chinese celebrities on Weibo and Facebook. *Chinese Language and Discourse, 13*(1), 7–27. DOI: 10.1075/cld.21031.lin

Liu, J. X., Cheng, J. R., Wang, Z. Y., Lou, C. Q., Shen, C. L., & Sheng, V. S. (2022). A Survey of Deep Learning for Named Entity Recognition in Chinese Social Media. *Artificial Intelligence and Security. Lecture Notes in Computer Science, 13338*(Pt I), 573–582. DOI: 10.1007/978-3-031-06794-5_46

Liu, Q., & Xia, Z. (2019, 21-22 Sept. 2019). Multi-layer LSTM Network Statement Generation Based on Mixed Input. *2019 Seventh International Conference on Advanced Cloud and Big Data (CBD)* DOI: 10.1109/CBD.2019.00048

Liu, S., Gui, D.-Y., Zuo, Y., & Dai, Y. (2019). Good Slang or Bad Slang? Embedding Internet Slang in Persuasive Advertising. *Frontiers in Psychology, 10*, 1251. DOI: 10.3389/fpsyg.2019.01251 PMID: 31231278

Liu, W., Wu, Y., & Gong, W. (2022). Measuring Internet Slang Style in the Marketing Context: Scale Development and Validation. *Frontiers in Psychology, 12*, 751806. Advance online publication. DOI: 10.3389/fpsyg.2021.751806 PMID: 35115982

ADDITIONAL READING

Agarwal, N., Ünlü, T., Wani, M. A., & Bours, P. (2021, October). Predatory conversation detection using transfer learning approach. In *International Conference on Machine Learning, Optimization, and Data Science* (pp. 488-499). Cham: Springer International Publishing.

Agarwal, N., Wani, M. A., & Bours, P. (2020). Lex-pos feature-based grammar error detection system for the English language. *Electronics (Basel), 9*(10), 1686. DOI: 10.3390/electronics9101686

Ahmad, P. N., Liu, Y., Ali, G., Wani, M. A., & ElAffendi, M. (2023). Robust benchmark for propagandist text detection and mining high-quality data. *Mathematics, 11*(12), 2668. DOI: 10.3390/math11122668

Hammad, M., Wani, M. A., Shakil, K. A., Shaiba, H., & Abd El-Latif, A. A. (2024). Deep cancelable multibiometric finger vein and fingerprint authentication with non-negative matrix factorization. *IEEE Access : Practical Innovations, Open Solutions, 12*, 120638–120660. DOI: 10.1109/ACCESS.2024.3450372

Imran, A. S., Hodnefjeld, H., Kastrati, Z., Fatima, N., Daudpota, S. M., & Wani, M. A. (2023). Classifying european court of human rights cases using transformer-based techniques. *IEEE Access : Practical Innovations, Open Solutions, 11*, 55664–55676. DOI: 10.1109/ACCESS.2023.3279034

Khairutdinov, R. R., Mukhametzyanova, F. G., & Gaysina, A. R. (2017). Socio-psychological characteristics of the subject use of slang and abbreviations in english-speaking social networks. *Turkish Online Journal of Design Art and Communication*, *7*, 832–839. DOI: 10.7456/1070ase/090

Matsumoto, K., Ren, F. J., Matsuoka, M., Yoshida, M., & Kita, K. (2019). Slang feature extraction by analysing topic change on social media. *CAAI Transactions on Intelligence Technology*, *4*(1), 64–71. DOI: 10.1049/trit.2018.1060

Mody, D., Huang, Y. D., & de Oliveira, T. E. A. (2023). A curated dataset for hate speech detection on social media text. *Data in Brief*, *46*, 108832. Advance online publication. DOI: 10.1016/j.dib.2022.108832 PMID: 36605500

Rawat, A., Wani, M. A., ElAffendi, M., Imran, A. S., Kastrati, Z., & Daudpota, S. M. (2022). Drug adverse event detection using text-based convolutional neural networks (TextCNN) technique. *Electronics (Basel)*, *11*(20), 3336. DOI: 10.3390/electronics11203336

Sedik, A., El-Latif, A. A. A., Wani, M. A., El-Samie, F. E. A., Bauomy, N. A. S., & Hashad, F. G. (2023). Efficient multi-biometric secure-storage scheme based on deep learning and crypto-mapping techniques. *Mathematics*, *11*(3), 703. DOI: 10.3390/math11030703

Shakil, K. A., Tabassum, K., Alqahtani, F. S., & Wani, M. A. (2021). Analyzing user digital emotions from a holy versus non-pilgrimage city in Saudi Arabia on Twitter Platform. *Applied Sciences (Basel, Switzerland)*, *11*(15), 6846. DOI: 10.3390/app11156846

Sundaram, A., Subramaniam, H., Hamid, S. H. A., & Nor, A. M. (2023). A Systematic Literature Review on Social Media Slang Analytics in Contemporary Discourse. *IEEE Access : Practical Innovations, Open Solutions*, *11*, 132457–132471. https://doi.org/https://doi.org/10.1109/access.2023.3334278. DOI: 10.1109/ACCESS.2023.3334278

Ul Haq, N., Ullah, M., Khan, R., Ahmad, A., Almogren, A., Hayat, B., & Shafi, B. (2020). USAD: An Intelligent System for Slang and Abusive Text Detection in PERSO-Arabic-Scripted Urdu. *Complexity*, *2020*, 6684995. Advance online publication. DOI: 10.1155/2020/6684995

Venkataraman, J., & Mohandoss, L. (2023). FBO-RNN: Fuzzy butterfly optimization-based RNN-LSTM for extracting sentiments from Twitter Emoji database. *Concurrency and Computation*, *35*(12), e7683. Advance online publication. DOI: 10.1002/cpe.7683

Wani, M. A., Bours, P., Agarwal, N., & Jabin, S. (2019). Emotion-based mining for gender prediction in online social networks. In *Proceedings of the ACM, International Conference on Machine Learning and Data Science*.

Wani, M. A., ELAffendi, M., Bours, P., Imran, A. S., Hussain, A., & Abd El-Latif, A. A. (2024). Codes: A deep learning framework for identifying covid-caused depression symptoms. *Cognitive Computation*, *16*(1), 305–325. DOI: 10.1007/s12559-023-10190-z

Wani, M. A., ElAffendi, M., & Shakil, K. A. (2024). AI-Generated Spam Review Detection Framework with Deep Learning Algorithms and Natural Language Processing. Computers (2073-431X), 13(10).

Wijayanti, R., & Arisal, A. (2021). Automatic Indonesian Sentiment Lexicon Curation with Sentiment Valence Tuning for Social Media Sentiment Analysis. *Acm Transactions on Asian and Low-Resource Language Information Processing, 20*(1).

KEY TERMS AND DEFINITIONS

Contextual Ambiguity: Uncertainty or lack of clarity in the meaning of a word or phrase due to an insufficient context, leading to multiple possible interpretations.

Data Anonymization: Process of removing personally identifiable information from a dataset to protect the privacy of individuals.

Emotion Lexicons: Words or terms specifically associated with various emotions that are categorized based on their emotional connotations.

Feature Analysis: In the context of machine learning, feature analysis involves evaluating the relevance and impact of individual features on the model's performance.

Linguistic Shifts: Changes or transformations in language usage, encompassing alterations in vocabulary, syntax, semantics, or overall linguistic conventions over a specific period or within a particular context.

Sentiment Analysis: It is a computational and natural language processing technique used to evaluate and determine the sentiment expressed in a piece of text, ascertaining whether the sentiment is positive, negative, or neutral.

Sentiment Attribution: Determining the origin or reason behind the positive, negative, or neutral emotions conveyed within a piece of language.

Slang: A type of informal language characterized by unconventional words, expressions, acronyms that often deviate from standard linguistic norms.

Slang Dictionaries: Reference works that compile and define words, expressions, and phrases belonging to informal, non-standard language usage.

Text Mining: Process of extracting valuable insights, patterns, and knowledge from large volumes of unstructured text data.

Chapter 4
Deep Mixed Activated Long Short-Term Memory-Restricted Boltzmann Recurrent Neural Network for Piano Melody Generation

Amartya Mukherjee
https://orcid.org/0000-0002-6535-1181
Institute of Engineering and Management, Kolkata, India

Snehan Biswas
IEMA R&D Pvt. Ltd., India

Ayan Kumar Panja
Institute of Engineering and Management, Kolkata, India

Satyajit Chakrabarti
Institute of Engineering and Management, Kolkata, India

Souvik Chatterjee
IEMA R&D Pvt. Ltd., India

Dhritesh Bhagat
Institute of Engineering and Management, Kolkata, India

DOI: 10.4018/979-8-3693-2935-1.ch004

ABSTRACT

This paper deals with,a very unique way of implementing the Long Short Term Memory Algorithm (LSTM) in the field of musical melody generation. We have used this LSTM in an advanced way which can be amalgamated with another special deep learning architecture, known as the Restricted Boltzmann Machine (RBM), thus giving rise to a completely new form of LSTM Algorithm for Musical Melody Generation, which we call the Deep Mixed Activated Long Short Term Memory Restricted Boltzmann Recurrent Neural Network Machine (DMA-LSTM-RBRNN). The DMA-LSTM-RBRNN can generate melodies with a corresponding training accuracy of 80.78%, validation accuracy of 81.52% and corresponding training loss of 0.5965, validation loss of 0.5634, and we see that the DMA-LSTM-RBRNN's validation accuracy is leading the training accuracy and the validation loss is lagging the training loss.

1 INTRODUCTION

Music Theory is the study of the practices and possibilities of music and also frequently concerned with describing how musicians and composers make music, including tuning systems and composition methods among other topics. Because of the ever-expanding conception of what constitutes music, a more inclusive definition can be concluded from past studies, i.e., Music Theory is the consideration of any sonic phenomena, including silence, as they relate to music. Music Theory as a practical discipline encompasses the methods and concepts composers and other musicians use in creating wonderful music and melodies. The development, preservation, and transmission of music theory in this sense may be found in oral and written music-making traditions, musical instruments, and other artifacts. The scholarly study of music theory in the 20th century has several different subfields, each of which takes a different perspective on what are the primary phenomenon of interest and the most useful methods for investigation.

- Analysis of Music Sheets (Attempt to answer the question about how the music works)
- Music Perception and Music Cognition (Psychology of Music, both Music-Psychology and Musicology)
- Genre and Technique (The types of music or the tune of music as well)
- Musical Mathematics (ComputationalMusic)
- Serial Composition and set theory
- Musical semiotics (Musical semiology, i.e., Semiotics, is the study of signs as they pertain to music on a variety of levels, the persons behind this idea were Roman Jakobson and Kofi Agawu
- Musical Research and Musical Careers

Defining a musical melody as the linear succession of musical tones that the listener perceives as a single entity. In its most literal sense, a musical melody is a combination of pitch and rhythm, while more figuratively, the term can include successions of other musical elements such as tonal color. It is the foreground to the background accompaniment. Melodies often consist of one or more musical phrases or motifs and are usually used to increase the listening perspective of any music. Some examples are given below about different melodies.Having used an awesome software known as Muse Score, which is used for Computational Music Theory and Music Information Retrieval.

Figure 1. A Diagrammatic Representation of a Piano Melody, viewed on Muse Score Software

The rest of the article has been arranged in the following flow. In section 2 we have discussed the related works, in section 3 we have proposed our state-of-the-art methodology, section 4 describes the entire result analysis, section 5 we have incorporated the discussion and we have concluded our work in section 6.

2 RELATED WORKS

Generating new melodies with the help of Deep Learning and Music Theory is a veritably unique way of pre-processing Music Data and algorithms for the generation of new melodies (Yang et al., 2021; Briot et al., 2020). Structuring machine learning models to classify, describe, or induce audio or music, involves concerning modelling tasks where input data are audio samples (Agarwal et al., 2018). Deep Learning can be used to pre-process musical datain a veritably unique manner and planting to understand a work which demonstrates the colorful exertion,performing with a Neuron for Musical Melody Generation and therefore understanding the power of deep learning in the field of Data Science (Lu & Su, 2018; Cuthbert, Ariza, & Friedland, 2011; Humphrey, Bello, & LeCun, 2012).

Hadjeres & Nielsen (2020) deals with data that's dependent on time, also known as time-series data, having prefer to use a type of neural network known as the Recurrent Neural Network (RNN). But when using only RNN for time data, came to lighta special type of neural networks known as the convolutional neural network, (CNN), but in an inimical way (Yang, Chou, & Yang, 2017). Having planting in sense that there can be numerous challenges encountered while dealing with audio samples and therefore,to suffer a veritably complicated pre-processing task (Carnovalini & Rodà, 2020).

In Python,reusing audio data in ". wav" format using "Librosa" (Cuthbert et al., 2011) and for ". krn, musicxml", "Music21" (Phon-Amnuaisuk, 2019). These audio samples are generally represented as time series, where the X-Axis represents the time period and the Y-Axis represents the Breadth of the Audio signal. The Breadth of the signal is generally measured as a function of the change in pressure around the microphone or receiver bias,using this bias to prize the main affair of the Audio Signal, and thereforeperforming numerous different operations upon the audio signal, performing Fourier Transform, performing Fast Fourier Transform, Mel Spectrograms, Log Spectrograms and so on (Amiot, 2016; Yust, 2017). Python plays a veritably vital part in any audio deep learning task, in python prizing spectrograms of different audio signals using Librosa, (McFee et al., 2015) and Matplotlib, (Hunter, 2007), also reusing the entire music data into a MIDI train (MacMillan, Droettboom, & Fujinaga, 2002; Brinkmann & Sekretariat, 2005). Further processing using LSTM, MIDI train conversion is again done by Python's Music21 Library (Arias-Vergara et al., 2021). Python's Librosa also helps us to induce a "Periodogram", a periodogram can be used to estimate the spectral viscosity of an audio signal and also allowing the periodogram to compass into different audio signals using Matplotlib and periodogram as data for deep literacy is yet another state-of-the- art operation (Cuthbert & Ariza, 2010; Cho & Jang, 2020). Generating a spectrogram helps us to fantasize the representation of the diapason of frequentness, of the signal as it varies with time. In a nutshell, a spectrogram is a piled view of multiple periodograms (Rodriguez et al., 2020). Python for the Processing of Audio, (Ringeval et al., 2019; Farrokhmanesh & Hamzeh, 2016) make it veritably readily for us to approach the particular problem-specific operations of Audio. Open-Source donation is a great gift for inventors to develop real- life AI grounded music operations.

3 PROPOSED METHODOLOGY

3.1 Motivation

To make an independent module for the generation of Music in an automated way is the main motivation of this work. To achieve this, we've proposed LSTM grounded RNN system. Our Deep LSTM RNN can predict these melodies using the MIDI format as specified in further notes. The proposed system is a veritably simple yet effective LSTM Architecture piled with Mixed activation function layers as well, followed by a Batch-Normalization subcaste and a Dropout well which increases the robustnessof the LSTM Model also proposed an awful conception using multiple LSTM Neuron in the form of an LSTM Neuron Layer, followed with two different types of activation functions along with Batch Normalization and Powerhouse Layers therefore performing in a new armature which we had named as the "Deep Mixed Actuated Long Short Term Memory Confined Boltzmann Intermittent Neural Network (DMA-LSTM-RBRNN).The term Confined Boltzmann is deduced from the motifs of Confined Boltzmann Machines, which are nothing but a stochastic way of representing the internal retired layers of a neural network. We havedemonstrated how an RBMS hidden architecture may look when we mound LSTM layers one after the other. Using an RBM armature with LSTM Layers makes the model not only deep and complex, but also will be suitable to understand much more complex sequences of melodies that we will be handed during training. Therefore, making a neural network deeper will help the network understand much more complicated patterns and melody sequences but with deeper networks comes the problem of overfitting and so we've applied an RBM conception along with stacked LSTM Layers, Mixed Activated Layers, Batch Normalization Layers, and Dropout layers as well. The usage of these mixed system would make the predictions of the LSTM layers much more robust and hence the prediction of the entire system can be scaled as per requirements. The entire system being depicted in later sections of this paper.

3.2 Objectives of the proposed system, The DMA-LSTM-RBRNN

1) Erecting machine learning models to classify, describe, or induce audio or music, involves modelling tasks where input data are audio samples. Thus, with the help of this proposed system, one can easily generate an infinite number of melodies regarding Piano Music and can accordingly mix them to produce new unseen melodious songs.
2) In deep learning when we want to deal with data that's dependent on time, I.e., time series data, we always prefer to use a type of neural network known as the intermittent neural network aka, RNN, but as RNNs tends to become a lot slower with increased amount of Data, so our proposed DMA-LSTM-RBRNN acts as a weapon to back RNNs by using different activation functions in a sequential manner, thus

reducing the chances of generating erroneous melodies and also the use of two different activation function leads to much more stabler gradients during training.

3) In Python we can exercise audio data in ". wav" format using "Librosa`` and" for ". krn, musicxml" we've"Music21 ``. The Breadth of the signal is generally measured as a function of the change in pressure around the microphone or receiver bias, we can use this bias to prize the main affair i.e., performing Fast Fourier Transform, Mel Spectrograms, Log Spectrograms and so on, thus making it easier for our proposed architecture to be used for multiple times as well as independent generation. The DMA-LSTM-RBRNN can also work on these images provided during the data pre-processing stages thus we can approach the problem of generating melodies in two different ways, by the help of using the single proposed architecture.
4) In Machine Learning, we love to involve statistics, and therefore, the statistical normal of a signal, when measured in terms of its frequency content, is known as Spectrum, therefore we've got another point of audio in which we can apply machine learning. Generating spectrograms help us to fantasize the representation of diapason of frequency, of the signal as it varies with time. In a nutshell, a spectrogram is a piled view of multiple periodograms. As mentioned earlier, the proposed system, DMA-LSTM-RBRNN takes around 2 epochs for getting fully trained, which is quite faster as compared to other methods.
5) The LSTM-RBRNN is capable enough to both work on pre-processed musical data as well as images of different musical properties and hence, the system can be used for automatic musical mixing, musicinformation retrieval and also the system can work at par with musical directors by guiding them through the process of Music Production.

3.3 Data Overview

This paper deals with we have used the data set for generating new melodies, for a good ample amount of data, we have tried to work with different custom data set, but the best outcome was from the "Humdrum" Data Set of melodies for different German Folk Songs. We have trained our model with around 600000 sequences of song melodies encoded in our MIDI format for better results. In the Humdrum data set, the songs were present in ". krn" format, I.e., songs of kernel format, so we had to first process the entire data in such a way so that the LSTM-RNN model can easily work on it and supply us our desired results. For this purpose, we have created an algorithm in which we would be encoding the songs from. krn to MIDI notations and then convert the entire songs into a single data set file in which all the songs will be present together sequences by sequences and hence our LSTM can work on it. The entire processing of the songs from ". krn" to MIDI notations is done using Python 3.7, NumPy, and Music21, a library for computational music theory and music information retrieval.

3.4 Methodology of the Melody Generation

The main motive behind the Data Flow Methodology is the processing of the original data in such a way that it becomes easy for our proposed architecture. In deep learning, LSTM-RNNs (Long Short Term Memory Recurrent Neural Networks), require time-series data, continuous-time data, or in other words sequential data, data that depends on time. LSTMs are quite advanced architecture that is capable to process time-series data.

We proposed this data flow modeling for the main purpose of converting our original data set into the time series format, Music Time Series Representation. In Music21 we can easily handle many different extensions for audio or music files, like ". krn", musicxml, MIDI, and many more.

Figure 2. (A) The mapping json File Figure 2. (B) The entire single file data set for the encoded song (songs in integer format)

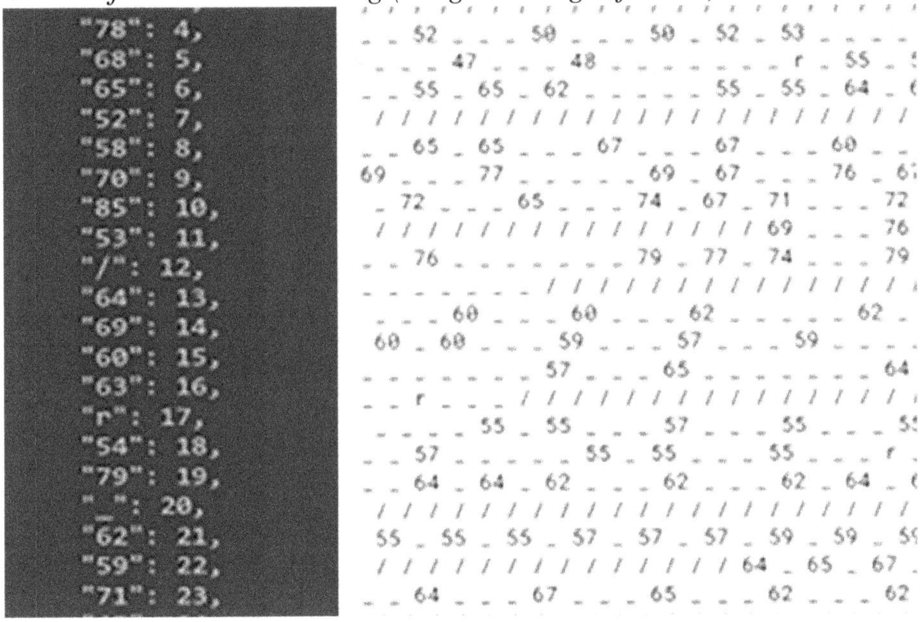

In Music21 we have many useful predefined functions that we have used in our data flow modeling. Some of the functions help us to check whether the songs were in the correct duration like 4/4 beats, 3/4 beats, and so on. Those songs which were not in our required duration format were simply ignored during the data flow modeling. Figure 2(A), is a brief description of how the mapping JSON file looks, and also Figure 2(B), is the description of the single-file data set that we have created.

Figure 3. The entire dataflow Modelling for the Melody Generating LSTM (How the folder with .krn files are changed to an integers representation for the LSTM

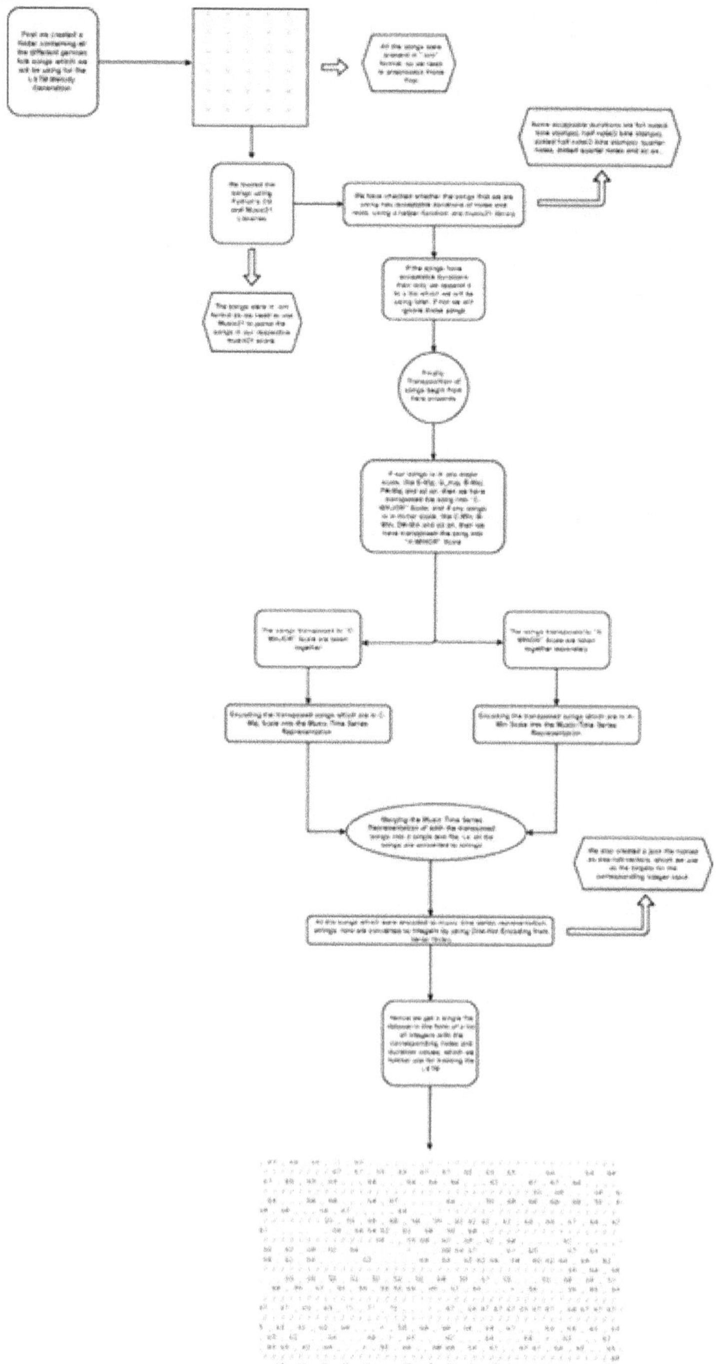

Figure 3, depicts the entire data inflow modelling of our work. We first created a brochure in which all the German Folk Songs were present together. Using OS's walk class and join a class we were suitable to load all the songs which were in. krn format into our python practitioner. In Python we've a wonderful library known as Music21 for Computational Music Proposition, in which we can reuse songs in a different format, like. krn, musicxml, midi, etc. In our case we target to render the songs in a MIDI time series representation, so Music21 serves with its stupendous features. All the songs in the data set were in unstable duration format, so we've created a coadjutor function that would just return a Boolean value of either true or false for the corresponding songs which will be having the needed respectable duration.

We've created a list of respectable duration, like 0.25,0.5, 1, 2, 3, 4, and so on, therefore the coadjutor function selects that song which has the respectable duration as mentioned in our, and again for this complicated task we can calculate on Music21 and Librosa for this purpose, in Librosa we can separate the entire songs as timestamps and we can fantasize the FFT of the entire songs and also MFCCs as well along with the spectrograms, but for that we've converted the. krn songs to. wav format using Python as well.

On widely checking the songs, those which have the respectable duration were used for farther preprocessing and rests were just ignored by our data pre-processing algorithm. Since we've in our hands those songs which have the needed respectable duration, now we can further continue the pre-processing, and therefore we end up transposing the songs in a veritably unique way. All those songs which were in any major scale, like B-Maj, G-Maj, F# Maj, etc., were transposed to "C-MAJOR" scale and contemporaneously those songs which were in any minor scale-such like, B-Min, G-Min, F-min, D#-Min, etc., were transposed to "A-MINOR" scale.

Again, this complicated task can be achieved using Music21 and Python. Therefore, we end up by getting the transposed songs in the C-Maj scale and A-Min scale and hence we continue the pre-processing and now begin the encoding of the songs independently in two different lines one for the decoded C-Major scale songs and the other for the A-Minor scale songs.

Figure 4. Brief working of the entire data flow modeling and the processing of the .krn files to a single integer file representing all the songs with certain delimiters

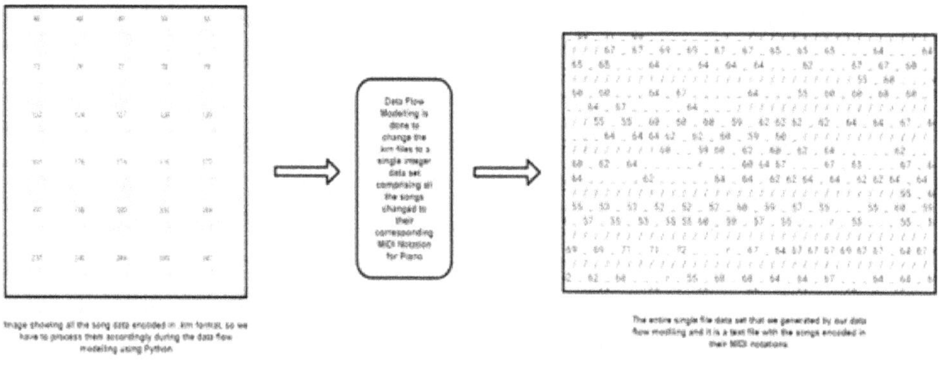

We have tried to demonstrate the entire motive behind our data flow modeling in a nutshell in Figure 4. Our data flow modeling serves the purpose of feature engineering and extraction as well, and thus providing us with data in our required format for the DMA-LSTM-RBRNN.

3.4.1 LSTM Neuron

In the LSTM, we use two activation functions, The Sigmoid Activation Function, and The Hyperbolic Tangent Activation Function. These activation functions play a major role in determining which of the input sequences must be kept as long-term memory and which input sequence must be kept for the short-term memory. These LSTM cells together can be placed or organized in many different ways, one such way is "The Multiple Input- Multiple Output LSTM Network" or in simple language we name it as the "Sequence to Sequence LSTM Network".

3.4.2 Data flow in LSTM neurons

LSTM was created as a solution to this problem as they have internal mechanisms called gates that can regulate the flow of information. These gates can learn which data in a sequence is important to keep or throw away. By doing that, it can pass relevant information down the long chain of sequences to make predictions i.e., in this case the long chain of melody. Before understanding the data flow in LSTM, we would understand the data flow in RNN with a quick analysis.

In an RNN the data gets transformed into machine-readable vectors and then it is processed one by one. While processing, it passes the previous hidden state to the next step in the sequence. This hidden state acts as the memory of the neural network. It holds the information about the previous data the network has seen before. First, the input and the previous hidden state are combined to form a vector that now has information on the current input and the previous inputs. This goes through the tanh activation, and the new hidden state output is released.

3.4.3 Mathematical Modelling of an LSTM

Let's take the LSTM Neuron as a reference to understand the mathematical formulation (feed-forward and the backpropagation with time).

Figure 5. Diagrammatically representing an LSTM Neuron

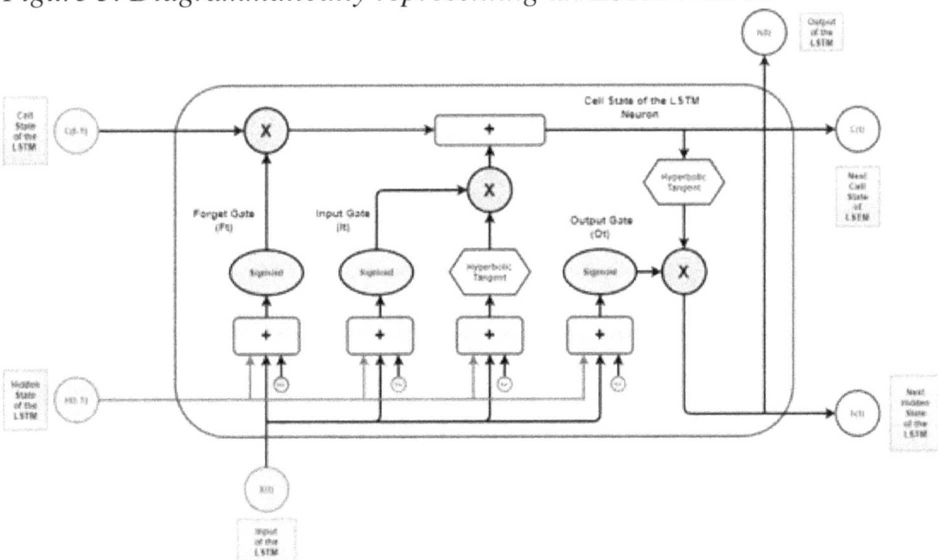

Notation

h_t, C_t: hidden layer vectors.
x_t: input vector.
b_f, b_i, b_c, b_o: bias vector.
W_f, W_i, W_c, W_o: parameter matrices
σ, h: activation functions

The feed-forward formulation of the neuron can be represented as:

$$f_t = \sigma\left(W_f \cdot [h_{t-1}, x_t] + b_f\right) \tag{1}$$

$$i_t = \sigma\left(W_i \cdot [h_{t-1}, x_t] + b_i\right) \tag{2}$$

$$o_t = \sigma\left(W_o \cdot [h_{t-1}, x_t] + b_o\right) \tag{3}$$

$$\widetilde{C}_t = tanhtanh\left(W_c \cdot [h_{t-1}, x_t] + b_c\right) \tag{4}$$

$$C_t = f_t \odot C_{t-1} + i_t \odot \widetilde{C}_t \tag{5}$$

$$h_t = o_t \odot tanh\left(C_t\right) \tag{6}$$

Now we will find out the output or the hidden state as a complete mathematical formula.

$$h_t = o_t \odot tanh\left(C_t\right)$$

Combining (4), (5), and (6), we get

$$h_t = o_t \odot tanh\left(f_t \odot C_{t-1} + i_t \odot tanh\left(W_c \cdot [h_{t-1}, x_t] + b_c\right)\right) \tag{7}$$

Now putting in (1), (2) in (7), we get

$$h_t = o_t \odot \tanh\left(\sigma\left(W_f \cdot [h_{t-1}, x_t] + b_f\right)\right.$$

$$\left.\odot C_{t-1} + \sigma\left(W_i \cdot [h_{t-1}, x_t] + b_i\right) \odot tanhtanh\left(W_c \cdot [h_{t-1}, x_t] + b_c\right)\right) \tag{8}$$

Now putting in (3) in (8)

$$h_t = \sigma(W_o \cdot [h_{t-1}, x_t] + b_o) \odot \tanh(\sigma(W_f \cdot [h_{t-1}, x_t] + b_f) \odot C_{t-1}$$

$$+ \sigma(W_i \cdot [h_{t-1}, x_t] + b_i) \odot tanh(W_c \cdot [h_{t-1}, x_t] + b_c)) \tag{9}$$

This equation 9 that we get is the final equation that the LSTM neuron would give us as an output.

3.4.4. The Deep Mixed Activated Long Short Term Memory Restricted Boltzmann Recurrent Neural Network (DMA-LSTM-RBRNN)

To understand the entire DMA-LSTM-RBRNN Architecture, we have to consider figure 12, the entire algorithm is being depicted in a color-coded format, we have used five different color coding for the architecture. This color-coding is associated with different components of our DMA-LSTM-RBRNN, in different colored rectangles. Cream color rectangle, Deep Blue Color rectangle, Sky Blue colored rectangle, Maroon Colored rectangle, and Deep Yellow-colored rectangle, representing LeakyReLU (Leaky Rectified Linear Unit) Activated Layer, ELU (Exponential Linear Unit) Activated Layer, Batch-normalization Layer, Dropout Layer, and LSTM layer respectively. The below figure depicts the first four-color coding, i.e, cream rectangle, deep blue rectangle, sky blue rectangle, and maroon rectangle,

Figure 6. The color coding for the entire DMA-LSTM-RBRNN Algorithm

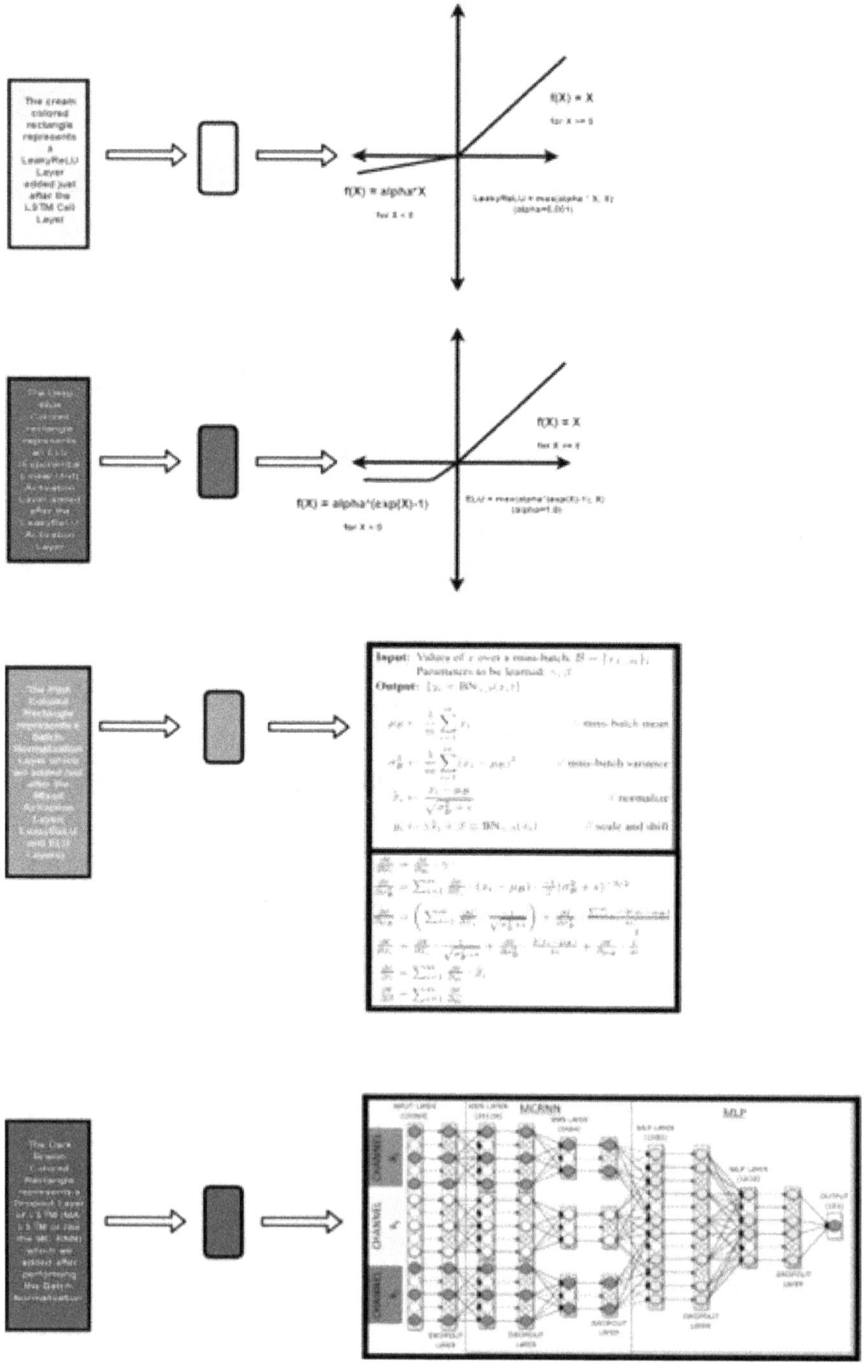

(These different colored rectangles will be making up an entire DMA-LSTM-RBRNN Model)

The rectangle marked with deep yellow represents an LSTM layer consisting of Multiple LSTM Cells for calculating and predicting the melody sequence on a given incomplete melody. We have made some hyper-parameter optimization upon these LSTM Cells by adding LSTM dropout and Recurrent Dropout simultaneously, also we have used "Hyperbolic Tangent (tanh activation) and "Sigmoid Activation", for the activation and recurrent activation respectively. The dropout parameters in each dropout layer are connected in like a sequence of number pattern, like 0.1, 0.1, 0.2, 0.3, 0.5, 0.8(in rare cases) etc. Therefore, figure 7 is illustrated for a better understanding of the LSTM Cell that we have used in our architecture,

Figure 7. An LSTM-RNN Neuron used in the DMA-LSTM-RBRNN Architecture is shown in detail (Long Short-Term Memory Recurrent Neural Network)

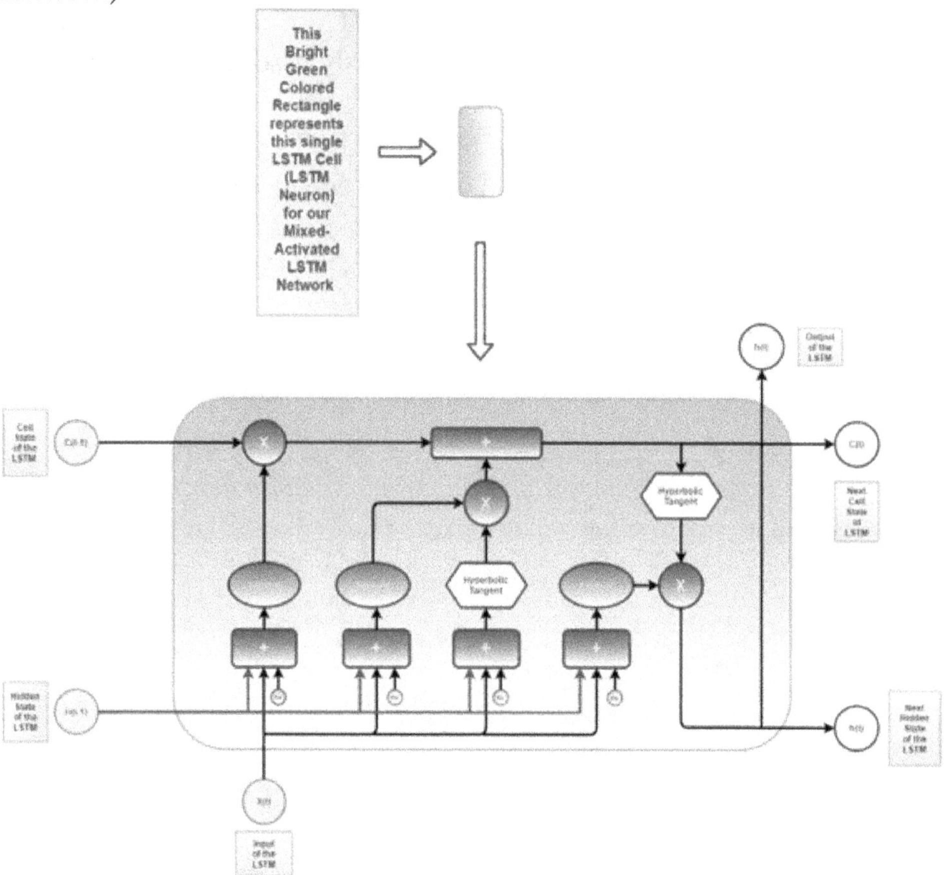

On understanding these respective color coding, we can now take a look at the DMA-LSTM-RBRNN Architecture, that we have proposed for the melody generation, do refer to figure 14. In our model, we have stacked layers of LSTM Cells one after the other just like an RBM (Restricted Boltzmann Machine) Architecture and along with these LSTM Layers, we have also added two different types of activation function which is again stacked one after the other followed with batch normalization and a dropout. The entire model can be treated as a Black Box and thus we can use these multiple black boxes accordingly for multiple music melody generations.

Figure 8. The Entire DeepMixedActivated LSTM architecture for melody generation

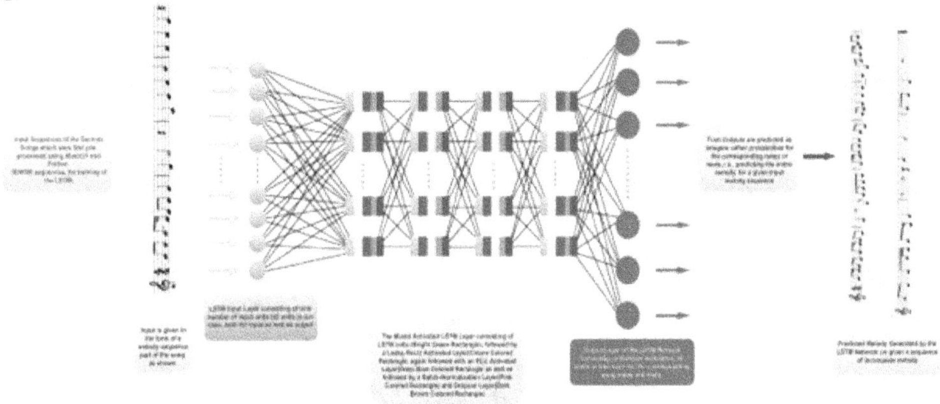

In figure 8, we have stacked different colored rectangles one after the other to form the entire DMA-LSTM-RBRNN Architecture for the generation of Piano Melodies. In figure 6.3 we can see that the input layer of the DMA-LSTM-RBRNN layer accepts an incomplete piano melody and after the calculation of the DMA-LSTM-RBRNN, the next prediction of notes (in MIDI score format) is given as output which we can hear via Muse Score. The main component of the DMA-LSTM-RBRNN architecture is the hidden DMA-LSTM layers that are stacked one after the other. Below is a picture of the DMA-LSTM-RBRNN's hidden layer,

Figure 9. The main component that forms the DMA-LSTM-RBRNN algorithm architecture (The Deep Mixed Activated Layer, I.e, LeakyReLU and ELU layers respectively)

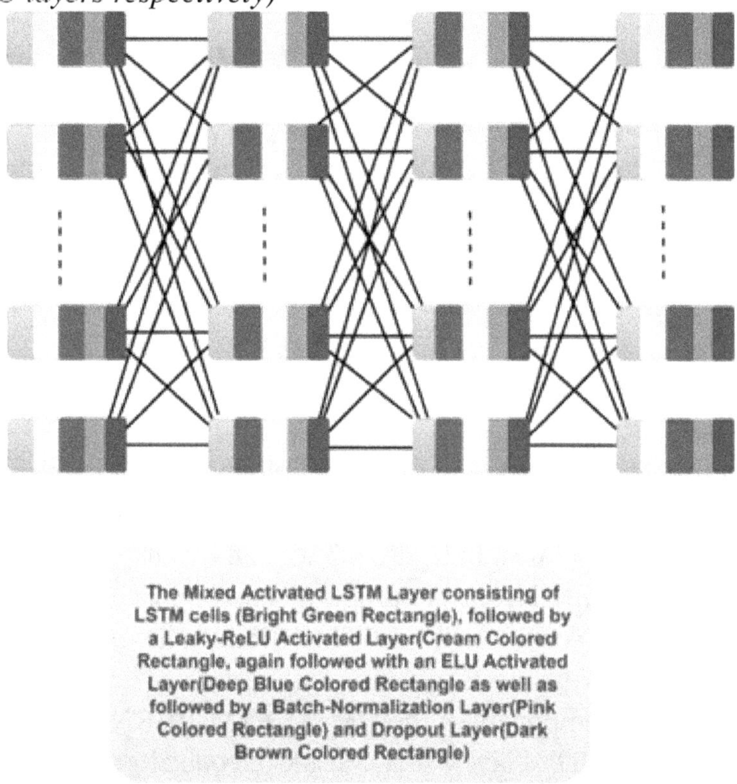

Figure 9, depicts the entire "Deep Mixed Activated Long Short Term Memory Restricted Boltzmann Recurrent Neural Network" (DMA-LSTM-RBRNN) is being depicted with the help of color-coding. We've the great advantage of having the LSTM Cell predefined in the TensorFlow module of Python which is greatly used in different artificial intelligence and Deep Literacy purposes. In our armature, we've used a veritably simple but yet effective conception of mounding layers one after the other, just like in an RBM (Restricted Boltzmann Machine). The DMA-LSTM-RBRNN uses this conception of RBM but with the primary focus of applying it on an LSTM Layer which is followed by a LeakyReLU Activation Function, which is in turn again connected to an ELU Activation Function, followed with Batch Normalization Layers and Powerhouse Layers as well. The

LeakyReLU and ELU Layers act as a wrapping to the value prognosticated by the LSTM cell, the LSTM Cell predicts a number between 0 and 1, which corresponds to the separate probability of the given input sample, and the probability distribution is therefore achieved and these numerical values pass on through the Mixed- Activated Function and therefore results in another numerical value which is important regularized and concurrent with the input.

This conception of mounding activation function layers one after the other makes the network more sophisticated and hence the chance of over-fitting is reduced to a great extent. In our case, we've used the mounding of the activation function layers in a veritably unique manner, in the first and the fourth DMA-LSTM-RBRNN Function, we've first used LeakyReLU activation and also followed by an ELU activation Function, along with Batch Normalization and Powerhouse independently. But for the alternate and third DMA-LSTM-RBRNN Function, we've first used ELU and also LeakyReLU, and hence we got much more promising prognostications of melody. Therefore, our final armature is comprised of four DMA-LSTM-RBRNN layers and two thick layers for the melody class vaticination. Therefore, in the end, we've relatively quantum of promising warbles which are relatively soothing and robust, and therefore with farther advancements, we can also induce songs as well which comprises of different melody melodies and beats. The DMA-LSTM-RBRNN uses such an armature that a Restricted Boltzmann Machine does, i.e., mounding up layers one after the other to form a veritably deep retired Function that can break retrogression purpose or bracket purpose consequently. The main advantage of having such a deep retired Function is to identify numerous complex features of a given input sequence.

With this unique way of using mixed activation function layers along with the Batch Normalization and Powerhouse layers, a veritably unique observation was made, the DMA-LSTM-RBRNN Network was suitable to achieve a veritably promising melody. On training the entire network with our data set, the training delicacy was getting impregnated at a value of 0.813 (I.e,81.3), along with a training loss of 0.325, while the corresponding confirmation delicacy was getting impregnated at a value of 0.8754 (I.e,87.54), along with a confirmation loss of 0.256. Therefore, the results were relatively robust and promising as well. Another veritably unique point of the DMA-LSTM-RBRNN algorithm is that just training the network for around 2 epochs, the results were relatively promising, the confirmation delicacy tends to lead the training delicacy and the confirmation loss is foot than that of the training loss. Therefore, the model isn't befitting neither it's under-fitting, it's generalizing the entire data in a veritably proper manner and also the Batch Normalization Function along with the Dropout Layer prevents the DMA-LSTM-RBRNN from getting over fitted while training.

3.4.5 Parameters of the DMA-LSTM-RNN

The Deep Mixed Activated Long Short-Term Memory Recurrent Neural Network (DMA-LSTM-RNN) uses a couple of several parameters which we have found out during the training phase of the entire model. If we further tune these parameters along with some other hyper-parameters as well. Hyper Parameter Optimization is a very important and useful way to determine the structural architecture of any custom model so that a specific purpose can be achieved. This paper deals with, we have tuned as many parameters as possible, so that the validation accuracy and the validation loss of the entire model attain a promising value. Hyper Parameter Optimization also helps the model to reduce the chance of over-fitting during the validation phase. Above is a list of parameters that were tuned during the training of the DMA-LSTM-RNN, provided in a tabular format. The table gives an idea about the parameters which were tuned during the training of the model and the corresponding data types of the parameters are provided as well.

Table 1. Various parameters of the DMA-LSTM-RBRNN

Parameter Name	Type of Parameter	Tuned Value of Parameter	Purpose of the tuning
LSTM Cell Layer Parameters	Integers and String values	LSTM Kernel Initializer (x1), LSTM Activation(A1), LSTM Recurrent Activation(A2), LSTM use_bias (B1),Recurrent Dropout(D1), LSTM Dropout (D2).	These parameters help the LSTM to reduce the chance of overfitting during the training. The LSTM Cell parameters play an important role in justifying the training phase and validation phase.
LSTM Dense Layer Parameters	String values	LSTM Dense Kernel Initializer (X2), LSTM Dense Layer use_bias (B2)	These parameters belong to the dense layers that are connected with the DMA-LSTM-RNN Network, the main purpose of tuning these parameters are again to reduce the chance of over fitting
DMA-LSTM-RNN Optimizer's Parameters	Integer values	Optimizer used were RMSProp (Root Mean Square Propagation) (Op1), Adam (Adaptive Moments Gradient Descent) (Op2) and Nadam (Nesterov Adaptive Moments Gradient Descent) (Op3)	Tuning of the values of any optimizer is very much intuitive and many calculations involves in this tuning. If we can correctly tune the best type of optimizer values, then no one can stop the neural network to perform in an outstanding way.
DMA-LSTM-RNN Training Parameters (Parameters involved during Epochs)	Integers and Strings	Training data (X_train, y_train), Validation data (X_validation, y_validation), Batch Size 1 (BS1), Batch Size 2 (BS2), Number of Epochs (NE1), Initial Epochs (IE1), Maximum Queue Size (MQ1)	These parameters justifies the entire training of our DMA-LSTM-RNN Architecture. During the training of the DMA-LSTM-RNN, these parameter guides the entire network to understand about the data, aka, Back Propagation with time

In table 1 all the tuned parameters are given but their corresponding values are not. So we have provided another table for all the values of the corresponding tuned parameters. Table 2 guides us to understand the types of values which we have passed during the programming phase.

Table 2. The values of the parameters that we have tuned to obtain the DMA-LSTM-RBRNN

Variable	Data Type	Values	Type of Layer Defined Together
LSTM Kernel Initializer (x1)	String	Glorot Uniform	LSTM Cell Layer Parameters List
LSTM Cell Activation (A1)	String	Hyperbolic Tangent (tanh) Activation Function	
LSTM Cell Recurrent Activation	String	Sigmoid Activation Function	
LSTM Cell use_bias (B1)	String	True	
Recurrent Dropout (D1)	Integer Value between 0 and 1	0.1 (for our work)	
LSTM Dropout (D2)	Integer Value between 0 and 0.5	0.1 (for our work)	
LSTM Dense Kernel Initializer (X2)	String	He_Normal	DMA-LSTM-RNN Dense Layer Parameters
Dense Layer use_bias (B2)	String	True	

The optimizers that were used to train the DMA-LSTM-RBRNN were RMSProp (Root Mean Square Propagation Optimizer), "Op1", along Adam Optimizer (Adaptive Moments Gradient Descent Optimizer), "Op2" and Nadam Optimizer (Nesterov's Adaptive Moments Gradient Descent Optimizer), "Op3". In some special cases we plant out the "Eve" optimizer also plays a veritably nice part along with "Adam", just an intuitive study. Some images were used to make the understanding a bit clear for the parameters. These update- rules are followed by the TensorFlow Back end during the programming phase and model training phase, out of these optimizers now we will be looking into our point of interest, i.e., RMSProp

(Op1), Adam (Op2), and Nadam (Op3), Math's has always been the heart of all deep literacy algorithms that exists till date.

All the optimizers are together handed in a irregular format below, we've also handed some of the shots of our program in which the optimizers were used during the model compendium period and therefore making the understanding a bit more intuitive. Each optimizer, Op1, Op2, and Op3 has its corresponding parameters, which we can consider as hyper-parameters to fine- tune the network for better results and robustness. Below are images of the three optimizers that were used by us in this work. The RMSProp Optimizer, in a veritably introductory way of perpetration, using Python3.7 and Keras using Google Collaboratory, the values of the parameters are "decay", a pier value that controls the literacy rate; "rho" a hyper-parameter that attenuates the influences of any once slants if present, its also a pier value. All the parameters that we've tuned for our DMA-LSTM-RBRNN network for better results during training and testing, again, "decay", "beta_1", "beta_2", and learning rate are all pier, with their matching purpose. Decay again handles the literacy rate, The hyperactive-parameters "beta_1" and "beta_2" of Adam are original decay rates used when estimating the first and alternate moments of the grade, which are multiplied by themselves (exponentially) at the end of each training step (batch).

Nadam means adding a Nesterov's fashion of enforcing the Adam Optimizer algorithm but with just some update to the "decay" parameter, in Nadam we use a term known as "schedule decay", this is the main suspicion behind Nadam Optimizer. The schedule decay also handles the literacy rate parameter and decreases or increases it gradationally depending on the verge of achieving the original minima or global minima. The DMA-LSTM-RBRNN also uses numerous other parameters, like the parameters for the different layers, parameters for the activation functions as well, so another table is handed in which we've given all the parameters that we've supplied to the algorithm for better results and also making the DMA-LSTM-RBRNN algorithm much more resistance to over-fitting. We've also performed hyper-parameter optimization using Randomized Search CV and Keras Tuner for determining the parameters for each sub-caste along with their impact on confirmation delicacy and confirmation loss. Our proposed armature was relatively good and robust as it can give delicacy up to 80 in its first time only when we're using the Nadam (Nesterov's Adaptive Moments Optimizer, aka Op. We proposed that one should always use Nadam Optimizer for this Melody Generation using DMA-LSTM-RBRNN for getting optimal delicacy in just a many 2 to 3 ages.

On the other hand, when we've used the RMSProp also we find that the model is gradationally learning the parameters and it's taking around 20 ages to reach the optimal value of delicacy both for training and for testing. The same happens when we tried to use Nesterov's Grade Descent with Momentum, and the results were the same as that of the RMSProp, so both in case of Nesterov's Momentum Gradient Descent and RMSProp, the DMA-LSTM-RBRNN took some quantum of time to give the optimal results, but yes the values of the criteria were more or less same with each other. Therefore we've handed all the graphs that we've generated after the entire training was over and yes as we've proposed to use Early Stopping as a Call Back, so the model was trained for around 67 ages and eventually stopping the training and therefore we conclude that introductory optimizers would take some time to give the optimal values but for Nadam, the effects can get a bit more mysterious. We've also tried numerous further optimizers, but none of them could match the speed and delicacy as that of Nadam Optimizer. So we propose to use Nadam Optimizer for this particular piece of the problem,I.e, Melody Generation. Table 3 represents the entire hyper-parameters of the DMA-LSTM-RBRNN.

Table 3. The hyper-parameter list of the DMA-LSTM-RBRNN

Layer Parameters	**Name of the parameter**	**Value After Hyper Parameter Optimization**
LSTM Layer 1	Units (Number of LSTM Neurons in the first LSTM Layer)	64 LSTM Neurons (64 Deep Yellow Rectangles)
LeakyReLU Layer 1	Alpha of LeakyReLU	0.23
ELU Layer 1	Alpha of ELU	0.87

continued on following page

Table 3. Continued

Layer Parameters	Name of the parameter	Value After Hyper Parameter Optimization
BatchNormalization Layer 1	1. The momentum of batch normalization	89%
	2. Re-norm Momentum of batch normalization	88.8%
	3. Epsilon of batch normalization	0.0015
Dropout Layer 1	Rate of Dropout	15%
LSTM Layer 2	Units (Number of LSTM Neurons in the second LSTM Layer)	128 LSTM Neurons (128 Deep Yellow Rectangles)
LeakyReLU Layer 2	Alpha of LeakyReLU	0.23
ELU Layer 2	Alpha of ELU	0.87
BatchNormalization Layer 2	1. The momentum of batch normalization	89%
	2. Re-norm Momentum of batch normalization	88.8%
	3. Epsilon of batch normalization	0.0015
Dropout Layer 2	Rate of Dropout	15%
LSTM Layer 3	Units (Number of LSTM Neurons in the third LSTM Layer)	256 LSTM Neurons (256 Deep Yellow Rectangles)
LeakyReLU Layer 3	Alpha of LeakyReLU	0.23
ELU Layer 3	Alpha of ELU	0.87
BatchNormalization Layer 3	1.Momentum of batch normalization	89%
	2.Re-norm Momentum of batch normalization	88.8%
	3.Epsilon of batch normalization	0.0015
Dropout Layer 3	Rate of Dropout	30%
LSTM Layer 4	Units (Number of LSTM Neurons in the third LSTM Layer)	512 LSTM Neurons (512 Deep Yellow Rectangles)

continued on following page

Table 3. Continued

Layer Parameters	Name of the parameter	Value After Hyper Parameter Optimization
LeakyReLU Layer 4	Alpha of LeakyReLU	0.23
ELU Layer 4	Alpha of ELU	0.87
BatchNormalization Layer 4	1.Momentum of batch normalization	89%
	2.Re-norm Momentum of batch normalization	88.8%
	3.Epsilon of batch normalization	0.0015
Dropout Layer 4	Rate of Dropout	30%

The DMA-LSTM-RBRNN algorithm was optimized using three different optimizers, the Adam Optimizer, The RMSProp Optimizer, and The Nadam Optimizer. These optimizers have their respective parameters which were also optimized during the hyper-parameter optimization of the DMA-LSTM-RBRNN algorithm. Table 4 is provided here for depicting all the hyper-parameter optimized values of the corresponding optimizers.

Table 4. Hyper Parameter Optimization for the three Optimizers for our DMA-LSTM-RBRNN

Name of Optimizer	Name of parameter	Hyper parameter optimized values
Root Mean Square Propagation Optimizer (Op1) (RMSProp)	1. Learning rate	0.00052
	2. Decay	0.004
	3. Rho	85%
Adaptive Moments Optimizer (Op2) (Adam)	1. Learning rate	0.00088
	2. Decay	0.004
	3. Beta 1	88%
	4. Beta 2	88.9%

continued on following page

Table 4. Continued

Name of Optimizer	Name of parameter	Hyper parameter optimized values
Nesterov's Adaptive Moments Optimizer (Op3) (Nadam)	1. Learning rate	0.002
	2. Schedule Decay	0.001
	3. Beta 1	50%
	4. Beta 2	60%

Thus from the above table, we can conclude that all the hyper-parameters for the optimizers also play a very vital role in justifying the DMA-LSTM-RBRNN's performance during evaluation and training. We have proposed all the possible hyper-parameters that we can tune to change the model's results and it is these optimizers hyper-parameters that govern the overall training of our DMA-LSTM-RBRNN algorithm and thus as we have said the main motive of using such a complicated architecture was to achieve very promising results in just some few epochs and our purpose was accordingly fulfilled successfully.

In every deep learning algorithm, we can perform hyper-parameter optimization to guide the model to achieve the best possible validation accuracy and also the lowest possible value for the validation loss, thus making the model more robust and prone to over-fitting while training. These hyperparameter optimizations are done using the help of Python and Keras Tuner along with Randomized Search CV. The hyperparameter optimization was performed on a workstation with quite a good amount of GPU power and time as well.

We have used Nvidia RTX 2080Ti along with a RAM of 64 GB. The more powerful GPU, we use, the less time will be taken by our DMA-LSTM-RBRNN Algorithm during the training, thus making the calculations faster and more robust and converge achieves a global minimum as well.

4 RESULT ANALYSIS

In this work we have used three different optimizers, the Adaptive Moments Optimizer (Adam), the Root Mean Square Propagation Optimizer (RMSProp), and the Nesterov's Adaptive Moments Optimizer aka, Nadam. The DMA-LSTM-RBRNN follows the principle of the "Back Propagation with Time" Algorithm. The network learns very quickly when we have used Nadam Optimizer, but with Adam and RMSProp, the results were also quite promising, just in the case of Adam, we had to run 3 epochs out of the 100 epochs and the model gave the same accuracy more or less and also for the RMSProp, the model also performed quite exactly just it took around 4 epochs out of 100 epochs to get a quite promising result. Figures 10, 11 have got after the training and validation phase is done.

Figure 10. The graph of training accuracy VS validation accuracy (testing accuracy) of the DMA-LSTM-RBRNN

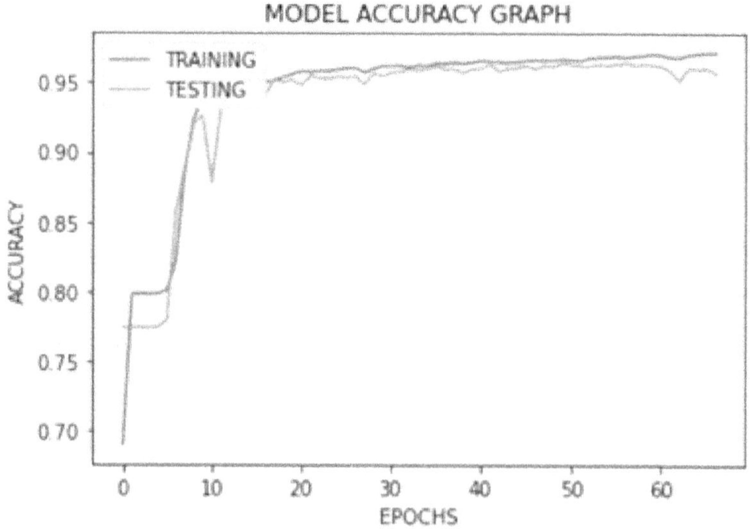

Figure 11. The graph of training loss VS validation loss (testing loss) of the DMA-LSTM-RBRNN

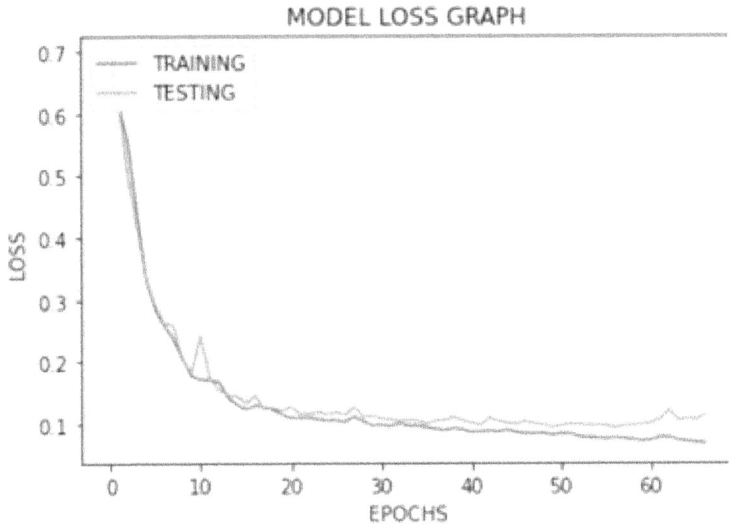

Figure 12 and Figure 13 were the graphs that were obtained while using the Nadam Optimizer, we can see that the validation accuracy leads to the training accuracy at just the beginning of the training procedure. The other two graphs were not quite promising as the graphs for Nadam. Figure 11 and Figure 13 are the graphs that we have obtained when we used the standard Nesterov's Momentum Gradient Descent with Momentum, and the graphs that were obtained seemed a bit mysterious, as we can see that the training accuracy leads the validation accuracy but the validation accuracy slowly increases and we can conclude from the graphs that it will be getting saturated to a very close value of the training accuracy.

Figure 12. The graph of training accuracy VS validation accuracy (testing accuracy) of the DMA-LSTM-RBRNN but using Nesterov's Momentum Gradient Descent Optimizer

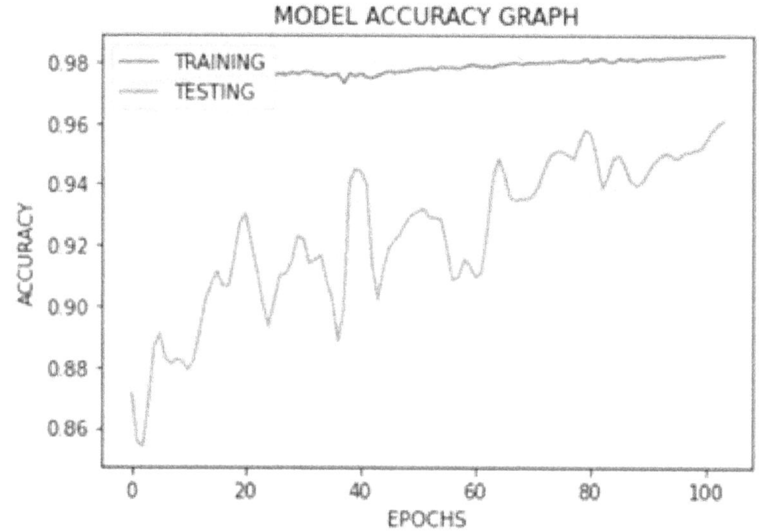

Figure 13. The graph of training loss VS validation loss (testing loss) of the DMA-LSTM-RBRNN but again using Nesterov's Momentum Gradient Descent Optimizer

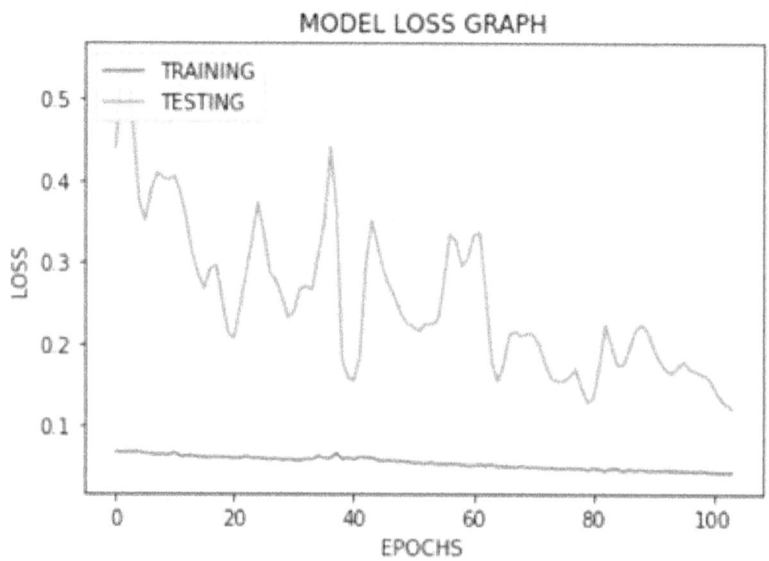

Thus, using Nesterov's Momentum Gradient Descent, we have concluded that the main things that help the DMA-LSTM-RBRNN to achieve such great results were the DMA-LSTM-RBRNN internal complex architecture and the type of optimizers that we are using as well. The Graphs tell us that the model was going to overfit at a certain epoch value but due to the early stopping, the model was saved from getting overfitted by the data, as the DMA-LSTM-RBRNN network is a very deep recurrent neural network, so it can sometimes get over fitted and hence we used early stopping to counteract the overfitting chances. The final accuracy and loss were calculated as the mean of all the accuracy and loss till the 67th epoch, and so it got justified correctly. We have also provided a comparison graph between different optimizers that we have used to perform the training, the best optimizer that we have concluded for this work is the Adam and Nadam Optimizers. But for intuitive understanding one must be using the very basic optimizers at the beginning to understand the DMA-LSTM-RBRNN Network for melody generation, if we use advanced optimizers like Nadam or Adam, then we can see that network is performing the best as the training accuracy is increasing drastically within the first few epochs, while others take quite an amount of time to reach such a phase.

Figure 14. The comparison among the different optimizers that we have used This paper deals with for the DMA-LSTM-RBRNN

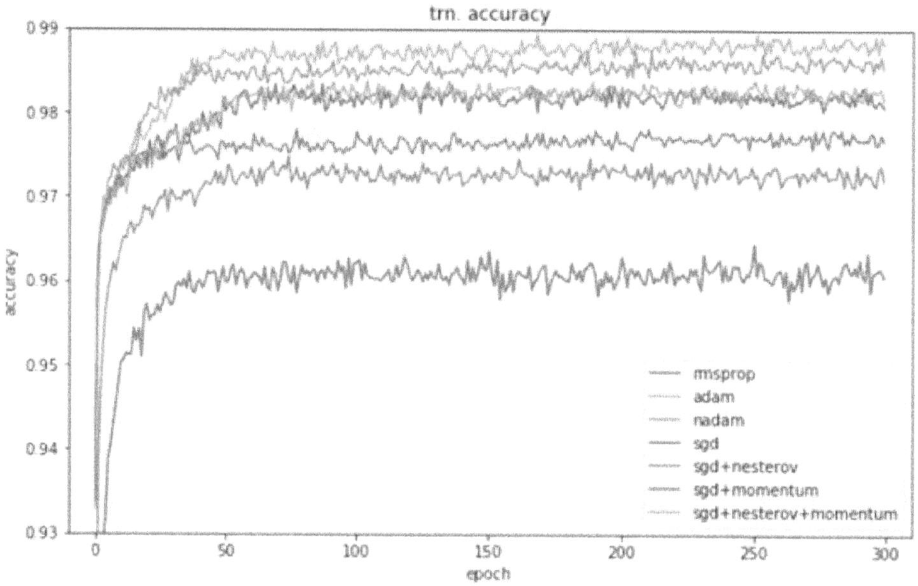

Figure 14 showing the comparison among the different optimizers that we have used This paper deals with. Optimizers play a very important role in any neural network as it is these optimizers, that helps the neural network to understand the errors that it is making during the training phase and as a result, the neural network can reach the Global Minima, and also the overall performance of the entire neural network depends somewhat upon the optimizer as well. In Deep Learning, optimizers can change the game for a particular neural network algorithm, and hence, without these optimizers, the field of deep learning would be just avoiding thing to study. Using these optimizers, the neural network can also justify the work that it is doing, either the regression problem or the classification problem. In any neural network, the last output that we get is nothing but just a function that gives a value that acts like a probability and thus the value lies between 0 and 1 and this value is calculated using the loss function that the neural network generates during the training and the Optimizer's task is to minimize this value of the loss function to converge to the Global Minima and thus we get the better results during the training of the DMA-LSTM-RBRNN Algorithm.

5 DISCUSSIONS

The DMA-LSTM-RBRNN was able to generate quite a good amount of melodies from given incomplete melody sequences. The output of the DMA-LSTM-RBRNN was just a single number that lies between 0 and 1, which justifies the probability of the corresponding given notes encoded in our Music Time Series Representation. These melodies which were generated by the DMA-LSTM-RBRNN were encoded in MIDI notation and which was later converted to a MIDI file. This MIDI file that was generated by the DMA-LSTM-RBRNN was viewed using a wonderful software known as Muse Score, which generally researchers use for Computational Music Theory and Music Information Retrieval. Our Network, The DMA-LSTM-RBRNN was able to correctly identify all the notes that were present in our entire song data set, and thus using those predefined song's knowledge, our network was able to generate quite a good amount of melodies which were not only perfectly matched but also were quite soothing for our ears to hear. We have provided the images of the inputted incomplete melody and the corresponding generated melody.

Figure 15. Image of an incomplete German Folk Song melody that is given as an input to our DMA-LSTM-RBRNN Algorithm

Figure 16.The Piano melody that was generated by the DMA-LSTM-RBRNN algorithm

The Generated Melodies were visualized and can be heard using Muse Score Software and we can also perform many preprocessing using the mentioned software (figure 15 (A), (B)). The DMA-LSTM-RBRNN Network can be used in a very broader aspect. We have used such a concept to create an outstanding outcome. We have created three DMA-LSTM-RBRNN Networks, naming them as BLACK BOX 1, BLACK BOX 2, and BLACK BOX 3.

These 3 Black BOXES aka, 3 DMA-LSTM-RBRNN Networks get 3 different incomplete melodies as input, they give their corresponding output predictions which are the list of 3 different probability distributions of the corresponding incomplete melody's MIDI notations, which we merge using Keras merging function and hence the 3 different predicted melody sequence can be used as an entire song made up of melodies of piano and also generated artificially using DMA-LSTM-RBRNN. A pictorial representation of our future scope of using such BLACK BOXES (DMA-LSTM-RBRNN Networks) is provided for reference do check it out in figure 16.

Figure 17. The Entire Future Scope of the DMA-LSTM-RBRNN is shown

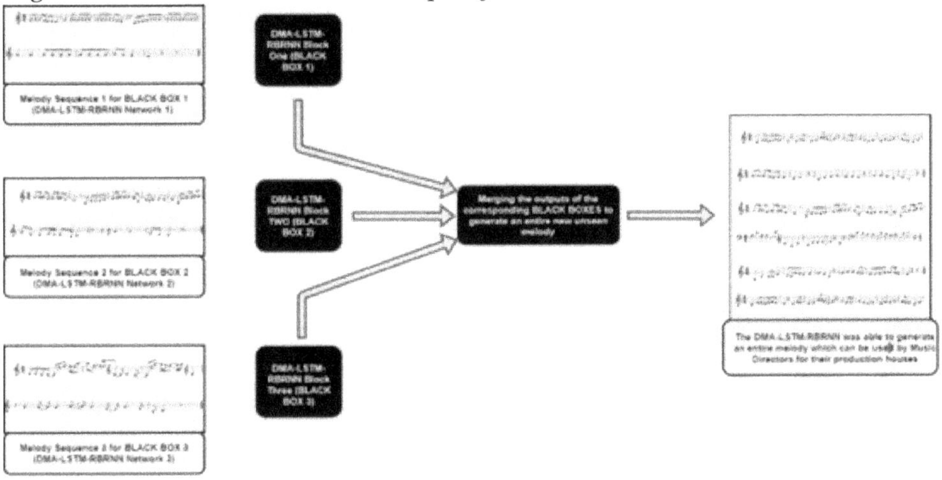

Here (figure 16) each BLACK BOX is acting as a separate DMA-LSTM-RBRNN Network with their corresponding incomplete melody input, but yes, we must be preprocessing the melodies using Python and Music21 for the respective input of the DMA-LSTM-RBRNN Network. Thus, our architecture can easily predict the remaining sequences and we can further merge them to form our entire song which is composed of piano melodies. Thus, Music Directors, Computational Music Specialists, Music Information Retrieval Engineers, Deep Learning Engineers of Audio Industries, Artificial Intelligent Specialists, and all the different multimedia specialists can use our proposed architecture to generate new melodious tones for different genre songs and hence can be a unique one. Our work shall bring great achievements regarding the field of Computational Music Theory, thus ending our work along with the references provided below which we have referred for executing this wonderful work successfully.

6 CONCLUSION

Thus,this paper deals with, we can conclude that deep learning can be applied to those fields in which we have a quality amount of data. Our main proposal was that of getting a neural network to learn more quickly.

This can be achieved by using a very deep complicated architecture like our DMA-LSTM-RBRNN. But we know that with very deep neural networks, the problem of overfitting comes into action, but this problem did not appear in our case, thus making the architecture much more intuitive and robust. Thus we conclude that the architecture of our DMA-LSTM-RBRNN is best suited for Melody Generation but yes with the help of Nadam Optimizer, which results in much more promising values of training accuracy and testing accuracy on the song dataset which we have used for the Melody Generation.

REFERENCES

Agarwal, S., Saxena, V., Singal, V., & Aggarwal, S. (2018, November). LSTM-based music generation with dataset preprocessing and reconstruction techniques. In *2018 IEEE Symposium Series on Computational Intelligence (SSCI)* (pp. 455–462). IEEE. DOI: 10.1109/SSCI.2018.8628712

Amiot, E. (2016). *Music through Fourier space*. Springer International Publishing. DOI: 10.1007/978-3-319-45581-5

Arias-Vergara, T., Klumpp, P., Vasquez-Correa, J. C., Nöth, E., Orozco-Arroyave, J. R., & Schuster, M. (2021). Multi-channel spectrograms for speech processing applications using deep learning methods. *Pattern Analysis & Applications*, *24*(2), 423–431. DOI: 10.1007/s10044-020-00921-5

Brinkmann, P., & Sekretariat, M. A. (2005). MidiKinesis—MIDI controllers for (almost) any purpose. In LAC2005 Proceedings (pp. 9–12).

Briot, J. P., & Pachet, F. (2020). Deep learning for music generation: Challenges and directions. *Neural Computing & Applications*, *32*(4), 981–993. DOI: 10.1007/s00521-018-3813-6

Carnovalini, F., & Rodà, A. (2020). Computational creativity and music generation systems: An introduction to the state of the art. *Frontiers in Artificial Intelligence*, *3*, 14. DOI: 10.3389/frai.2020.00014 PMID: 33733133

Cho, K. O., & Jang, H. J. (2020). Comparison of different input modalities and network structures for deep learning-based seizure detection. *Scientific Reports*, *10*(1), 1–11. DOI: 10.1038/s41598-019-56958-y PMID: 31924842

Cuthbert, M. S., & Ariza, C. (2010). music21: A toolkit for computer-aided musicology and symbolic music data.

Cuthbert, M. S., Ariza, C., Cabal-Ugaz, J., Hadley, B., & Parikh, N. (2011). Hidden beyond MIDI's reach: Feature extraction and machine learning with rich symbolic formats in music21. In *Proceedings of the NIPS 2011 Workshop on Music and Machine Learning*.

Cuthbert, M. S., Ariza, C., & Friedland, L. (2011, October). Feature extraction and machine learning on symbolic music using the music21 toolkit. In ISMIR (pp. 387–392).

Farrokhmanesh, M., & Hamzeh, A. (2016, April). A novel method for malware detection using audio signal processing techniques. In 2016 Artificial Intelligence and Robotics (IRANOPEN) (pp. 85–91). IEEE.

Hadjeres, G., & Nielsen, F. (2020). Anticipation-RNN: Enforcing unary constraints in sequence generation, with application to interactive music generation. *Neural Computing & Applications*, *32*(4), 995–1005. DOI: 10.1007/s00521-018-3868-4

Humphrey, E. J., Bello, J. P., & LeCun, Y. (2012, October). Moving beyond feature design: Deep architectures and automatic feature learning in music informatics. In ISMIR (pp. 403–408).

Hunter, J. D. (2007). Matplotlib: A 2D graphics environment. *IEEE Annals of the History of Computing*, *9*(03), 90–95.

Lu, W. T., & Su, L. (2018, November). Deep learning models for melody perception: An investigation on symbolic music data. In 2018 Asia-Pacific Signal and Information Processing Association Annual Summit and Conference (APSIPA ASC) (pp. 1620–1625). IEEE.

MacMillan, K., Droettboom, M., & Fujinaga, I. (2002). Gamera: Optical music recognition in a new shell. In ICMC.

McFee, B., Raffel, C., Liang, D., Ellis, D. P., McVicar, M., Battenberg, E., & Nieto, O. (2015, July). Librosa: Audio and music signal analysis in Python. In *Proceedings of the 14th Python in Science Conference* (Vol. 8, pp. 18–25). DOI: 10.25080/Majora-7b98e3ed-003

Phon-Amnuaisuk, S. (2019, July). Exploring Music21 and Gensim for music data analysis and visualization. In *International Conference on Data Mining and Big Data* (pp. 3–12). Springer, Singapore. DOI: 10.1007/978-981-32-9563-6_1

Ringeval, F., Schuller, B., Valstar, M., Cummins, N., Cowie, R., Tavabi, L., Schmitt, M., Alisamir, S., Amiriparian, S., Messner, E. M., & Song, S. (2019, October). AVEC 2019 workshop and challenge: State-of-mind, detecting depression with AI, and cross-cultural affect recognition. In Proceedings of the 9th International on Audio/Visual Emotion Challenge and Workshop (pp. 3–12).

Rodriguez, C. R., Angeles, D., Chafloque, R., Kaseng, F., & Pandey, B. (2020, September). Deep learning audio spectrograms processing to the early COVID-19 detection. In 2020 12th International Conference on Computational Intelligence and Communication Networks (CICN) (pp. 429–434). IEEE.

Yang, L. C., Chou, S. Y., & Yang, Y. H. (2017). MidiNet: A convolutional generative adversarial network for symbolic-domain music generation. arXiv preprint arXiv:1703.10847.

Yu, Y., Srivastava, A., & Canales, S. (2021). Conditional LSTM-GAN for melody generation from lyrics. [TOMM]. *ACM Transactions on Multimedia Computing Communications and Applications*, *17*(1), 1–20. DOI: 10.1145/3424116

Yust, J. (2017). Review of Emmanuel Amiot, Music through Fourier Space: Discrete Fourier Transform in Music Theory (Springer, 2016). Music Theory Online, 23(3).

Chapter 5
Enlarged Artificial intelligence and Deep Learning in Big Data Analytics and Intelligent Interactive Multimedia Systems for m-Healthcare Applications:
Rapidly Changing Lives of Humans through Smart Healthcare Techniques

Bhupinder Singh
https://orcid.org/0009-0006-4779-2553
Sharda University, India

Saurabh Chandra
https://orcid.org/0000-0003-4172-9968
Bennett University, Greater Noida, India

DOI: 10.4018/979-8-3693-2935-1.ch005

ABSTRACT

Mobile health (m-health) refers to the practice of monitoring health using mobile phones and patient monitoring devices, and it is considered a significant technological breakthrough in the contemporary era. Recently, the integration of artificial intelligence (AI) and big data analytics has been introduced in m-health to enhance the efficiency of healthcare systems. Modern medical research utilizes various types of data, including electronic health records (EHRs), medical images, and complex text, which are diverse, poorly interpreted and extensively unorganized. It conducts a systematic analysis of the application of AI and big data analytics to enhance the m-health system. It discusses various AI-based algorithms and big data frameworks which considering the source of data, techniques applied and the areas of application. This chapter explores how AI and big data analytics provide insights to users, aiding them in planning and addressing specific challenges in m-health. Also, it proposes a model based on AI and big data analytics for m-health.

1. INTRODUCTION

Artificial Intelligence (AI), Deep Learning (DL) integrated with Big Data Analytics and Intelligent Interactive Multimedia Systems are bringing a new paradigm shift in m-Healthcare applications, which represent the next big thing in delivering/using healthcare services. This intersection of modern technologies is not just an improvement in computation but a changing force that alters human existence by means of smart healthcare techniques. Using such innovations, m-Healthcare programs facilitate customized, forecasted and accurate health professional practices on grounds of eliminating gaps in standard healthcare supply systems. Whether it is for health insurance providers, doctors or patients; AI has become an integral aspect of healthcare with its computing power being able to sift through torrents of unstructured data and generate actionable insight in short order (Batalden et al., 2023). When combined with DL, which imitates the neural networks of own brains, these technologies achieve massively better results in terms of pattern recognition and predictions.

This is especially true within m-Healthcare, where the volume and variety of health data (fromEHR to wearable sensors) require significant computational resources for processing and analysis. AI and DL convert these data sources to knowledge, which helps health care providers with decision support by providing the right element at the right place and time while delivering customized solutions for patient care.

Big Data Analytics is a key component that manages the tremendous volume, velocity and variety of enormous healthcare data, in this ecosystem. Whether it is genomic sequences or wearable metrics reflecting the peculiarities of an individual's lifestyle, such a varied data spanning the entire spectrum must be analyzed to derive holistic healthcare solutions. Big Data Analytics leverages these datasets to find trends and anomalies that improve the accuracy of disease prediction models, minimize diagnostic errors and facilitate better resource allocation in healthcare facilities. Coupled with AI and DL, it takes m–Healthcare into a whole new world of efficiency and accuracy (Balarajan et al., 2021).

These technologies along with Intelligent Interactive Multimedia Systems make a greater impact by providing user engagement and accessibility. The systems that combine multimedia content like video, audio, and interactive graphics along with an intuitive interface are more accessible to both patients and healthcare providers. That is, leveraging AI and natural language processing (NLP)-based virtual health assistants such that it allows for an easy two-way communication between the patient and guide thereby gaining trust to have the patient adhere better by following guidelines of treatment recommendations. In addition, immersive technologies such as augmented reality (AR) and virtual reality (VR) have found application in the field of rehabilitation therapies providing new options for addressing physical and mental health issues. The union of these technologies is especially disruptive to mobile healthcare, which inherently is both accessible and scalable. Text m-Healthcare apps democratize access to medical knowledge with borders free and all underserved group included. Whether remote patient monitoring, telemedicine or personalized treatment plans implementation; All of these applications on technology really show us that we can achieve global health equity with the help of it.

At the same time, the growing use of AI, DL and Big Data Analytics in healthcare comes with challenges such as data privacy, ethical issues and needs for regulation. It is imperative to respond these challenges in order to achieve the sustainable expansion of smart healthcare systems. It extensively explores the existing as well as newer and novel interlinked components of AI, DL, Big Data Analytics and Intelligent Interactive Multimedia Systems in m-Healthcare ecosystem (Godman et al., 2020). In that spirit, the following report explore how these technologies are impacting lives–some through healthcare delivery and some through innovative research in ways it had not been able to do until now.

Figure 1. shows the Dimensions of Introduction Section (Source- Self Prepared- Original)

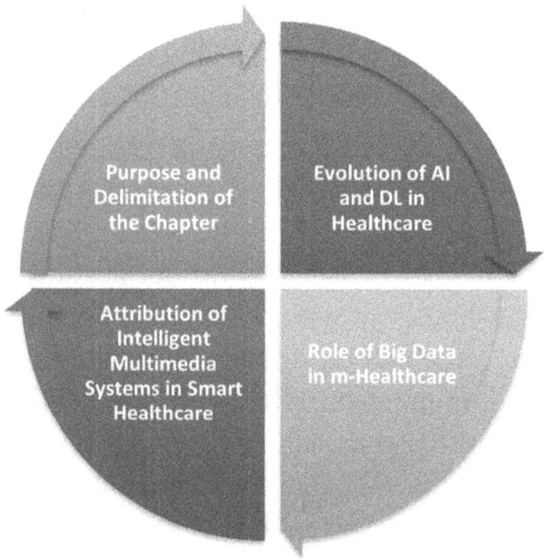

1.1. Evolution of AI and DL in Healthcare

The implementation of Artificial Intelligence (AI) and Deep Learning (DL) has changed the healthcare domain entirely, making it proactive rather than reactive as well as predictive in nature. Primitive uses of AI, like rule-based expert systems, relied on static programming and narrow data integration. The arrival of DL referred to training of neural networks that can learn the structures of complex/sparse data has transformed healthcare applications such as medical imaging, prediction of diseases and personalized medicine (Gandhi et al., 2018). Recent advances like CNNs on diagnostics and NLP on clinical notes have equipped clinicians with new tools to make better decisions. AI and DL have matured as integral building blocks of smart healthcare that can provide unprecedented levels of precision and efficiency in solving various health issues.

1.2 Role of Big Data in m-Healthcare

Mobile healthcare (m-Healthcare) benefits from Big Data, a huge pool of mostly unstructured data available from several sources like electronic health record (EHR), smart devices, and IoT systems. Big Data has a role to play because its strength is in offering real-time insights, predictive analytics and population health management tools In m-Healthcare, this translates into customized care plans, improved resource allocation, and disease detection at an early stage. Big Data using AI and DL further allows continuous monitoring, predictive modeling, and individualized interventions with the potential of vastly improved patient outcomes in more remote or underserved areas.

1.3 Attribution of Intelligent Multimedia Systems in Smart Healthcare

Audio, video, and graphical interface components are essential in intelligent multimedia systems for healthcare they improve patient engagement and make effective health delivery possible. These systems give users friendly platforms into their hands for managing well-being knowledge, virtual consultations, and therapy instruments. Augmented reality (AR) and virtual reality (VR) help to create immersive environments for rehabilitation; AI-driven virtual assistants also provide 24/7 assistance, enhancing care adherence and patient satisfaction.

1.4 Purpose and Delimitation of the Chapter

This chapter intends to study the synergy of AI, DL, Big Data Analytics and intelligent multimedia systems within m-Healthcare. Focusing on their evolution, roles and transformative ability this chapter outlines the potential of these technologies in solving modern healthcare challenges, namely accessibility, efficiency and personalization.

2. BIG DATA ANALYTICS IN M-HEALTHCARE

Big data (BD) analytics serves as a foundational pillar of m-Healthcare, enabling the process by which medical data can be collected, processed and transformed into meaningful information to improve health outcomes. Massive, heterogeneous and continually growing datasets such as electronic health records (EHRs), wearable devices and Internet of Things (IoT) sensors are main pillars for the m-Healthcare ecosystem. And this real-time and predictive analytics capability has essentially expanded the horizons of healthcare delivery by facilitating precision medicine, personalized care, and enhanced resource allocation (American Diabetes Association, 2015).

The size of health data created by millions of devices, sensors and clinical interactions every day. Within the Variety, it includes more structured data or lab results, and less structured like doctor's notes, medical images and patient-reported outcome measures. Velocity refers to how quickly this data is generated and must be processed for finding insight. These features offer a marriage of value but also means that Big Data Analytics is pivotal to m-Healthcare given its ability, to process and analyze vast datasets at previously unimagined speeds in order to create actionable insights.

2.1 Data Sources in m-Healthcare

Electronic Health Records (EHRs): EHRs give a near-immediate, holistic impression of the patient's medical history that can have significant implications on how invasive or extensive treatment may need to be; these records often include data such as past diagnoses and treatments performed with their outcomes.

Wearable Devices and IoT Sensors: Smartwatches and fitness bands monitor vital signs such as heart rate, oxygen level, sleep data on a continuous basis. They provide streams of data that allow for continuous monitoring of health and rapid detection of anomalies.

Genomics and Personal Medicine: The genomic sequencing which is derived from so many data sets can be created to customize treatment for an individual based on a genetic profile. The backbone of m-Healthcare is these data sources, which enable evidence-based and patient-centric care.

2.2 Big Data Analytics in m-Health Care Applications

The role predictive analytics has played in studying disease patterns and forecasting health risk is remarkable. Such predictive models can, for example, estimate the risk of developing chronic conditions include diabetes or cardiovascular disease from longitudinal health data, allowing early interventions. Through Big Data Analytics, treatment plans can be personalized for a patient based on their individual health history (Hassan et al., 2024). The synthesis of data from EHRs, genomics and wearable devices allows healthcare providers to formulate patient-specific treatment plans that help minimize adverse effects whilst maximizing efficacy. IoT devices and real-time analytics enables remote monitoring of patients that offer improved care for chronic patients. Such systems monitor key indicators, notify medical professionals in case of incoming catastrophes and provide the opportunity for preventive steps remotely rather than face-to-face. With big data we can find trends in health of groups/populations and this information helps policy makers and clinicians use resources wisely. As an example, you can use Big Data Analytics to monitor disease outbreaks and implement containment strategies during pandemic times.

This means Big Data Analytics can help hospitals improve the patient experience by analyzing things like wait times, resource utilization and treatment outcomes to bail out streamlining hospital operations for better patient flow and staffing optimization. Big Data Analytics in m-Healthcare promises transformational potential; however, there are number of challenges still being faced. Treating health data needs proper security in order to avoid breaches but also regulation with laws like GDPR or HIPAA (Gan et al., 2020). More interesting factor will be the quality of insights yielded from Big Data, depending on how accurate or reliable the underlying data are. Inconsistent or wrong data can result in misleading analyses and results. The high sums needed for advanced Big Data solutions, their infrastructure, means of mass storage as well as skilled personnel and maintenance burden many healthcare systems that lack sufficient resources.

AI and ML extend the power of Big Data Analytics by automating data processing and uncovering deeper insights. These algorithms can analyze vast amounts of data in order to identify patterns, correlations and anomalies that might not be immediately obvious.

Federated learning and real-time edge analytics are major trends in Big Data Analytics for m-Healthcare in the future, which enable collaborative data analysis with privacy preservation and on-device local processing respectively. Such advancements will continue to make high-quality healthcare accessible to people around the world including those in underserved and rural communities. Thus, Big Data Analytics are not just a technological step forward but a real catalyst for change in m-Healthcare. Utilizing its functionalities, healthcare providers will be able to provide successful, tailored medicine and treatment that improves the lives of patients while making care more accessible across the globe.

2.3 Features of Big Data in Healthcare

The Volume consists of large amounts of data produced around the world every day from multiple sources like electronic health record (EHR) systems, imaging systems, wearable devices and IoT sensors. Such an unprecedented scale requires higher levels of analytics to be effectively processed and utilized. Variety is the diversity of healthcare data types structured data (lab results), semi-structured(universal health insurance claims), and unstructured clinical/discharge notes or radiological images. Integrating these disparate formats is essential to complete health care insights. Velocity emphasizes the speedy generation and streaming of health data, especially from IoT devices and Mobile apps (Fang et al., 2019). For example, in the case of the health domain where timely decision-making is important for critical scenarios, it is imperative to process this high velocity data in near real time environment. Also, the Veracity of data, that is about its reliability and correctness, also comes into play with these increasingly tightening scales. Together these characteristics help Big Data Analytics become a high power tool drive solution for complexities of healthcare.

2.4 Data Sources: EHR, Wearables and IoT Devices

Healthcare data comes from many different sources, each of which provides information that is unique. Electronic Health Records (EHRs) are a comprehensive medical history of patients that includes information such as the diagnosis, medications, allergies and treatment plans. They are probably the most critical for long-term health observation and decision-making. Wearable devices such as fitness trackers and smartwatches provide patients with real-time continuous data on vital signs, physical activity, and sleep stages. These devices enable patients to play an active role in managing their health while clinicians can monitor them remotely. Internet of Things (IoT) devices such as smart medical appliances and environmental sensors facilitate the remote monitoring of an individual in various settings by collating information on environmental conditions and patient status (Bergwerk et al., 2021). They provide a very integral perspective of patient health together and encourages personalized and preventive care to bridge the last mile gap in healthcare delivery systems.

2.5 Quality of Decision Support in Real-Time Analytics

With allowing for the immediate processing and analysis of massive amounts of data, real-time analytics has completely transformed the way that clinical decisions are made. This is especially crucial in healthcare, where emergency situations arise and rapid insights can be the difference between life and death. For example, you may have seen that analytics from wearables or IoT sensors are notifying a provider about deviations such as an irregular heart rhythm or drop in oxygen saturation. Real-time analytics is also godsend in the intensive care units (ICUs), where streams of crucial data flow through continuous monitoring of patients.

When combined with CDSS (clinical decision support systems), real-time analytics provide actionable insights to healthcare providers and enable them to optimize the treatment strategy. Apart from clinical use, real-time analytics helps boost operational efficiency by predicting patient inflow, resource allocation and hospital wait time minimization. All these capabilities provide m-Healthcare real-time analytics, where the reactive care ranges to proactive and preventive healthcare.

2.6 Predictive Modeling for Disease Management

The predictive modeling of patient data enables the use of Big Data and machine learning algorithms to predict risks and outcomes for diseases. Using historical health records, genetic information, and lifestyle data, predictive models can identify patterns and risk factors for chronic conditions including diabetes, hypertension, and cardiovascular diseases. By analyzing workloads, the models can predict health events which enables better management of potential hospitalization if evidence sources such as a wearable data on physical activity and vital signs integrator are integrated with EHRs for actionable outcome. Another important aspect of epidemic control involves predictive modeling, evidenced by the role these tools played in recent pandemics forecasting the locations and intensity of infections along with clinical resource utilization. Predictive models in oncology help in personalizing treatment by predicting tumor growth and response to therapies (Tomas et al., 2023). Ditching the patient and looking at population level health management these models can assist local and national policy makers when it comes to resource allocation and primary care prevention planning. With predictive modeling, healthcare gives its providers a look into the future allowing them to take on a more proactive role in preventing illness and disease management leading toward better outcomes for patients and lower costs for everyone.

3. DEEP LEARNING TECHNIQUES IN M-HEALTHCARE

DL techniques have recently become stunning tools in mobile, healthcare (m-Healthcare) by providing innovative solutions for diagnosis, treatment, and management. DL or deep learning, which is a subfield of artificial intelligence (AI), uses neural networks that mimic the brain to analyse massive datasets and discover patterns with great precision. These approaches are used in m-Healthcare to solve the complicated problems from medical imaging to personalize care enabling future enhancement of quality and recovery in healthcare services. Medical imaging is among the most significant applications of DL in m-Healthcare. Approaches such as convolutional neural networks (CNNs) are powerful for analysing visual data, such as X-rays, MRIs or CT scans. Help with Early Diagnosis CNNs identify slight anomalies that a human eye might overlook and in turn aids for the timely detection of diseases such as cancers, heart ailments, and neurological disorders. Now, mobile applications exploiting DL allow patients and healthcare providers to take diagnostic tests at home without ever visiting a doctor ensuring timely intervention for people living in underserved or remote locations (Runciman et al., 2017).

Therefore, Natural Language Processing (NLP) goes a step further in improving the efficiency of processing unstructured clinical data with it being backed by deep learning. DL algorithms reveal useful information for better decision making by analyzing texts from electronic health records (EHR), medical notes and patient reports. Such as, analysis of patient reviews can reveal the areas needing improvement, while entity-recognition tools assist in creating a summary of clinical histories for accurate treatments. The power of deep learning models in predictive analytics enables health care providers to predict health problems and take preventive measures. Because they are specifically designed for sequential data, Recurrent Neural Network (RNNs) and Long Short-Term Memory (LSTM) networks have the potential to be very useful when you want to follow a patient's health over time. These models use longitudinal data from wearable devices to predict outcomes, like the risk of a heart attack or chronic disease progression, allowing for early intervention and individualized treatment strategies.

Genomic data analyzed through DL techniques are revolutionizing personalized medicine by allowing us to design treatments based on someone's DNA sequence. DL systems can incorporate patient health records and multi-omics data to determine the optimal therapies, which reduces side effects and enhances outcomes. Also, for drug discovery, DL algorithms such as GANs, also accelerate the process of finding new compounds by reducing both time and cost needed in traditional research methods. Tools powered by DL also aid remote patient monitoring as well as remote virtual care (Li et al., 2018). As an example DL models assess live information from IoT devices and wearables to identify anomalies so that the healthcare providers can be contacted. DU springdows, virtual health assistants powered by DL algorithms provide tailored dietary recommendations, medication reminders, and mental health assistance while they remain engaged with patients throughout the treatment process.

DL in m-Healthcare has many challenges, such as data privacy and algorithm interpretability, which must be overcome to fulfil the promise of accurate DL solutions that care for their users with high-quality training datasets. Ongoing focus on regulatory compliance, e.g., GDPR, HIPAA vs. model performance. On the positive side, developments in federated finding out, explainable AI and secure multi-party computation are setting the stage for stronger and ethical DL use circumstances ultimately. Deep learning techniques redefined m-Healthcare by providing scalability, efficiency and personalization. As the technology continues to progress, it will undoubtedly help fill significant gaps in health care delivery–especially for those with limited options and resources more broadly, likely changing the lives of many patients globally.

4. AI-POWERED INTELLIGENT INTERACTIVE MULTIMEDIA SYSTEMS

The emergence of AI-powered IIM Systems is transforming the interaction between human beings and technology enabling deeper, richer and more personalized experiences in fields such as healthcare, education, entertainment and business. They use artificial intelligence to analyze large amounts of data, adjust to the user, and respond in real time which results in dynamic environments with high immersiveness. Despite the continuing challenges of data privacy and technical complexity, improvement in AI, computing power and network infrastructure continues to unleash more areas for development. AI-backed (yes, more and more of this) IIMS serve as a missing link in the interaction between man and machine that will envelope these machines into human lives, industries & enhancing liveability too (Bowman, 2023).

Such systems, together with an AI-enabled logo and advanced multimedia technologies allow users to experience interaction between the user and machine dynamically by providing more customized services customized experiences with rich interaction. It is not only changing the way this view our media content, but also moving us away from traditional static delivery to responsive, adaptive and intelligent media environments.

Figure 2. specifies the Points on AI-Powered Intelligent Interactive Multimedia Systems (Source- Self Prepared- Original)

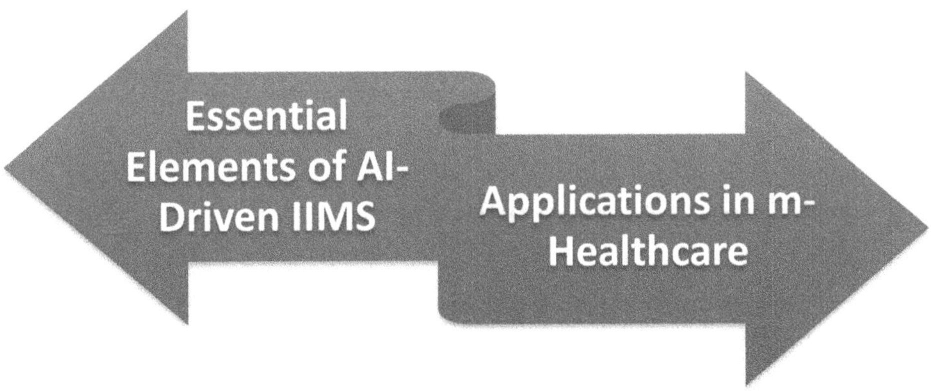

4.1 Essential Elements of AI-Driven IIMS

AI-Powered IIMS have a set of key technologies that they rely on to perform:

Natural Language Processing (NLP): It allows systems to comprehend human language and process it, making multimedia applications work with voice commands, chatbots, real-time translation.

Computer Vision: Its interpretation of visual data (images, videos) adds features like facial recognition, object detection and content recommendation for media.

ML and DL algorithms enable the system to learn and evolve over time, providing tailored content delivery and dynamic responses.

Augmented Reality (AR) and Virtual Reality (VR): AR and VR tools offer multi-sensory experiences that can replace or augment the original physical reality, delivering different types of virtual content to users who interact with 3D objects, simulated environments and scenarios in real-time.

Speech Recognition and Synthesis: AI allows multimedia systems to recognize and synthesize human speech, which is essential for interactive applications such as virtual assistants and language learning platforms. By combining these pieces together, AI-based IIMS provide people with the real interactivity, intelligence and involvement to them.

4.2 Applications in m-Healthcare

Especially in the mobile healthcare (m-Healthcare) domain, AI-powered intelligent information management system (IIMS) play a transformative role. Use of multimedia tools such as video, audio, and text to support diagnostics, patient engagement, and medical training in these systems. An AI multimedia system can further integrate video conferencing with AI diagnostics to facilitate virtual consultations. As an example, systems assess voice and facial expressions during video-conference calls to identify markers of certain neurological or psychological symptoms in patients (Watts et al., 2023).

Remote Monitoring: The multimedia architecture with the combination of IoMT sensors and wearable devices provides real time data about the patients vital signs. With these updates, presented as dashboards through AI tools on his smartphone or tablet whenever necessary in the hospital so that timely prevention can be carried out by caregivers.

Medical Training & Simulations: Using VR and AR, multimedia systems provides virtual immersive training environments for medical professionals. To help practitioners hone their skills, AI tools provide simulations for strategic behavior that can be highly intricate while in a risk-free environment.

Patient Education: Interactive multimedia tools that educate patients about their specific conditions and treatment options through videos, infographics, or AI-based chat interfaces will lead to a better understanding of the patient which would promote health literacy and adherence to the care plans.

In the education sector, even AI-powered IIMS are changing the entire landscape of learning by making it more engaging, challenging and accessible. AI analyzes learners from multiple points of view, such as their strengths and weaknesses, preferences to customize educational content. Interactive platforms modify lessons to suit the learner's level and give them personalized feedback so that they learn well. These include the creation of virtual classrooms through AR and VR that enable students to engage with 3D models, historical recreations or simulated experiments. Such as a biology student, can check out human anatomy in a virtual lab. Speech Recognition and Synthesis systems can help you learn a foreign language (Chartier, 2024). Interactive tools offer immediate feedback on things such as: pronunciation, grammar, and vocabulary use. Smart multimedia systems can be particularly useful for students with disabilities who will need real-time captioning, sign language interpretation, and text-to-speech conversion.

AI-powered IIMS are crafting a new form of entertainment for the entertainment industry, providing users with personalized and interactive experiences. Using advanced AI algorithms to analyze users preferences and consumption patterns, we can recommend a movie, music or game that will match individual tastes. Multimedia systems allow users to participate in the story creation process, enabling them to choose their own adventure. Powered by AI, it alters the storyline according to user inputs collecting throughout the story. AI-based multimedia systems elevate gaming by means of adaptive difficulty levels, realistic graphics, and voice-controlled gameplay. Virtual reality gaming environments provide the player with an immersive, realistic simulation. AI integrates real-time analytics as well as audience interaction elements into live streams, which significantly increases engagement in the course of an event by providing personalized content recommendations. The same goes for commercial spaces where IIMS with the assistance of AI are reforming different departments like marketing, customer service and decision making.

AI-enabled multimedia systems design interactive ads that change according to user behavior, improving both engagement and conversion rates. Leverage AR and VR to provide customers with virtual showrooms where they can experience their products, like dressing up in a suit or simply scanning the clothes or previewing furniture in a simulated room. AI-powered intelligent chatbots and multimedia systems ensure 24/7 delivery of customer service by responding to queries via text, voice, or even video. AI based multimedia tools convert complicated data set into interactive visualisation to assist business minds in taking better decisions (Ogugua et al., 2024).

5. ETHICAL AND LEGAL CHALLENGES IN SMART HEALTHCARE

While this integration of artificial intelligence and digital technologies in smart healthcare is ground-breaking, it can also result in ethical and legal challenges. With the rise of m-Healthcare solutions, it is essential to guarantee that these are not implemented irresponsibly at the cost of patient rights and trust. Concerns such as data privacy and security, fairness of AI models, compliance to regulation, accountability etc. To have an equitable, efficient and sustainable healthcare ecosystem it is important that we address these challenges.

5.1. Data Privacy and Security Issues

The foremost ethical challenge is data privacy and security. Sensitive patient data such as medical histories, genetic information, and real-time health metrics from wearables and IoT devices countryside into m-healthcare applications (American Diabetes Association, 2014). Since this data is collected, stored and processed to certain degree they become a target for unauthorize access, data breaches and misuse.

Strict regulations such as GDPR (General Data Protection Regulation) and HIPAA (Health Insurance Portability and Accountability Act), must be adhered to by healthcare providers and technological developers. These frameworks require data minimization, consent before processing, and encryption standards to protect patient records. Even with these protections, ensuring compliance on a global scale is no small feat. Looking into finding solutions, things like blockchain to help with security of the data. Using Blockchain essentially helps keep records permanent and transparent which gives the patients control over their own data. Likewise, with federated learning models, it can use decentralized data to learn while preserving privacy for every single respondent. To deploy these technologies, though, there are technical and organizational hurdles to overcome (Sikka et al., 2020).

5.2. AI Models Bias and Fairness

AI models involved in m-Healthcare suffer from biases due to unrepresentative or incomplete training data. Such biases risk misdiagnosis, unequal treatment suggestions, and disparate results for marginalized populations. If an AI has been trained mostly on data of one subpopulation, it can work poorly for other groups and further entrench health inequities. If AI is to be fair, it needs to build measures for that while developing the models themselves. Biases can be mitigated by techniques such as data augmentation, re-sampling, and fairness-aware algorithms. Also, training dataset must include populations of various ages/genders/ethnicities/socio-economic backgrounds etc. However, healthcare applications of AI will require ethical oversight committees at a higher rate than other areas as faced by law enforcement and militaries around the globe today or we risk allowing future decision-making to be dictated solely by biased datasets (Music, 2022). Acting in this manner, e.g., by openly reporting on performance metrics such as error rates for various demographics can improve trust and accountability.

5.3. AI Regulation in m-Healthcare

This has prompted international organizations and governments to consider how they should develop AI, with some developing AI-specific guidelines. One such regulation is the European Union's Artificial Intelligence Act, which aims to regulate the design, development and deployment of AI systems, considering healthcare as a high-risk domain. Along these lines, the U.S. Food and Drug Administration (FDA) has also laid out a proposed framework to regulate AIdriven devices with emphasis on safety, effectiveness, and transparency. Well, m-Healthcare is evolving quickly but the provision of regulation governing this area is lagging behind that evolution including so-called AI frameworks. While existing data protection regulations like GDPR and HIPAA are applicable at a high level, they tend not to contain provisions specifically tailored for systems driven by AI. Such a lack of regulation leaves developers, healthcare providers and patients in the dark. Striking the right balance between innovation and patient safety is a major hurdle in regulatory compliance. As we evaluate new regulations, the challenge is to avoid regulating innovation out of existence while not allowing practices that could put patients at risk. Finding this equilibrium will require collaboration between regulators and industry stakeholders, as well as healthcare professionals (Knagg et al., 2024).

5.4. Accountability, Transparency and Good Faith

To enable trust in such an AI-based smart healthcare system, transparency and accountability are more important. It's crucial for patients and providers alike to understand how AI systems derive their recommendations, especially in the case of diagnosis or treatment plans where such decisions can be life-changing. But the very nature of AI algorithms, in particular deep learning models, tends to render them as opaque systems. However, the challenge of explainability brings users to suspicion and reluctance.

This is a growing challenge that can be solved through Explainable AI (XAI) clarifying and rendering visible how an AI model operates on information. For example, some XAI tools can illustrate what exactly led to a diagnostic conclusion in many instances this can be a particular feature found in medical imaging (Pool et al., 2024).

Identifying accountability points for errors committed by an AI system is difficult, especially with multiple players involved the developers, healthcare providers, device manufacturers, etc. If harm caused by an AI system occurs then patients should have the same rights and access to legal redress as that derived from legislation governing equitable liability. A mixture of ethical codes of conduct, along with legal obligations for transparency, can also improve accountability. External audits and AI certification processes can help ensure adherence to ethical and legal requirements. The ethical and legal challenges in smart healthcare can be complex in nature, and will need to be taken more with a coordinated response (Goldsteen et al., 2024). CII highlights data privacy and security, bias in AI models, regulatory frameworks, transparency as areas that require focus. Focus on these areas will guarantee that m-Healthcare solutions are innovative, equitable, secure and trusted. Finding the balance between beneficial use of this technology and ensuring equitable access is critical, and will require collaboration between governments, organisations and members of the public alike to realise a future where AI-driven healthcare systems serve all sections of society.

6. CHALLENGES AND OPPORTUNITIES

AI and smart technologies hold immense potential to transform healthcare. Yet, there are challenges and opportunities in achieving this potential. Taking advantage of this emerging opportunity means tackling the technical barriers, adoption issues and make room for a sustainable, equitable and efficient m-Healthcare ecosystem.

6.1. Technical Hurdles in Integrating Reading Data

The integration of diverse data sources and system interoperability is one of the prominent technical challenges in smart healthcare. Multiple platforms generate healthcare data, including Electronic Health Records (EHR), wearable devices, Internet of Things (IoT) sensors, and diagnostic imaging systems. Driven by the diversity of these data sources, integration remains complex due to dissimilar formats, standards and protocols (Slaunwhite et al., 2024).

Emergency room teams may not be able to get a sense of what else might have been going on with the patient, as well; interoperability issues make it difficult to adequately exchange information between providers, leading to gaps when it comes time for decision making and continuity of care. As an example, if a patient moves from one hospital to another, their health records may not be shared seamlessly because of proprietary systems or non-standardized data formats. The unintegrated state means that diagnosis and treatments are delayed leading to poor patient outcomes. Technical solutions like Health Level Seven (HL7) standards and Fast Healthcare Interoperability Resources (FHIR) seek to solve these problems. But not all regions and organizations will pick up such standards quickly. Centralized data platforms and secure data transfer utilizing advanced technologies such as blockchain can be used to help minimize issues caused by interoperability (Fuse Brown & Hall, 2024).

6.2. Obstacles to Adoption: Both Infrastructure and Cost Implications

AI-based m-Healthcare solutions will drive Modernization at the Healthcare organizations and need huge infrastructural investment and thus, higher cost implications. High-throughput IT backbone and connectivity due to cloud computing, AI-enabled devices requiring near real time data processing systems are hardly ever available universally, especially in rural or other underserved locations. The other major impediment is the cost of smart healthcare systems. The investment needed for AI solution acquisition, the training of health professionals, and long-term maintenance of technological infrastructure can become expensive overwhelming for many small healthcare providers or emerging economies. The ROI for these technologies may not be clear upfront and would therefore further deter adoption (Singh & Kaunert, 2025).

Overcoming these barriers calls for shared responsibility from both governments, private sector and health care organizations. Public-private partnerships have an important role to play in subsidizing costs, enabling deployment to underserved areas and bridging residents digital divide. Low-cost AI models and scalable solutions designed for low-resource contexts can similarly promote greater usage.

6.3. Areas of AI-Enabled Innovation with Room to Grow

Though continuing obstacles exist, the potential for AI-powered development in underserved sectors is tremendous. There are indeed many regions, especially in the developing world that find themselves lacking on healthcare workers associated with hospitals, laboratories and other diagnostics and treatment solutions. These gaps can be filled with AI-based solutions that provide healthcare services, efficiently making them more accessible and affordable. Telemedicine platforms, for example, are able to use AI and connect patients in remote areas with specialists at urban centers and facilitate the consultations over video calls so that in-person consultations can be avoided. Likewise, artificial intelligence-powered diagnostic solutions like smartphone-based imaging for diabetic retinopathy are cost-effective substitutes for conventional diagnoses (Singh et al., 2025).

Wearable devices and IoT-powered sensors can monitor chronic conditions in real-time, enabling patients to manage their health while reducing the load on healthcare facilities. This is especially useful for diseases that are continuous, such as high blood pressure and diabetes. AI enables predictive analytics to help healthcare providers predict disease outbreaks and allocate resources. Machine learning models that process climatic, demographic and historical data can predict above-normal malaria transmission risk two to three months in advance hence paving the way for preemptive control measures guided by targeted interventions specific to high-risk areas. In various communities AI-based language translation tools could help with the gap there holds linguistic barriers, to bridging communication among people and access proper healthcare information/service (Singh et al., 2025). These tools can work together as part of telehealth platforms to allow patients and healthcare providers who speak different languages to communicate with one another.

While the challenges of infusing AI and smart technologies into healthcare are high, it is not impossible (Singh & Kaunert, 2025). Overcoming technical obstacles involves the standardization of data protocols, investments in interoperable systems, and scaling-up through international frameworks. Likewise, addressing infrastructure and cost constraints requires strategic partnerships and scalable, cost-effective solutions designed for resource-limited environments. The promise of AI to tackle healthcare inequities, especially in under-resourced areas, demonstrates its capacity for good (Singh & Kaunert, 2024). AI and healthcare goes hand in hand, because AI is changing the way we deliver health care from virtual diagnostics to predictive analytics to patient-specific care (Singh & Kaunert, 2025). Through the collective effort of stakeholders, smart healthcare systems can catalyse a paradigm shift to create an equitable, fast and sustainable health ecosystem for everyone.

7. CONCLUSION AND FUTURE SCOPE

This is a new phase of digital smart healthcare opening up by the three magnets of Artificial Intelligence (AI), Deep Learning (DL), Big Data Analytics, and Intelligent Interactive Multimedia Systems that play revolutionary roles in m-Healthcare applications. The new technologies play a vital role to improve the precision of diagnosis, individualized treatment and better patient involvement that leads towards improved health outcomes. M-Healthcare solutions utilise data analytics, predictive models and interactive tools facilitate health care delivery, especially in remote areas or underserved regions. Even though such advancements have happened, data privacy, interoperability and adoption barriers are still critical fields that need addressing. These challenges will need to be overcome with the co-operation of governments, healthcare providers and technology developers. Political will and policy choice, as much as technological advancement, will dictate what the future may hold for AI and DL healthcare applications; ethical considerations and strong regulatory frameworks will be critical to ensure responsible and equitable implementation of AI- and DL-oriented healthcare solutions.

This field has infinite potential in the future as the AI and DL in telemedicine, precision medicine and population health management is huge. This will help to localize the m-healthcare systems even better, increasing the speed of decision making and patient remaining active connected. This will also enable building transparent and trusted AI-driven healthcare systems by developing explainable AI (XAI) models. With these technologies developing, the focus should be on scalability and affordability for wide diverse populations. Though, if we continuously innovate while acting ethically responsible, the future of m-Healthcare is not only going to add up in our lives but it might change the course of how healthcare systems are administered globally by providing health equity and sustainability.

REFERENCES

Agarwal, N., Ünlü, T., Wani, M. A., & Bours, P. (2021, October). Predatory conversation detection using transfer learning approach. In *International Conference on Machine Learning, Optimization, and Data Science* (pp. 488-499). Cham: Springer International Publishing.

Agarwal, N., Wani, M. A., & Bours, P. (2020). Lex-pos feature-based grammar error detection system for the English language. *Electronics (Basel), 9*(10), 1686. DOI: 10.3390/electronics9101686

Ahmad, P. N., Liu, Y., Ali, G., Wani, M. A., & ElAffendi, M. (2023). Robust benchmark for propagandist text detection and mining high-quality data. *Mathematics, 11*(12), 2668. DOI: 10.3390/math11122668

American Diabetes Association. (2014). Standards of medical care in diabetes—2014. *Diabetes Care, 37*(Supplement_1), S14–S80. DOI: 10.2337/dc14-S014 PMID: 24357209

American Diabetes Association. (2015). Standards of medical care in diabetes—2015 abridged for primary care providers. *Clinical Diabetes : a Publication of the American Diabetes Association, 33*(2), 97–111. DOI: 10.2337/diaclin.33.2.97 PMID: 25897193

Balarajan, Y., Selvaraj, S., & Subramanian, S. V. (2021). Health care and equity in India. *Lancet, 377*(9764), 505–515. DOI: 10.1016/S0140-6736(10)61894-6 PMID: 21227492

Batalden, M., Batalden, P., Margolis, P., Seid, M., Armstrong, G., Opipari-Arrigan, L., & Hartung, H. (2023). Coproduction of healthcare service. *BMJ Quality & Safety*. PMID: 26376674

Bergwerk, M., Gonen, T., Lustig, Y., Amit, S., Lipsitch, M., Cohen, C., Mandelboim, M., Levin, E. G., Rubin, C., Indenbaum, V., Tal, I., Zavitan, M., Zuckerman, N., Bar-Chaim, A., Kreiss, Y., & Regev-Yochay, G. (2021). Covid-19 breakthrough infections in vaccinated health care workers. *The New England Journal of Medicine, 385*(16), 1474–1484. DOI: 10.1056/NEJMoa2109072 PMID: 34320281

Bowman, S. (2023). Impact of electronic health record systems on information integrity: Quality and safety implications. *Perspectives in Health Information Management, 10*(Fall). PMID: 24159271

Chartier, Y. (Ed.). (2024). *Safe management of wastes from health-care activities*. World Health Organization.

Fang, H., Eggleston, K., Hanson, K., & Wu, M. (2019). Enhancing financial protection under China's social health insurance to achieve universal health coverage. *bmj, 365*.

Fuse Brown, E. C., & Hall, M. A. (2024). Private Equity and the Corporatization of Health Care. *Stanford Law Review*, •••, 76.

Gan, W. H., Lim, J. W., & Koh, D. (2020). Preventing intra-hospital infection and transmission of coronavirus disease 2019 in health-care workers. *Safety and Health at Work, 11*(2), 241–243. DOI: 10.1016/j.shaw.2020.03.001 PMID: 32292622

Gandhi, T. K., Kaplan, G. S., Leape, L., Berwick, D. M., Edgman-Levitan, S., Edmondson, A., Meyer, G. S., Michaels, D., Morath, J. M., Vincent, C., & Wachter, R. (2018). Transforming concepts in patient safety: A progress report. *BMJ Quality & Safety, 27*(12), 1019–1026. DOI: 10.1136/bmjqs-2017-007756 PMID: 30018115

Godman, B., Haque, M., Islam, S., Iqbal, S., Urmi, U. L., Kamal, Z. M., Shuvo, S. A., Rahman, A., Kamal, M., Haque, M., Jahan, I., Islam, M. Z., Hossain, M. M., Munzur-E-Murshid, , Kumar, S., Charan, J., Bhatt, R., Dutta, S., Abhayanand, J. P., & Sefah, I. (2020). Rapid assessment of price instability and paucity of medicines and protection for COVID-19 across Asia: Findings and public health implications for the future. *Frontiers in Public Health, 8*, 585832. DOI: 10.3389/fpubh.2020.585832 PMID: 33381485

. Goldsteen, R. L., Goldsteen, K., & Dwelle, T. (2024). Introduction to public health: promises and practices.

Hammad, M., Wani, M. A., Shakil, K. A., Shaiba, H., & Abd El-Latif, A. A. (2024). Deep cancelable multibiometric finger vein and fingerprint authentication with non-negative matrix factorization. *IEEE Access : Practical Innovations, Open Solutions*, *12*, 120638–120660. DOI: 10.1109/ACCESS.2024.3450372

Hassan, I., Chisty, A., & Bui, T. (2024). Structural and Social Determinants of Health. In *Leading an Academic Medical Practice* (pp. 343–355). Springer International Publishing.

Imran, A. S., Hodnefjeld, H., Kastrati, Z., Fatima, N., Daudpota, S. M., & Wani, M. A. (2023). Classifying european court of human rights cases using transformer-based techniques. *IEEE Access : Practical Innovations, Open Solutions*, *11*, 55664–55676. DOI: 10.1109/ACCESS.2023.3279034

Knagg, R., Dorey, J., Evans, R., & Hitchman, J. (2024). Sustainability in healthcare: Patient and public perspectives. *Anaesthesia*, *79*(3), 278–283. DOI: 10.1111/anae.16159 PMID: 38205532

Li, Y., Wang, H., Jin, X. R., Li, X., Pender, M., Song, C. P., Tang, S.-L., Cao, J., Wu, H., & Wang, Y. G. (2018). Experiences and challenges in the health protection of medical teams in the Chinese Ebola treatment center, Liberia: A qualitative study. *Infectious Diseases of Poverty*, *7*(1), 1–12. DOI: 10.1186/s40249-018-0468-6 PMID: 30134982

Music, T. (2022). Protecting patients, protecting healthcare workers: A review of the role of influenza vaccination. *International Nursing Review*, *59*(2), 161–167. DOI: 10.1111/j.1466-7657.2011.00961.x PMID: 22591085

Ogugua, J. O., Anyanwu, E. C., Olorunsogo, T., Maduka, C. P., & Ayo-Farai, O. (2024). Ethics and strategy in vaccination: A review of public health policies and practices. *International Journal of Science and Research Archive*, *11*(1), 883–895. DOI: 10.30574/ijsra.2024.11.1.0141

Pool, J., Akhlaghpour, S., Fatehi, F., & Burton-Jones, A. (2024). A systematic analysis of failures in protecting personal health data: A scoping review. *International Journal of Information Management*, *74*, 102719. DOI: 10.1016/j.ijinfomgt.2023.102719

Rawat, A., Wani, M. A., ElAffendi, M., Imran, A. S., Kastrati, Z., & Daudpota, S. M. (2022). Drug adverse event detection using text-based convolutional neural networks (TextCNN) technique. *Electronics (Basel), 11*(20), 3336. DOI: 10.3390/electronics11203336

Runciman, B., Merry, A., & Walton, M. (2017). *Safety and ethics in healthcare: a guide to getting it right*. CRC Press.

Sedik, A., El-Latif, A. A. A., Wani, M. A., El-Samie, F. E. A., Bauomy, N. A. S., & Hashad, F. G. (2023). Efficient multi-biometric secure-storage scheme based on deep learning and crypto-mapping techniques. *Mathematics, 11*(3), 703. DOI: 10.3390/math11030703

Shakil, K. A., Tabassum, K., Alqahtani, F. S., & Wani, M. A. (2021). Analyzing user digital emotions from a holy versus non-pilgrimage city in Saudi Arabia on Twitter Platform. *Applied Sciences (Basel, Switzerland), 11*(15), 6846. DOI: 10.3390/app11156846

Sikka, R., Morath, J. M., & Leape, L. (2020). The quadruple aim: Care, health, cost and meaning in work. *BMJ Quality & Safety, 24*(10), 608–610. DOI: 10.1136/bmjqs-2015-004160 PMID: 26038586

Singh, B., & Kaunert, C. (2024). Adventure in High Altitude of Mountainous Topographies and Health Impacts: Lensing Tourism Sustainability via Reducing Ecological and Sociocultural Footprint and Health Emergency and Medical Assistance Management. In Meraj, G., Hashimoto, S., & Kumar, P. (Eds.), *Navigating Natural Hazards in Mountainous Topographies. Disaster Risk Reduction*. Springer., DOI: 10.1007/978-3-031-65862-4_15

Singh, B., & Kaunert, C. (2025). Leveraging IoT for Patient Monitoring and Smart Healthcare: Connected Healthcare System. In B. S & S. Kadry (Eds.), *Revolutionizing Healthcare Systems Through Cloud Computing and IoT* (pp. 27-46). IGI Global. https://doi.org/DOI: 10.4018/979-8-3693-7225-8.ch002

Singh, B., & Kaunert, C. (2025). Cloud Computing and IoMT in Disease Screening and Diagnosis: AI Approaches in Transmuting Healthier Homes. In B. S & S. Kadry (Eds.), *Revolutionizing Healthcare Systems Through Cloud Computing and IoT* (pp. 99-120). IGI Global. DOI: 10.4018/979-8-3693-7225-8.ch005

Singh, B., & Kaunert, C. (2025). Featuring Healthcare, Environment, and Human Rights: Applications of Artificial Intelligence in the Health Domain. In Chakraborty, S., & Satapathy, S. (Eds.), *Gender, Environment, and Human Rights: An Intersectional Exploration* (pp. 45–74). IGI Global., DOI: 10.4018/979-8-3693-6069-9.ch004

Singh, B., Kaunert, C., & Singh, G. (2025). Scaling Legal Framework for Plastic Pollution and Advancing Cutting Edge Water Governance: Reducing and Eliminating Marine Pollution in Alignment With SDG 14 (Life Below Water). In Gaur, N., Sharma, E., Nguyen, T., Bilal, M., & Melkania, N. (Eds.), *Societal and Environmental Ramifications of Plastic Pollution* (pp. 197–222). IGI Global., DOI: 10.4018/979-8-3693-9163-1.ch010

Singh, B., Lal, S., Arora, M. K., & Kaunert, C. (2025). Mounting Legal-Driven Solutions for Plastic Pollution Focusing on Environment and Coastal Management: Eradicating Marine Pollution in Alignment With SDG 14 (Life Below Water). In Gaur, N., Sharma, E., Nguyen, T., Bilal, M., & Melkania, N. (Eds.), *Societal and Environmental Ramifications of Plastic Pollution* (pp. 223–252). IGI Global., DOI: 10.4018/979-8-3693-9163-1.ch011

. Slaunwhite, A., Min, J. E., Palis, H., Urbanoski, K., Pauly, B., Barker, B., ... & Nosyk, B. (2024). Effect of Risk Mitigation Guidance opioid and stimulant dispensations on mortality and acute care visits during dual public health emergencies: retrospective cohort study. *bmj, 384*.

Tomas, M. E., Kundrapu, S., Thota, P., Sunkesula, V. C., Cadnum, J. L., Mana, T. S. C., Jencson, A., O'Donnell, M., Zabarsky, T. F., Hecker, M. T., Ray, A. J., Wilson, B. M., & Donskey, C. J. (2023). Contamination of health care personnel during removal of personal protective equipment. *JAMA Internal Medicine, 175*(12), 1904–1910. DOI: 10.1001/jamainternmed.2015.4535 PMID: 26457544

Wani, M. A., Bours, P., Agarwal, N., & Jabin, S. (2019). Emotion-based mining for gender prediction in online social networks. In *Proceedings of the ACM, International Conference on Machine Learning and Data Science*.

Wani, M. A., ELAffendi, M., Bours, P., Imran, A. S., Hussain, A., & Abd El-Latif, A. A. (2024). Codes: A deep learning framework for identifying covid-caused depression symptoms. *Cognitive Computation*, *16*(1), 305–325. DOI: 10.1007/s12559-023-10190-z

. Wani, M. A., ElAffendi, M., & Shakil, K. A. (2024). AI-Generated Spam Review Detection Framework with Deep Learning Algorithms and Natural Language Processing. Computers (2073-431X), 13(10).

Watts, N., Adger, W. N., Agnolucci, P., Blackstock, J., Byass, P., Cai, W., Chaytor, S., Colbourn, T., Collins, M., Cooper, A., Cox, P. M., Depledge, J., Drummond, P., Ekins, P., Galaz, V., Grace, D., Graham, H., Grubb, M., Haines, A., & Costello, A. (2023). Health and climate change: Policy responses to protect public health. *Lancet*, *386*(10006), 1861–1914. DOI: 10.1016/S0140-6736(15)60854-6 PMID: 26111439

Chapter 6
Facial Emotion-Based Music Player

Sudha Senthilkumar
https://orcid.org/0000-0003-3132-000X
VIT University, India

Tanya Gupta
VIT University, India

Rishabh Saboo
VIT University, India

Raj Anand
VIT University, India

ABSTRACT

Artificial Intelligence has applied in many significant fields in which expression and emotion detection is one of them. To detect a facial expression, the system should analyze various variability of human faces like colour, posture, expression, orientation, lighting, etc. Detecting facial features is a prerequisite to facial emotion recognition. One of the applications of this input can be for extracting the information to deduce the mood of an individual. This data can then be used to get a list of songs that comply with the "mood" derived from the input provided earlier. This eliminates

DOI: 10.4018/979-8-3693-2935-1.ch006

the time-consuming and tedious task of manually segregating or grouping songs into different lists and helps in generating an appropriate playlist based on an individual's emotional features. Facial Expression Based Music System aims at scanning and interpreting the data and accordingly creating a playlist based on the parameters provided. Thus our proposed system focuses on detecting human emotions for developing emotion-based music players. This is achieved by observing the parts of the face, like eyes, lips movement, etc. These are then classified and compared to trained sets of data. In this research, a human facial expression recognition system will be modelled using the eigenface approach. The proposed method will use the HAAR Cascade classifier to detect the face in an image. Fisher Faces calculation can be utilized for decreasing the high dimensionality of the Eigen space and after that anticipating the test picture upon the Eigen space and computing the Euclidean separation between the test picture and meaning of the Eigen faces. The grayscale image of the face is used by the system to classify five basic emotions such as surprise, disgust, neutral, anger, and happiness.

1. INTRODUCTION

Human face detection plays an important role in applications such as video surveillance, human-computer interface, face recognition, and face image database management. Facial expressions are important cues for nonverbal communication among human beings. This is only possible because humans can recognize emotions quite accurately and efficiently. Automatic facial emotion recognition has many commercial uses and can be used as a biological model for cognitive processing and analysis of the human brain. Collectively they can enhance their applications like monitoring and surveillance analysis, biomedical image, smart rooms intelligent robots, human- computer interfaces, and driver's alertness systems and can play a vital role in the field of security and crime investigations.

The Fisher face classifier and CNN algorithms are mostly used for recognizing faces. The Fisher Face Classifier algorithm is based on Principal Component Analysis (PCA). These eigenvalues are the eigenvectors associated with the largest eigenvalues in the training data covariance matrix.

In fact, this is a powerful way to represent the sample data, as it ensures that input data's variance is maintained while eliminating unwanted existing correlations between the original features (dimensions) in the sample vector. After the eigenfaces of the selected test image are retrieved, the Euclidean distance of is calculated using the eigenface averages of the training dataset. The Euclidean distance is then compared to the eigenvalues of the eigenvector. It is measured as the distance between the unique faces of the training dataset and their average images. Training images that correspond to different distances from the average image are labeled with expressions such as happiness, sadness, fear, surprise, and anger, and the Euclidean distance between the eigenface of the test image and the average image is the distance of the average image. In the eigenface of the training dataset, emotions are categorized and named according to the labeled train picture.

Convolutional Neural Network: In machine learning, convolutional neural networks (CNN or ConvNet) are a class of deep feed forward artificial neural networks that have been used to analyze visual images. CNN uses a variant of the Multilayer Perceptron designed to require minimal pre- treatment. They are also called shift-invariant or space-invariant artificial neural networks (SINNs) based on the shared weight architecture and translational invariant properties. Convolutional networks are inspired by biological processes, and the patterns of connections between neurons are inspired by the tissues of the animal's visual cortex. Individual cortical neurons respond to stimuli only in a restricted area of the visual field known as the receptive field. The receptive fields of different neurons partially overlap and thus cover the entire visual field. They apply to image and video recognition, recommender systems, and natural language processing.

2. LITERATURE REVIEW

In the article (Gilda et al., 2017) the multi-layer convolutional neural network is programmed to evaluate the characteristics of the user's image. A convolutional neural network includes an input layer, some convolutional layers, a ReLU layer, a pooling layer, some high density layers (fully connected layers), and an output layer. Describes the steps used to identify the association between each song and its mood. Extract the acoustic characteristics of the song using LibROSA, aubiopitch, and other state-of-the-art audio extraction algorithms. Based on these features, we will train an artificial neural network that successfully classifies songs into 4 classes with 97.69 percent accuracy.

The system proposed in article (Ramanathan et al., 2017) uses a video capture object to access the webcam of your computer. Multiple images are captured by the webcam. Multiple facial images may be needed to accurately predict emotions. Blurred images can cause errors (especially in dark places), so average multiple images to get one image without blur. Histogram equalization is an image processing technique used to improve the contrast of an image by normalizing the image over the entire range. This image is then cropped and converted to grayscale, leaving only the foreground of the image and reducing ambiguity.

Emotion detection based facial expressions proposed in article (Abdat, Maaoui, & Pruski, 2011) is a very powerful tool for human-machine interaction applications, as the camera enables unobtrusive applications. This article describes controlling a music player based on the emotions of a computer user. The person is in front of the computer's built-in camera, and real-time emotion detection is performed with our approach based on distance changes and SVM classifiers. The purpose of this application is to change the music as the user's emotions change.

This article (Arora, Kaul, & Mittal, 2019) describes various algorithms based on classification, i) classifies songs into 4 mood categories, ii) detects user mood based on facial expressions, and combines the two into a custom music playlist. It provides a clear way to create. The songs are categorized according to two approaches. Use the audio features of your choice to train your model directly, namely KNNs, Support Vector Machines (SVMs), Random Forests, and MLPs, and use these audio features to predict song excitation and valence values. The former approach achieves a maximum accuracy of 70 percent in MLP and the latter achieves 81.6 percent accuracy in SVM regression. A facial mood classifier with HAAR classifier and Fisher Face algorithm achieves 92percent accuracy.

The proposed system in article (Alrihaili et al., 2019) detects emotions, and if the subject has negative emotions, a specific playlist is presented, while if the detected emotions are positive, the appropriate playlist is provided. The proposed recommended system implementation is done using the Viola Jonze algorithm and the Principal Component Analysis (PCA) method. The proposed system was successfully implemented in MATLAB.

This paper (Altieri et al., 2019) introduces a new system that can adaptively manage multimedia content (music, video clips, etc.) and lighting scenarios based on the detected emotional state of the user. The system captures the emotions of the user's facial expressions, maps them to the 2D value space where the multimedia content is mapped, and maps them to the colours of the lights. Preliminary test results show that the proposed system can recognize the user's emotional state and manage proper music and bright colors in a symbiotic way.

In the article (Nguyen et al., 2017) uses two traditional approaches, a regression-based approach and a template matching approach, can be used to detect facial clues in facial images. The regression-based method iteratively refines the initial initialization of landmark locations and uses image features to make explicit predictions by regression. The template matching approach, on the other hand, does not require you to infer facial features first, but instead establishes a facial template that matches the input image.

The article proposed method (Ahmad, Najam, & Ahmed, 2013) to evaluate various face detection and recognition methods and provide an all-in-one image-based face detection and recognition solution with higher accuracy and better response rate as the first step in video surveillance. That is. This solution is proposed based on tests performed on a rich database of different faces in terms of subject, pose, emotion, race and light.

Although significant advances have been made in the areas of facial recognition and recognition for the purposes of security, identification, and attendance, there are still issues that impede progress in reaching or exceeding human-level accuracy. These problems are changes in the appearance of the human face, such as: various lighting conditions, face image noise, scaling, poses, etc. This research paper (Bah & Ming, 2020) presents a new way to use the Local Binary Pattern (LBP) algorithm in combination with advanced image processing techniques such as contrast adjustment, bilateral filters, and histogram equalization. Some of the issues that affect the accuracy of face recognition improve the LBP code and improve the accuracy of the entire face recognition system.

This review paper (Lal et al., 2018) sought to explain the most difficult facial features such as postural invariance, aging, lighting, and partial obstruction. They are considered an integral part of facial recognition systems when implemented through facial images. Computers are used in a variety of application pyramids, from simple methods to complex problem-solving methods. In such posts, facial recognition technology has emerged as a useful tool for detecting facial features based on unique features. And it is one of the most studied areas in the field of pattern recognition and computer vision.

To improve the security level of access systems, smart home security systems have been proposed in article (Lal et al., 2018) that uses facial recognition algorithms with a local binary pattern histogram (LBPH). Facial recognition is an interesting but challenging area of machine learning, affecting critical applications in many areas, including: Face rendering shows how a face is modelled using LBPH detection and recognition algorithms. The most useful and unique features of facial images are extracted during the feature extraction phase. Face recognition compares a new face image with an image that has already been extracted and stored in the database. Facial recognition and recognition methods have been applied to allow and prevent eligible residents and guests from entering the home (Dagar et al., 2016)

3. PROPOSED WORK

Figure 1. Proposed System Architecture

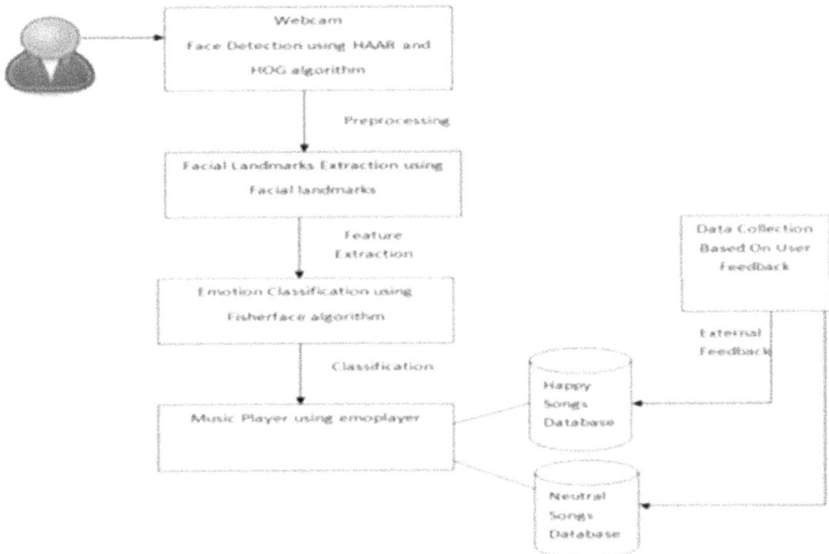

The Figure 1 shows the system architecture for proposed method. It involves the following steps.

1. Gathering the dataset.
2. Face Detection - Standardized techniques like HOG, LBP and HAAR cascades will be used to detect faces from the standard images or in any real time videos.
3. Face Recognition - Luminosity Algorithm - LBPH (Local Binary Pattern Histogram)

LBPH (Local Binary Pattern Histogram): Local Binary Pattern (LBP) is a simple yet very efficient texture operator which labels the pixels of an image by thresholding the neighborhood of each pixel and considers the result as a binary number.

i. The parameters used in the LBPH are
   (a) Radius: the radius is used to build the circular local binarypattern and represents the radius around the central pixel. It is usually set to 1.
   (b) Neighbors: the number of sample points to build the circular local binary pattern. Keep in mind: the more sample points you include, the higher the computational cost. It is usually set to 8.
   (c) Grid X: the number of cells in the horizontal direction. The more cells, the finer the grid, the higher the dimensionality of the resulting feature vector. It is usually set to 8.
   (d) Grid Y: the number of cells in the vertical direction. The more cells, the finer the grid, the higher the dimensionality of the resulting feature vector. It is usually set to 8.

4. Emotion Recognition – The Fisher face classifiers and Convolutional Neural Networks are used for emotion recognition in the input face images.

Fisher face classifiers: Fisher face classifiers considered to be a more effective algorithm compared to eigen face method in classifying the face based on emotions. Mainly the fisher face algorithm removes the principle components which are responsible for light intensity changes. This feature helps the algorithm to classify the images better than the other existing approaches. The fisher face classifiers are integrated with convolutional neural networks to produce the efficient emotion recognition outcome.

The above steps can be summarized into Training phase, Applying the LBP operation, Extracting the Histograms and Facial recognization.

Training the Algorithm: First, we need to train the algorithm. To do so, we need to use a dataset with the facial images of the people we want to recognize. We also need to set an ID (it may be a number or the name of the person) for each image, so the algorithm will use this information to recognize an input image and give you an output. Images of the same person must have the same ID.

Applying the LBP operation: The first computational step of the LBPH is to create an intermediate image that describes the original image in a better way, by highlighting the facial characteristics. To do so, the algorithm uses a concept of a sliding window, based on the parameter's radius and neighbors.

Extracting the Histograms: Now, the usage of the picture generated with inside the remaining step, we will use the Grid X and Grid Y parameters to divide the picture into more than one grids and make histograms of every grid. As we've an picture in grayscale, every histogram (from every grid) will comprise only 256 positions (0 255) representing the occurrences of every pixel intensity. Then, we want to concatenate every histogram to create a brand new and larger histogram. Supposing we've 8x8 grids, we can have 8x8x256=16.384 positions with inside the very last histogram. The very last histogram represents the traits of the picture unique picture

Facial recognition: The algorithm is already trained with the necessary amount of dataset. Each histogram created based on the above steps are used to represents each image from the training dataset. So finally the algorithm designed in such a way that given an input image, the same steps can be performed again for the new image and creates a histogram which represents the image.

4. RESULTS AND DISCUSSION

The Music Arena consists of a total of 3 languages i.e., Hindi, Tamil, Telugu and 3 player modes i.e, Queue Mode, Emotion Mode and Random Mode. The Figure 2 shows the list of songs in Hindi language for different types of emotions and it can be displayed under the Queue, Emotion and Random mode. The various category of song selection in different language is listed out in the below figures.

Figure 2. Songs lists in Hindi language

The Figure 3 shows the list of songs categorized under Tamil language with selection of different modes such as Queue mode, Random mode and Emotion mode.

Figure 3. Songs lists in Tamil language

The Figure 4 displays the list of songs categorized under Telugu language with selection of different modes such as Queue mode, Random mode and Emotion mode.

Figure 4. Songs lists in Telugu language

This user interface can be expanded to support various national languages in India to extend the model to support the different native language users.

Further the user face is captured using the various algorithms as mentioned in the proposed system and then their emotions are recognized using the hybrid of Fisher face classifiers and Convolutional Neural Networks algorithm. Finally the songs are played automatically according to the emotions of the user. The Figure 5 shows automatic play of songs for happy mode in Hindi language according to the user preference.

Figure 5. Song selection in Hindi language for Happy mode.

The results are evaluated using the various performance metrics such as Accuracy, Precision, Recall and F1-score. Those evaluation metrics are discussed in detail below (Yang et al., 2017; Saba et al., 2014; Li et al., 2020).

Accuracy: This metric used to measure the how frequently the model used to predict the correct outcome.

Accuracy = Correct predictions/ All predictions

Precision: The precision metric used to find out the true positive values from set of possible predictions by any algorithm. This metric is really useful to identify when the cost of false positive is high in any prediction model.

Precision = (True positive)/(True positive + False positive)

Recall: Recall metric used to measure how frequently ML model correctly classifies the positive instances from all the actual positive samples present in the dataset.

Recall = (True positive)/(True positive + False negative)

F1-score: The F1-score metric is used when balance between precision and Recall metrics should be obtained. It can be represented in terms of precision and recall as shown below

F1 = 2 * (Precision * Recall)/(Precision + Recall)

True Negatives (TN): The results obtained in the samples are categorized as not correctly belonging to the expected class.

False Negatives (FN): The sample classification is mistakenly categorized as not belonging to the expected class.

True Positives (TP): The data in the given sample are correctly categorized as belonging to the expected class.

False Positives (FP): The data in the given samples are classified incorrectly as belonging to the target class.

The Table 1 shows the outcome of various performance metrics discussed above results for emotions such as anger, happy, sad and Neutral in percentage. Using the hybrid method the accuracy, precision, Recall and F1 score for anger emotion comes around 94.2, 93.2, 95.1 and 96.7 percentages. The algorithm produces the output of 95.1, 95.3, 95.6 and 96% for happy mood. The accuracy, precision, recall and F1-Score come around 92.3, 96.2, 94.3 and 97% for Sad emotion. Similarly for Neutral the algorithm produces the outcome of 90.4 93.4, 93.1 and 94.6 percentage. The algorithm output better Accuracy, Precision, Recall and F1-score for Anger, Happy and Sad emotion compare to Neutral emotion.

Table 1. Results of various Performance metrics

Emotion	**Accuracy**	**Precision**	**Recall**	**F1-score**
Anger	94.2	93.2	95.1	96.7
Happy	95.1	95.3	95.6	96.0
Sad	92.3	96.2	94.3	97
Neutral	90.4	93.4	93.1	94.6

5. CONCLUSION AND FUTURE WORK

Facial expression recognition is a challenging problem in the field of image analysis and computer vision that has received a great deal of attention over the last few years because of its many applications in various domains. This paper proposes a human facial expression recognition model based on the eigen-face approach in which the various emotions are recognized by calculating the Euclidean distance between the input test image and the mean of the Eigen faces of the training dataset. Further based on the recognized emotions the music playlist will be selected and played automatically.

This project focuses on directly transforming the dataset images to their eigenfaces so as to depict a general sense in which these expressions are formed. The training is done by the fisher face classifier and despite the size of the dataset accuracy overall above 93% is achieved for different emotions. In order to optimize the training, we omitted 4 emotions out of 7 namely fear, surprise, contempt, and disgust. We can expand the rest of the emotions with greater datasets for future work. These emotions can be recognized with greater accuracy when a dataset with more images is used. This would also help us in expanding the size of our songs database and better matching of songs depending on the user.

REFERENCES

Abdat, F., Maaoui, C., & Pruski, A. (2011, November). Human-computer interaction using emotion recognition from facial expression. In 2011 UKSim 5th European Symposium on Computer Modeling and Simulation (pp. 196-201). IEEE. DOI: 10.1109/EMS.2011.20

Ahmad, F., Najam, A., & Ahmed, Z. (2013). Image-based face detection and recognition:" state of the art". arXiv preprint arXiv:1302.6379.

Alrihaili, A., Alsaedi, A., Albalawi, K., & Syed, L. (2019, October). Music recommender system for users based on emotion detection through facial features. In 2019 12th International Conference on Developments in eSystems Engineering (DeSE) (pp. 1014-1019). IEEE. DOI: 10.1109/DeSE.2019.00188

Altieri, A., Ceccacci, S., Ciabattoni, L., Generosi, A., Talipu, A., Turri, G., & Mengoni, M. (2019, January). An Adaptive System to Manage Playlists and Lighting Scenarios Based on the User's Emotions. In *2019 IEEE International Conference on Consumer Electronics (ICCE)* (pp. 1-2). IEEE. DOI: 10.1109/ICCE.2019.8662061

Arora, A., Kaul, A., & Mittal, V. (2019, March). Mood based music player. In *2019 International Conference on Signal Processing and Communication (ICSC)* (pp. 333-337). IEEE. DOI: 10.1109/ICSC45622.2019.8938384

Bah, S. M., & Ming, F. (2020). An improved face recognition algorithm and its application in attendance management system. *Array (New York, N.Y.)*, *5*, 100014. DOI: 10.1016/j.array.2019.100014

Dagar, D., Hudait, A., Tripathy, H. K., & Das, M. N. (2016, May). Automatic emotion detection model from facial expression. In *2016 International Conference on Advanced Communication Control and Computing Technologies (ICACCCT)* (pp. 77-85). IEEE. DOI: 10.1109/ICACCCT.2016.7831605

Gilda, S., Zafar, H., Soni, C., & Waghurdekar, K. (2017, March). Smart music player integrating facial emotion recognition and music mood recommendation. In 2017 international conference on wireless communications, signal processing and networking (wispnet) (pp. 154-158). IEEE.

Lal, M., Kumar, K., Arain, R. H., Maitlo, A., Ruk, S. A., & Shaikh, H. (2018). Study of face recognition techniques: A survey. *International Journal of Advanced Computer Science and Applications*, *9*(6). Advance online publication. DOI: 10.14569/IJACSA.2018.090606

Li, K., Jin, Y., Akram, M. W., Han, R., & Chen, J. (2020). Facial expression recognition with convolutional neural networks via a new face cropping and rotation strategy. *The Visual Computer*, *36*(2), 391–404. DOI: 10.1007/s00371-019-01627-4

Nguyen, B. T., Trinh, M. H., Phan, T. V., & Nguyen, H. D. (2017, April). An efficient real-time emotion detection using camera and facial landmarks. In 2017 seventh international conference on information science and technology (ICIST) (pp. 251-255). IEEE. DOI: 10.1109/ICIST.2017.7926765

Ramanathan, R., Kumaran, R., Rohan, R. R., Gupta, R., & Prabhu, V. (2017, December). An intelligent music player based on emotion recognition. In 2017 2nd International Conference on Computational Systems and Information Technology for Sustainable Solution (CSITSS) (pp. 1-5). IEEE. DOI: 10.1109/CSITSS.2017.8447743

Saba, T., Rehman, A., Al-Dhelaan, A., & Al-Rodhaan, M. (2014). Evaluation of current documents image denoising techniques: A comparative study. *Applied Artificial Intelligence*, *28*(9), 879–887. DOI: 10.1080/08839514.2014.954344

Yang, B., Cao, J. M., Jiang, D. P., & Lv, J. D. (2017). Facial expression recognition based on dual-feature fusion and improved random forest classifier. *Multimedia Tools and Applications*, *9*, 20477–20499.

Chapter 7
NLP in Social Media Data Processing

N. S. Saba
RV College of Engineering, India

Kumari Anjali
RV College of Engineering, India

Akansha Tanu
RV College of Engineering, India

Aryan Porwal
RV College of Engineering, India

Ahan Tejaswi
https://orcid.org/0009-0006-2356-4118
RV College of Engineering, India

R. Sindhu Rajendran
RV College of Engineering, India

ABSTRACT

Natural Language Processing (NLP) represents a cross-disciplinary domain that merges computer science with linguistics, empowering machines to comprehend, interpret, and generate human language. Its significance extends to transformative applications like chatbots, language translation, and sentiment analysis, thereby reshaping the landscape of human-computer interaction. Within the context of social media data analysis, NLP is indispensable for gleaning valuable insights from unstructured text data present on platforms such as Twitter, Facebook and Instagram. NLP serves as a linchpin in sentiment analysis, unraveling emotions in posts and comments. It aids businesses in understanding public opinion, customer satisfaction, and brand perception. Additionally, NLP facilitates trend analysis, user engagement, and personalized marketing by dissecting

DOI: 10.4018/979-8-3693-2935-1.ch007

user-generated content. A notable trend is the fusion of NLP with image and video processing, ushering in multimodal analysis. Explainable AI (XAI) enhances transparency in NLP models, contributing to accountable decision-making. NLP also plays an important role in combating misinformation on social media and assisting companies in refining their engagement strategies. The chapter explores the future of NLP in social media data analysis. It also involves advancements in contextual understanding, accuracy, and adaptability. It also includes incorporation of multimodal analysis and real-time data processing promises deeper insights and informed decision-making. The evolving landscape of NLP in social media analysis ensures refined analyses, responsible implementation, and informed decisions across diverse industries and societal contexts.

1.0.INTRODUCTION

In recent years, the field of Natural Language Processing (NLP) has undergone remarkable advancements, particularly in its application to social media data processing. These developments have revolutionized the analysis of vast amounts of unstructured data, offering insights into user behavior, sentiment trends, and emerging topics. This introduction delves into the evolution of NLP, its indispensable role in navigating the complexities of social media data, and the profound impact it has on both user experiences and organizational strategies.

The evolution of NLP is marked by significant strides in various subfields, including sentiment analysis, aspect-based sentiment analysis, Named Entity Recognition (NER), dynamic topic modeling, and multimodal analysis. These advancements have transcended basic text classification, enabling the nuanced understanding of emotions, opinions, and structured information within social media content. By leveraging sophisticated deep learning models and contextual embeddings, NLP has emerged as a powerful tool for extracting actionable insights from the ever-expanding digital discourse.

NLP integrates artificial intelligence with linguistic principles, acting as a crucial bridge between human language and machine comprehension. Its fundamental features cover a wide range of functions, including speech and sound recognition, translation, information retrieval, man-machine communication, and language interpretation and production. Not only do these fundamental elements allow machines to produce and understand language similar to that of humans, but they also make it easier for users to communicate with intelligent systems in a variety of contexts, such as chatbots, virtual assistants, and sentiment analysis tools.

NLP is used in social media data analysis in a variety of ways, addressing possibilities and constraints that are unique to the digital world. NLP algorithms probe deeply into the complexities of user-generated information by improving content understanding; this allows them to reveal hidden intentions, attitudes, and contextual nuances(Jiang, K., & Lu, X. 2020).

Furthermore, NLP enables efficient content moderation, empowering social media platforms to swiftly identify and mitigate improper or harmful content.

NLP algorithms modify information and recommendations to user preferences through personalized user experiences, increasing user satisfaction and engagement. Additionally, NLP makes trend analysis and tracking easier and gives businesses instant access to insightful information about conversations and subjects that are just starting to gain traction. Furthermore, sentiment analysis driven by NLP techniques provides complex viewpoints on how consumers perceive a brand, empowering businesses to make wise judgments and modify their approaches in response to changing customer sentiment.

1.1 Evolution of NLP

Notable advancements have been made in a number of NLP subfields throughout the years, such as dynamic topic modeling, Named Entity Recognition (NER), sentiment analysis, aspect-based sentiment analysis, and multimodal analysis. These developments go beyond simple text categorization and allow for the sophisticated interpretation of sentiments, viewpoints, and organized data in social media content.

Through the use of contextual embeddings and advanced deep learning models, natural language processing (NLP) has become a potent tool for gleaning insights from the rapidly growing digital discourse. With the help of these models, large volumes of unstructured data can now be analyzed and interpreted with greater accuracy. Sentiment analysis and aspect-based sentiment analysis can now capture complex emotions like surprise, delight, and wrath (Kanan, T., et al. 2019).

With the use of sophisticated deep learning models and contextual embeddings, Named Entity Recognition (NER) has significantly improved, allowing for the accurate extraction of structured data from social media material, such as names, dates, and locations. For many applications, such as trend analysis and event detection, this feature is essential.

Real-time tracking of shifting topics and conversations on social media platforms has been made possible by dynamic topic modeling, which has produced informative data on emerging trends and shifts in public debate. Text, image, and video processing combined with multimodal analysis provides a comprehensive understanding of social media posts with multimedia content, enhancing the ability to analyze user-generated content from a holistic viewpoint.

Explainable AI (XAI) has grown in significance in NLP applications, ensuring transparency and reliability. Techniques like SHAP (SHapley Additive exPlanations) and LIME (Local Interpretable Model-agnostic Explanations) offer insights into the decision-making processes of complicated NLP models, contributing to more complex and precise social media data processing.

1.2 Requirements of NLP

NLP integrates artificial intelligence with linguistic principles, acting as a crucial bridge between human language and machine comprehension. Its fundamental features cover a wide range of functions, including speech and sound recognition, translation, information retrieval, man-machine communication, and language interpretation and production.While language generation creates coherent and contextually appropriate human-like writing for chatbots and content production, language understanding allows robots to analyze natural language, improving user-computer interaction. By translating text between languages, machine translation lowers language barriers and promotes international communication and information exchange.

Speech recognition translates spoken words into text for voice prompts and keyboard input, allowing hands-free device engagements. In speech analysis and security, sound recognition plays a crucial role by identifying and interpreting sounds. Artificial sounds are produced via sound synthesis, which aids in voice synthesis and multimedia applications.

Information Retrieval extracts relevant information from extensive datasets, enhancing search engines' capability to provide accurate and timely results. Term Database manages and organizes a database of terms and concepts for precise information retrieval, ensuring efficient data processing and analysis.Optical Character Recognition (OCR) converts printed or handwritten text into machine-encoded text, facilitating document digitization and text extraction. Man-Machine Dialogue facilitates natural and interactive conversations between humans and machines, enhancing user experience across various applications.These components collectively enable machines to understand, interpret, and produce human-like language, bridging the gap between human communication and machine understanding across diverse domains and applications.

Figure 1. Applications of NLP

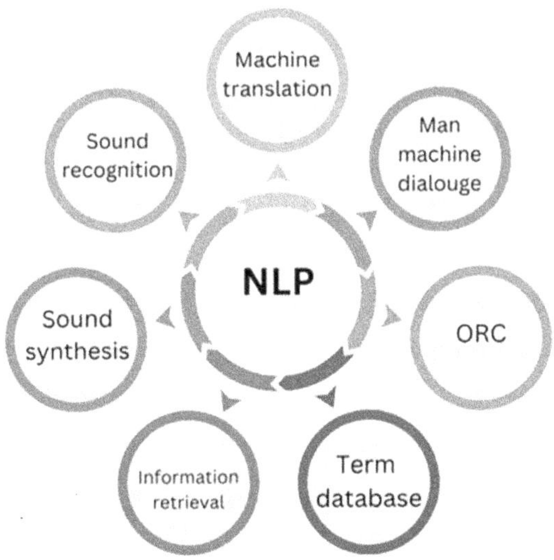

In Figure 1, a comprehensive overview of NLP applications unfolds. NLP's versatility is evident through its pivotal role in text analysis, sentiment assessment, and insightful information extraction. Furthermore, it extends to transforming spoken language into text, enabling seamless communication through speech recognition and transcription services. The figure also highlights NLP's impact on creating intelligent chatbots and virtual assistants, elevating user interactions through natural language understanding and fostering enhanced customer experiences.

1.3 Importance of NLP in Social Media Data Processing

Examining the complex field of NLP and how it relates to social media data processing reveals the significant influence NLP has on creating a more intelligent and sophisticated user experience. NLP essentially plays the role of an advanced interpreter, interpreting the complex web of user-generated content to reveal hidden user intentions, attitudes, and contextual nuances(Gelbukh, A., 2005).Its capacity to sort through the vast amount of unstructured data and turn it into useful insights that are extremely valuable for organizations and individuals navigating the ever-changing world of social media is indicative of its revolutionary power.

NLP is more than text analysis; It is important to improve user experience on social media platforms. NLP helps provide a personalized and tailored approach by understanding the nuances of language. Whether it is personalized recommendations or ads relevant to the user's interests, NLP can increase overall engagement by creating an environment tailored to each user, based on the user's unique characteristics and preferences. NLP has emerged as a transformative force that leads to better understanding and extraction of useful messages from the abundance of unnecessary content that exists on social media.While NLP is recognized for its transformative role in social media, its practical applications delve deeper into several key areas:

1. Improved Content Understanding

Algorithms are important to NLP because they improve the understanding of social media content. By leveraging NLP capabilities, these systems can explore the subtleties of customer behavior to gain a deeper understanding of emotions, context, and user preferences. This allows for detailed analysis that goes beyond the data surface, connecting the nuances of the user guide to present a bigger picture of the content landscape.

2. Efficient Content Moderation

Social media networks can use incredibly effective content filtering tactics due to NLP capabilities.Leveraging these skills, platforms can automatically identify and reduce improper or dangerous content, helping to the construction of a safer online environment. By incorporating NLP into content moderation procedures, platforms can detect infractions more quickly and accurately, allowing them to take rapid action against user-generated content that might be in violation of community norms. In addition to streamlining moderation operations, this cutting-edge strategy helps to promote a safer and more favorable user experience within the online community.

3. Personalized User Experiences

NLP algorithms are essential for creating individualized user experiences on social media. These algorithms enable social media sites to present customized user interfaces, adverts, and content recommendations by examining user behaviors and preferences. By guaranteeing that material is tailored to each user's unique preferences, this degree of personalization raises user satisfaction and engagement levels all around. Social media platforms may create a more dynamic and user-centric environment by tailoring content distribution to each individual user's specific requirements and interests, due to deep understanding of user behavior provided by NLP.

4. Trend Analysis and Monitoring

New trends and conversations on social media platforms can be monitored and analyzed instantly using NLP. NLP provides individuals and organizations with valuable insight into popular topics and conversations through rapid analysis of large amounts of data. This capability allows organizations to understand and adapt to changes in the social media landscape, enabling policy change. With NLP-focused research, organizations can become aware of current trends and establish timely and meaningful interactions with their target audiences. Qualitative analysis of various topics demonstrates the flexibility of NLP to provide a good understanding of the decision-making process in social media transformation(Surabhi, M. C. 2013).

5. Sentiment Analysis for Brand Perception

Sentiment analysis techniques, which make use of natural NLP, are essential for evaluating the opinions people have about a product or brand on social media. These resources give companies perceptive views into public opinion, allowing for tactical changes to enhance brand reputation. NLP-driven sentiment analysis provides a thorough grasp of brand perception by examining user-generated material, reviews, and comments. In the ever-changing world of social media, this actionable intelligence enables organizations to address issues, capitalize on positive sentiment, and make well-informed decisions—all of which help to improve brand perception.

More importantly, the importance of NLP goes beyond traditional text analysis and becomes the basis for improving user experience on social media platforms. NLP facilitates personalization and customization by recognizing the nuances of language. Through recommendations or targeted advertising tailored to the user's interests, NLP can increase overall engagement by creating an environment tailored to each user's needs, specific characteristics and preferences. In essence, NLP becomes a powerful tool that helps better understand and extract useful information from the lot of irrelevant content that exists on social media. Its development continues to drive innovation, highlighting its important role in shaping the future of digital communication and interaction(Shayaa, S., et al., 2018).

The following content explores modern NLP applications in social media data processing, starting with the unique characteristics of social media data such as informal language, user-generated content, multimodality, and high volume and velocity. These traits necessitate specialized preprocessing techniques for accurate analysis. The discussion then shifts to essential preprocessing steps, including data cleansing, handling missing values, standardization and dealing with categorical and text data. Advanced text cleaning methods like stemming and lemmatization are detailed, followed by an examination of data processing techniques such as tokenization, named entity recognition and part-of-speech tagging. The challenges inherent in social media data processing, including noise, redundancy, and sentiment analysis complexity are also addressed. The various data representation methods such as Bag of Words, TF-IDF, word embeddings, document embeddings and topic modeling are emphasizing their importance in transforming raw text into meaningful numerical formats for machine learning models. This structured approach ensures thorough understanding and effective processing of social media data for diverse NLP applications(Chiramel et al., 2020).

2. MODERN NLP APPLICATIONS IN SOCIAL MEDIA DATA PROCESSING

2.1 Characteristics of Social Media Data

The unique characteristics of social media data necessitate careful text preprocessing. These characteristics have a major impact on the techniques used for preparing data and doing subsequent analysis. Some of the important characteristics of social media data are described below.

Informal Language

Social media content is characterized by informal language, including slang, abbreviations, and emoticons. This informal tone, reflective of conversational interactions, poses challenges for conventional preprocessing methods. Specialized techniques are required to accurately interpret and analyze the informal nuances embedded in the language.

User-generated Content

User-driven content results in diverse writing styles, tones, and perspectives. This diversity challenges text preprocessing, necessitating adaptable methods to handle the array of voices and expressions present in social media data. Recognizing and accommodating this variability is essential for maintaining the authenticity of user-generated content.

Multimodality

Social media incorporates a mix of text, images, videos, and emojis. This multimodal nature adds complexity to preprocessing, demanding methods that can effectively process and extract relevant information from diverse media types. Integrating such capabilities into preprocessing ensures a comprehensive analysis of varied content forms.

Volume and Velocity

The sheer amount and real-time nature of social media data need efficient preprocessing solutions. Preprocessing techniques that are scalable and timely are essential due to the constant generation of enormous volumes of data. These techniques ought to control the flood of data, guaranteeing that studies proceed at the quick speed at which new data is being created.

2.2 Techniques Used for Pre-processing Data Cleansing and Limiting

Given its increasing importance in aiding operations and guiding business decisions, poor data can harm an organization's efficiency and effectiveness(Ridzuan et al., 2019). Data quality issues make it difficult to use good data because impure data can lead to poor decision making. Error detection, error correction and error analysis are the main tasks of the data cleaning process. Although it is necessary to analyze data quickly, the process of cleaning data is complex and time-consuming, but data cleaning is more effective.

The data cleansing process unfolds in the following stages as shown Figure 2:

1. *Understanding and Profiling the Data*

Conducting a thorough exploration of the dataset is a vital aspect of data analysis. This entails examining the distribution of data, exploring correlations between variables, and grasping the context in which the data was collected. It is imperative to detect any anomalies or irregularities that could have implications for the data cleansing process or subsequent analyses.

In the field of data analysis, a critical step involves delving into statistics. This encompasses the scrutiny of distributional skewness, the identification of outliers, and an appreciation of the importance of multivariate data. For a more profound understanding, utilize visualization tools like boxplots and histograms to visually represent the data. These tools play a crucial role in unveiling patterns, trends, and potential issues within the dataset, thereby contributing to a more enlightened and efficient data analysis process(Wangikar et al., 2011).

2. *Handling Missing Values and Duplicate Detection and Elimination*

Variables are examined for Missing value patterns to determine whether their presence is sporadic or systematic.Sophisticated techniques such as Levenshtein distance can be used for detecting duplicate records.

3. *Typos, Inconsistencies and Data Type Conversion*

A systematic approach for addressing typos and inconsistencies needs to be developed. Methods such as string matching or employing regular expressions are utilized to efficiently detect and rectify errors. Scrutinize the effects of data type conversions on further analysis, especially regarding numerical representations for categorical variables. Consider the interpretability of original data types(Smith et al., 2023).

4. Standardization and Normalization

Examine statistical properties when standardizing numerical features. Evaluate the suitability of normalization methods based on data distribution. Understand the impact on machine learning model performance.

5. *Handling Categorical Information*

Investigate categorical variables thoroughly, considering the cardinality of characteristics. Choose encoding techniques like label or one-hot encoding(Haldaret al., 2011).

6. *Text Data Cleaning*

Beyond special character removal, employ NLP techniques like lemmatization or stemming for consistent word representations. Entity recognition or sentiment analysis to be considered if required.

7. *Time Series Data Cleaning*

Look beyond missing value correction in time series data. Implement advanced techniques like trend smoothing or decomposition. Account for daylight-saving time changes and time zone variations.

8. *Data Quality Evaluation*

Conduct a comprehensive analysis of outliers, missing values, and inconsistencies. Develop quality metrics specific to dataset features. Assess how overall data quality impacts analysis reliability.

9. *Documentation*

Comprehensive documentation goes beyond recording modifications. Provide background for each decision made during the cleaning process. Note the rationale behind choosing cleaning methods and their impact on subsequent analysis. Consider compiling an extensive data dictionary for future use.

10. *Iterative Methodology*

Emphasize strategic re-evaluation over simple revisitation in the iterative process. Create a feedback loop, iterating based on earlier learnings. Adopt an agile strategy for ongoing improvement of the cleaning procedure (Someswararao et al., 2012).

Figure 2. Steps involved in Data Cleansing and Limiting

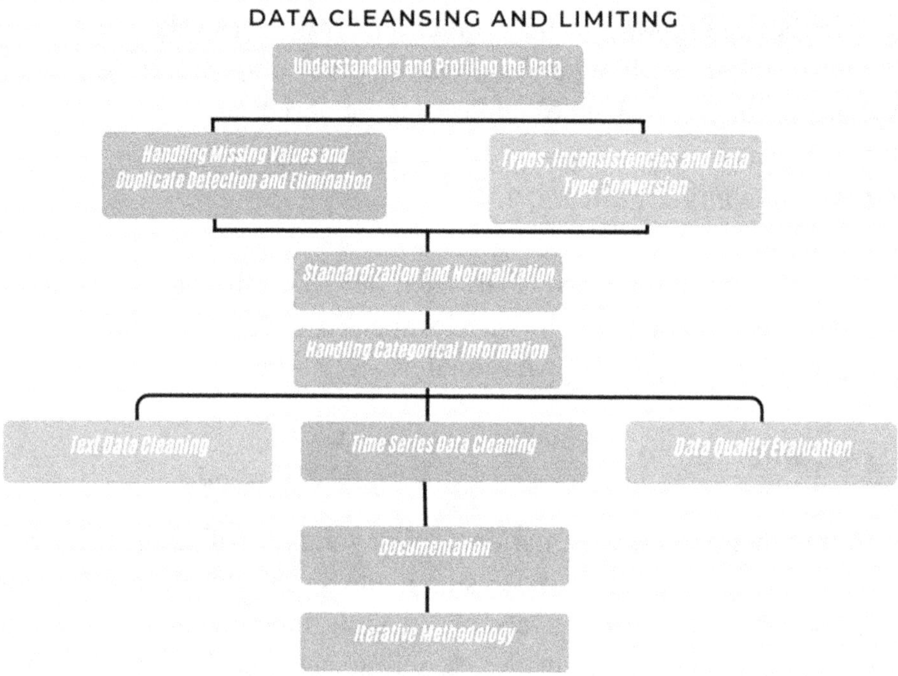

2.3 Text Cleaning Methods for NLP

NLP is the application of computational methods for analyzing and synthesizing natural language and speech. The initial step involves translating the text from English into a machine-understandable language to facilitate computational tasks in this domain.

The subsequent steps outline common methods for preparing textual data for NLP.

1. *Converting Text to Lowercase*

After obtaining the text data, the normalization process begins by converting all text to lowercase. This ensures equal treatment of all text, allowing comprehensive analysis.

2. *Removing HTML Tags*

HTML tags, which are the elements used for structuring content on the web, are often deemed unnecessary when extracting data through techniques like web scraping. Removing them helps filter out irrelevant information and streamline the collected data. This step retains relevant text for subsequent analysis.

3. *Removing Accented Characters*

Standardizing and converting accented characters to ASCII characters is essential, enhancing consistency in the dataset, especially in English language analyses.

4. *Expanding Contractions*

Contractions, shortened forms of words or syllables, are expanded to their original form, aiding in text normalization for improved analysis.

5. *Removing Special Characters*

Non-alphanumeric or numeric characters are removed using regular expressions, reducing interference in unstructured text.

6. *Correction of Typos*

Dictionary usage is used to map words to their correct forms based on resemblance, which improves data accuracy and corrects typographical errors.

7. *Standardization*

Through text standardization, terms that are not present in common dictionaries—like hashtags or acronyms—are restored to their regular form by using Python regular expressions or data dictionaries.

8. *Normalization*

The process of transforming tokens into their base forms involves removing inflections. Examples include converting "am," "are, " and "is" to "be." This reduces noise, streamlining language data for machine comprehension(Clarka, E., Arakia, K., 2011).

9. *Stop Words*

Frequently occurring words with minimal information are removed as stop words, reducing noise, especially in text classification tasks. Care must be taken in certain cases to avoid altering the meaning of the text.

10. *Stemming*

Cutting words down to their simplest form—"change," "changes," "changed," and "changing"—as seen in Figure 3 is the process of stemming. In linguistic data, this lowers noise and data dimensionality. Effective text data preparation, noise reduction, increased analysis efficiency, and accurate machine learning model performance in NLP are all taken care by these preprocessing stages(Cesar et al., 2023).

Figure 3. Word Stem and its Inflections

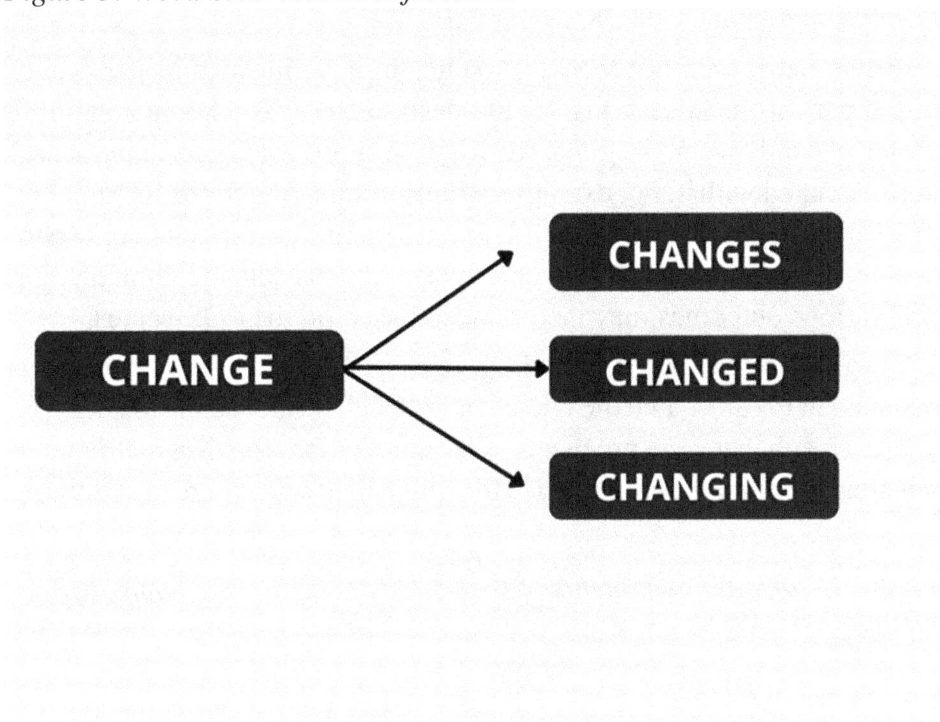

Stemming is a heuristic method aimed at removing word suffixes and prefixes to achieve the goal mentioned earlier. While the Stemming Algorithm is useful for obtaining word stems, it is considered a rough technique. However, stemming can sometimes result in non-dictionary words, making it less desirable as a normalization technique.

11. Lemmatization

While lemmatization and stemming both aim to reduce words to their most basic form, lemmatization is thought to be a more sophisticated technique. Lemmatization, in contrast to stemming, is a methodical, sequential procedure that includes in-depth morphological study to accurately identify a word's root, or "lemma." This method makes use of both morphological analyses—which take into account word structure and grammatical relations—and vocabulary—which takes into account a word's dictionary value(Khyani et al., 2021).

In lemmatization, the process is systematic, allowing for the specification of the part of the speech tag for the desired term. The lemmatization is performed only when the given word has an appropriate part of the speech tag associated with it. For example, when lemmatizing the term "running" as a verb, it maps to "run," but if lemmatizing it as a noun, no conversion occurs. Part-of-speech (POS) values play a crucial role in lemmatization, and various outcomes may be produced based on the POS values.

During lemmatization, four POS options are typically considered as depicted in Figure 4, and the choice of POS can influence the results. This approach enhances the precision of lemmatization, making it a more sophisticated technique compared to the rough heuristic nature of stemming.

Figure 4. Various components of speech that contribute to lemmatization efficacy.

Verb (v)
Examples : Study, Play, Learn, Am, Is, Are...
Noun (n)
Examples : Doctor, Engineer, Farm, Physiotherapist,Towards AI...
Adjective (a)
Examples : Beautiful, Elegant, Angry, Polite, Repulsive...
Adverb (r)
Examples : Badly, Slowly, Peacefully, Very, Extremely, Occasionally...

12. Chunking and Chinking

Chunking is a technique used in extracting relevant phrases from text-based, unstructured data. Finding relevant information might be difficult when working with tokenized texts or articles. As seen in Figure 5, chunking essentially entails dividing plain text into phrases that express more significant information than single words.

Figure 5. Steps involved in the breaking down of a Sentence

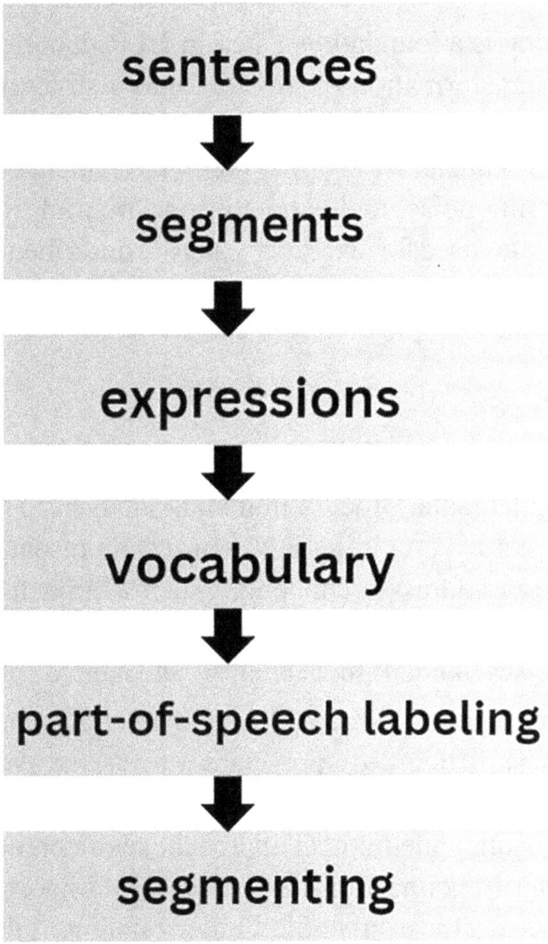

Chinking involves excluding specific segments from a chunk of text. This practice arises when it becomes necessary to remove certain portions from the entire text or chunk, preventing the output of advanced extractions from containing irrelevant data. Chinking plays a crucial role in such situations by omitting particular passages from the chunked text.

2.4 Data Processing

Text processing is a foundational step in NLP, encompassing the manipulation and transformation of raw text into a structured and analyzable format. It involves employing a range of techniques to enhance the efficiency of subsequent NLP tasks, tackling challenges like linguistic variations, reducing noise, and extracting meaningful information from text data.Techniques used for text Processing are described below(Mikolov et al., 2013).

Tokenization

Breaking down text into manageable units, whether they be words or phrases, is a fundamental process in textual analysis. This process aids various NLP tasks by providing a structured representation of textual data. Tokenization addresses challenges such as punctuation handling, word separation, special character management, laying the foundation for subsequent analyses like sentiment analysis and named entity recognition.

This procedure is crucial because it establishes the foundation for future investigation. It is difficult to appreciate a text's intricacies and derive important insights without a deep understanding of the various parts that make it up. By using a methodical approach, segmentation enables analysts to find patterns, connections, and contextual importance in the text. It is, in short, a crucial instrument for understanding of the language and involves a key role in revealing the levels of meaning that are present in any given textual communication.

Removal of Stop Words

They can be best described as common words that carry little meaning and can be safely disregarded without impacting the overall message of the text. Eliminating stop words is a crucial preprocessing step in NLP, reducing noise and dimensionality, thereby enhancing the efficiency of tasks like classification of texts and information retrieval.

Named Entity Recognition (NER)

Identifying entities within text involves recognizing specific elements .i.e names and locations embedded in a given linguistic context. This process, often referred to as entity recognition, helps in extracting and categorizing information from raw data.

Entity identification is significant because it is important to understand huge volumes of textual data. Finding relevant patterns in unstructured data—content without a preset format—is made possible by the ability to identify entities. Analysts can arrange and structure the data to enable a more methodical and effective study by recognizing and classifying names, places, and other items. This procedure is especially useful in domains like data mining and NLP, where the ability to recognise and classify items improves overall understanding and use of various textual data sources(Žukov-Gregorič etal., 2018). Entity identification is essentially a key instrument for turning unstructured data into meaningful, well-organized information.

Part-of-Speech Tagging

Part-of-speech tagging assigns grammatical labels (e.g., noun, verb, adjective) to each word in a text, enhancing understanding of sentence structure and semantics. This tagging is valuable for tasks such as syntactic parsing, NER and machine translation, improving subsequent NLP model performance by providing additional linguistic context.

Beyond syntax, grammatical classification is crucial since it is the foundation for deriving meaning from language. This process is essential to understanding the intended meaning of a text since it links words to their grammatical functions, such as distinguishing subjects and objects. In essence, grammatical classification is a vital instrument that connects the structural and semantic facets of language, promoting a more profound understanding of spoken or written communication.

2.4.1 Challenges in Data Preprocessing

The study of media information poses many challenges that primarily affect the accuracy and operation of subsequent analyses. Acknowledging and addressing these issues is crucial to ensuring reliable understanding of social media content. The challenges encountered in processing social media data are explained below.

Noise and Redundancy

Social media data has extensive noise, irrelevant information, and redundancies that can impede meaningful analysis. Tackling this challenge involves preprocessing techniques focused on noise reduction, eliminating irrelevant content, and handling redundancy to enhance the quality of the dataset.

Entity Recognition

The informal nature of messages on social media makes corporate recognition difficult. Identifying sources, such as citing people, places, and events; It is complicated by the use of nicknames, abbreviations and negative words.

Sentiment Analysis Complexity

The diverse and nuanced expressions found in social media content amplify the complexity of sentiment analysis. Preprocessing efforts must involve fine-tuning sentiment analysis models to capture the emotions precisely being expressed in informal language, ensuring a more accurate representation of user sentiments.

Short Texts and Abbreviations

Social media posts are often short and to the point, and users often use abbreviations. This poses a challenge to standard NLP models for longer texts. Customized preprocessing methods, including maintaining summaries and considering the content in the summaries, are important for accurate analysis.

Privacy Concerns

Protecting user privacy during data processing is especially important when processing personal or sensitive data. Complying with privacy laws, using anonymization techniques, and maintaining data security practices are important aspects of addressing privacy issues on social media.Understanding the complexity of information on social media and solving features and problems in advance forms the basis for the dissemination of useful insights in the fields of digital dynamics and ensures the credibility of the same(Marrero, M., et al., 2013).

2.5 Data Representation

Text representation involves converting textual data into a format easily understood and manipulated by machine learning algorithms, facilitating effective processing . The goal is to transform raw text into numerical or vector representations, enabling computational models to work with the data efficiently(Jurafsky et al.,2008). Various models play crucial roles in this process, each offering distinct advantages in capturing different aspects of linguistic information which are described below:

Bag of Words (BoW) Model

The Bag of Words model represents a document as an unordered set of words, disregarding grammar and word order but preserving word frequency (Pennington, J., Socher, R., & Manning, C, 2014). This model converts a document into a numerical vector, where each dimension represents a distinct word in the corpus. BoW finds extensive application in tasks such as document classification and clustering, laying the groundwork for more sophisticated approaches like TF-IDF and document embeddings.

Term Frequency-Inverse Document Frequency (TF-IDF)

TF-IDF is a numerical statistic reflecting the importance of a distinct word in a document relative to its frequency across a document collection. Combining term frequency (TF) and inverse document frequency

(IDF), TF-IDF is instrumental in information retrieval, text mining, and document similarity analysis.

Word Embeddings

Word embeddings, demonstrated by models like Word2Vec and GloVe, portray words as compact vectors within a continuous vector space, capturing semantic connections. These embeddings encapsulate semantic knowledge acquired from extensive text datasets, enhancing the performance of NLP models in activities such as sentiment analysis and machine translation(Le, Quoc & Mikolov, Tomas, 2014).

Document Embeddings

Extending the concept of word embeddings to entire documents, document embeddings captures the semantic information of the entire text. Techniques like Doc2Vec and TF-IDF weighted word embeddings model the overall meaning of documents, facilitating tasks for example, document classification, clustering, and information retrieval. Document embeddings plays a role in capturing the context and semantics of entire documents, making them invaluable for various NLP applications.

Topic Modeling

Discovering thematic patterns in document collections requires identifying and analyzing recurring themes or topics within a group of documents. This procedure is crucial for systematically categorizing and organizing textual data.

The significance of identifying themes stems from its function in organizing and interpreting vast amounts of data. Analysts can classify and arrange documents according to their content by spotting recurring themes, which makes the retrieval and analysis process run more smoothly. This is especially helpful in domains where systematic document classification improves accessibility and speeds up knowledge extraction, like academic research, content management, and information retrieval. Thematic analysis is a useful technique for extracting significant insights from a variety of textual sources, which helps analysts, researchers, and decision-makers navigate and comprehend the complex web of data found in document collections. In summary, a more structured and perceptive examination of textual data is facilitated by the methodical discovery of theme patterns.

3. ANALYZING SENTIMENTS IN SOCIAL MEDIA

In the context of social media, sentiment analysis plays a pivotal role in deciphering the attitudes, opinions, and emotions conveyed by users. It provides valuable insights into the collective sentiment of online communities, enabling businesses, researchers, and policymakers to gauge public opinion.

1.Major Challenges

Sentiment analysis encounters distinctive challenges when applied to social media data. The first challenge arises from the noisy and informal nature of language used in social media posts. Users often incorporate slang, abbreviations, and unconventional expressions, making it essential for sentiment analysis models to adapt to this linguistic diversity. The second challenge revolves around contextual understanding, as posts in social media are frequently terse and may lack explicit context. Deciphering sentiment within the broader conversation becomes pivotal to accurately interpreting the intended meaning. The third challenge involves the nuanced nature of sentiments, particularly when dealing with sarcasm and irony. Traditional sentiment analysis models may struggle to discern the true sentiment behind such expressions, requiring advanced approaches to capture subtleties and contextual cues.

2.Techniques and Approaches in Analysis

Various methods and strategies are utilized to tackle the inherent challenges in social media sentiment analysis. NLP methods, including tokenization and part-of-speech tagging, are pivotal in deconstructing text into meaningful units, enabling a more nuanced comprehension of words expressing sentiment (Kyunghyun Cho et al.,2014). NER improves sentiment analysis by identifying entities such as names and locations, adding extra context for sentiment interpretation. Machine learning models, encompassing both supervised and unsupervised learning, offer adaptability in handling diverse datasets. While supervised learning is effective for sentiment classification, unsupervised approaches, especially those relying on lexicons, prove beneficial in scenarios where labeled data is scarce.

3.Ethical Considerations in Social Media Sentiment Analysis

Analyzing sentiments on social media, which involves scrutinizing user-generated content, brings forth notable privacy concerns. Users might be unaware that their posts undergo sentiment analysis, potentially resulting in privacy violations. Ethical practices in sentiment analysis involve transparent disclosure and obtaining consent from users before analyzing their content. Striking a balance between extracting valuable insights and respecting user privacy is crucial to maintain ethical standards.

Users need to be informed that their posts undergo sentiment analysis, and organizations should obtain permission before utilizing their content for analysis. Respecting user privacy is not only an ethical obligation but also contributes to building trust between users and organizations leveraging sentiment analysis for decision-making.

4. NER in Social Media

NER serves as a critical component within the broader field of NLP. At its core, NER is a super important subtask of information extraction, aiming to automatically identify and categorize entities within unstructured text. Entities, in this context, refer to specific pieces of information that can be categorized into predefined classes. The primary categories usually include

- Persons: Which refers to the names of individuals.

- Organizations: Identifies names of companies, institutions, or any organized groups.
- Locations: Recognizes places, whether they are countries, cities, or specific geographical points.
- Dates: Involves extracting references to time, including dates and durations.

By employing sophisticated advanced algorithms, leveraging ML models, and analyzing linguistic patterns, NER systems can analyze and annotate text to identify these entities accurately. This process significantly contributes to enhancing the understanding of the content and context of textual data. NER plays a huge, massive role in breaking down the complexity of natural language by pinpointing specific pieces of very important information. This is a really useful feature for a lot of different applications, such as the analysis of sentiment and retrieval of information.

NER is especially important in the social media space since user-generated content is informal and dynamic. The accuracy with which entities are identified in an ever-changing environment greatly improves sentiment analysis, trend identification, and content comprehension. Examining NER's difficulties and uses concerning social media highlights how revolutionary this technology is for extracting meaningful insights from the vast amounts of textual data produced on these platforms(Sharma et al.,2018).

4.1 Navigating NER in the Realm of Social Media

As user-generated content has unique properties, applying NER to social media data presents new hurdles. These challenges stem from the informal nature of language, the prevalence of abbreviations, frequent misspellings, and the ever-evolving vocabulary influenced by trends and memes. Herein, we expound upon the challenges associated with Named Entity Recognition (NER) in the context of social media:

Informal Language

Social media platforms are hubs for casual communication where users often employ informal language, including slang, colloquialisms, and emojis. This informal language usage poses a challenge for NER systems that are trained on more formal language structures.

The presence of informal language can lead to misinterpretation by NER algorithms, potentially resulting in the misclassification or overlooking of entities. For instance, the entity "cool tech" in informal language may not be recognized as an organization or product by traditional NER models.

Abbreviations

The use of acronyms and abbreviations is frequently preferred by users because they are highly convenient, concise, and straightforward. A special problem exists, though, since these acronyms might differ throughout communities or even alter on the fly during a discussion. Similar to figuring out a riddle, this unpredictability adds a layer of intricacy. Furthermore, the subtlety of these abbreviations presents a major obstacle for NER systems, making it more difficult for them to correctly comprehend and classify the wide variety of abbreviations found in natural language.

The inability to correctly interpret and decode acronyms can have serious consequences, perhaps descending into chaos. Imagine a terrifying scenario in which important entities are either mislabeled or completely missed. As an example, the acronym "USA" could refer to a specific geographic area. In the absence of accurate information, a NER system can experience a significant malfunction and be unable to classify it correctly. This emphasizes how crucial it is to handle abbreviations with extreme care to avoid mistakes and guarantee precise entity identification.

Misspellings

Users often make spelling mistakes intentionally or unintentionally. Misspellings can be driven by the desire for brevity, the use of phonetic spellings, or intentional alterations to convey a particular tone or style.

Traditional NER models trained on grammatically correct text may struggle to handle misspellings. Incorrectly spelled entities might go unrecognized, affecting the overall accuracy of the NER system. For instance, "thx" instead of "thanks" could be a challenge for recognizing expressions of gratitude.

Evolving Vocabulary and Trends

The dynamic settings of social media platforms are marked by the quick emergence of new terms, expressions, and memes. Because of this dynamic nature, Named Entity Recognition (NER) models face significant challenges in quickly adjusting to changing language that is affected by pop culture and current trends.

NER models that are outdated or static may have difficulties recognizing entities associated with new trends or cultural events, which limits their ability to effectively capture up-to-date information. For example, a model trained on old data may not correctly identify a popular hashtag or meme. This constraint emphasizes how crucial it is to use current and dynamic NER models to guarantee information extraction accuracy, particularly in light of the quickly changing linguistic and internet cultures.

Adaptive NER models are being developed and improved by researchers in order to accommodate the constantly evolving linguistic environment of social media. These models are always learning and changing to keep up with the changing linguistic trends in social media. To ensure accurate and dependable NER performance, they make use of context-aware algorithms and machine learning techniques that take into account the variety in language use(Acheampong, Francisca et al., 2020).

In the region of NLP, NER and NLP together are a formidable combo. As researchers and developers delve deeper into the intricacies of adaptive NER models, significant advancements in tasks like sentiment analysis, document classification, and machine translation can be expected. By leveraging the synergy between NER and NLP, systems can effectively comprehend and derive valuable insights from diverse textual data, opening up numerous possibilities for improving various applications.

5. NLP MODELS TAILORED FOR SOCIAL MEDIA ANALYSIS

Online platforms have evolved into hubs of communication, generating massive amounts of unstructured textual data daily. The goal of NLP models created especially for social media is to solve the particular difficulties brought about by the colloquial language, acronyms, and quickly evolving trends that are common on these platforms.

5.1 Introduction to the Models

NLP models designed for social media are specific algorithms and methodologies that are adapted to the particular features of textual data coming from online sites. Even if classic NLP models are adept at processing formal, structured language, the predominance of informal language, emoticons, hashtags, abbreviations, and the ever-changing nature of expressions on social media provides a number of challenges that need to be addressed.

Social media-specific NLP techniques are essential for understanding the complex nature of user-generated information on the internet. Conventional NLP models are excellent at interpreting formal, structured language; nevertheless, the informal idioms, emoticons, hashtags, acronyms, and changing vernacular of social media provide difficulties. These specialist NLP models navigate the intricacies of internet speech like superheroes. Utilizing traditional methods such as tokenization, parsing, and part-of-speech analysis their distinctive advantage is their ability to adjust to the fluid and non-formal nature of social media content (Hutto, C. J., et al. 2014). Prominent models are those with proficiency in online platform analysis, demonstrating their ability to decipher the various and constantly evolving expressions found in this virtual space.

1. BERT:
    - BERT is a highly advanced transformer-based model that has been pre-initialized to comprehend relationships and information in text. It is extensively employed in many NLP applications, such as named entity identification, analysis of sentiment, and comprehension of language in online platforms.

Transformer Architecture

- The motor armature serves as the basis for BERT. In order to gather contextual information from both the left and right surrounds in a series of words, Mills uses tone-attention mechanisms. The comprehension of the meaning of words in the surroundings is largely dependent on this bidirectional environment modeling.

Pre-training

- BERT is pre-initialized on large quantities of unlabeled textbook data. By taking into account the context provided by the girding words, the model gains the ability to predict missing words in a judgment during pre-training. This is done through the masked language model(MLM) ideal, where a certain chance of words in each input sequence is aimlessly masked, and the model is trained to predict these masked words.

Lexicalization

- BERT tokenizer inputs textbooks into subwords or WordPieces, creating a vocabulary of subword commemoratives. This subword tokenization allows BERT to handle out-of-vocabulary words and prisoner morphological variations more effectively (Han, B. 2014).

Layers and Attention Heads

- BERT consists of multiple layers, generally using a mound of motor encoder layers. Each subcaste contains multiple attention heads. These attention heads singly attend to different corridors of the input sequence, landing different contextual information.

Attention Medium

- Each commemoration in the sequence, equipped with diverse attention weights, is capable of attending to every other commemoration through BERT's attention mechanism. With the use of this medium, the model may determine long-range dependencies by evaluating the importance of various words in relation to the word that is currently being reused.

Fine-tuning

- After pre-training, BERT can be fine-tuned for specific downstream tasks similar to sentiment analysis, named reality recognition, or question answering. Fine-tuning involves training the model on a lower-labeled dataset related to the target task.

Roberta (Robustly optimized BERT approach):

- Roberta is another motor-grounded model like BERT but is trained with different hyperparameters and on a larger dataset.

2.BERTweet:

- BERTweet is a specialized version of BERT that is pre-trained on a large corpus of tweets. It is designed to capture the unique characteristics and language nuances of Twitter, making it particularly suitable for sentiment analysis and other NLP tasks on Twitter data.

3. VADER (Valence Aware Dictionary and sentiment Reasoner):

- VADER is a rule-grounded sentiment analysis tool designed specifically for online platforms. Developed by experimenters at the Georgia Institute of Technology, VADER is particularly useful for assaying sentiment in short and informal textbooks, which are common in platforms like Twitter and other social media.

Crucial Features of VADER

Lexicon- Grounded Approach

- VADER employs a wordbook-grounded strategy, using predetermined sentiment scores for words to conduct nuanced sentiment analysis in the dynamic and informal language of social media. This approach facilitates effective environment mindfulness, making it well-suited for landing the craft of stoner-generated content.

Opposition Scores:

- For each judgment or document, VADER calculates an emulsion opposition score, which represents the overall sentiment. The emulsion score is a combination of the individual sentiment scores of content in the textbooks, considering both the intensity and environment.

Valence and Intensity:

- VADER considers the valence (positive, negative, or neutral) and intensity of words to provide a more nuanced sentiment analysis. For example, words like "happy" and "ecstatic" might both be positive, but the latter has a higher intensity.

Handling Punctuation and Capitalization:

- VADER takes into account the impact of punctuation marks (e.g., exclamation points) and capitalization on sentiment intensity. A word with several exclamation points or all caps, for example, can increase the intensity score.

Negation Handling:

- VADER considers the effect of negations on sentiment. For example, it understands that "not good" has a negative sentiment, even though the word "good" itself is positive (Mikolov et al., 2013).

4. Generative AI:

With the help of models like GPT-3, generative AI has several real-world uses in social media that improve user experience, content quality, and company productivity. Here are a few sensible applications of generative AI in this field:

Content Generation:

- Automated Posts: AI can create interesting content for social media platforms that are suited to certain populations and trends. This helps companies be active on social media without requiring continual human labor. AI supports the creation of creative material, including slogans, captions, and stories, that complement a brand's voice and prevailing trends.

Client Interaction:

- AI-generated individualized responses to user messages and comments enhance customer happiness and interactivity, particularly for large quantities of questions.

Moderating Content:

- Identifying and Reporting Unsuitable Information: Artificial intelligence (AI) contributes to the preservation of a secure online environment by recognizing and reporting offensive or dangerous information. Automated Moderation Reactions AI is capable of producing suitable reactions to content that has been moderated, guaranteeing polite and constant conversation.

Trend Research and Perspectives:

- Trend Prediction: Artificial intelligence (AI) can forecast new trends and subjects by examining vast databases. This allows influencers and companies to modify their content marketing plans appropriately.

Synopsis of Content:

- AI summarizes lengthy discussion threads to make it easier for users to catch up and for businesses to process comments more effectively. AI generates digests of significant talks and subjects on a daily or weekly basis, offering succinct synopses of pertinent data.

5. Word Embeddings (Word2Vec, GloVe, Emoji2Vec:):

- Word embeddings are pre-trained vector representations of words that capture semantic connections. In social media analysis, models such as the word2Vec and GloVe models are commonly used for understanding the context and meaning of content created by drug users for recreational purposes.
- Emojis play a significant part in conveying sentiment and feelings in a social media textbook. Emoji2Vec is a model that generates vector representations for emojis, facilitating a deeper comprehension of the emotional tenor of social media material.

It's crucial to take into account both the type of material and the unique features of the platform (such as Facebook, Instagram, and Twitter) while working with online data. Pre-processing and model fine-tuning may be needed to address sphere-specific challenges and verbal variations in social media textbooks.

6. APPLICATIONS OF NLP IN SOCIAL MEDIA

NLP stands at the van of revolutionizing the way of interaction and excerpt meaningful perceptivity from the vast realms of social media. Its vital part extends beyond bare textbook analysis, recapitulating a diapason of operations that elevate the stoner experience, empower businesses, and unravel precious patterns within the ever-expanding geography of social platforms. In this dynamic digital terrain, NLP catalyzes invention, offering a multifaceted toolkit to decode sentiments, curate substantiated content, and foster flawless communication across different verbal geographies. The operations of NLP in social media and its capabilities unfold to shape a more engaging, perceptive, and connected online experience.

1. *Content Recommendation*

NLP algorithms can dissect stoner preferences and actions to give substantiated happy recommendations. This enhances stoner engagement by delivering content that's more likely to be of interest to individual druggies.

2. *Chatbots and Virtual Sidekicks*

Social media platforms frequently use chatbots for client support, information reclamation, and engagement. NLP enables these chatbots to understand and respond to stoner queries in a natural language, perfecting the stoner experience.

3. *NER*

NLP can identify and prize named realities similar to people, associations, locales, and more from social media content. This information is precious for trend analysis, stoner profiling, and targeted advertising.

4. *Content Modeling*

NLP helps in grading and organizing large volumes of social media content into motifs. This can be useful for content temperance, trend analysis and understanding the interests of stoner communities.

5. *Language Translation*

Social media platforms connect people encyclopedically and NLP-powered language restatement facilitates communication between individuals who speak different languages. This is particularly important for platforms with a different stoner base.

6. *Emotion Discovery*

NLP algorithms can identify and dissect emotional tones expressed in social media posts. This information is precious for understanding stoner responses, perfecting client service, and conforming marketing strategies.

7. *Automatic Summarization*

NLP can be used to automatically induce summaries of lengthy social media posts or papers. This helps druggies snappily grasp the main points and facilitates content consumption.

8. *Content temperance*

To automatically identify and remove objectionable or unwanted content from social media sites, content moderation uses NLP. This helps to create a safer and more positive environment.

9. *Event Discovery and Trend Analysis*

NLP algorithms can dissect social media content to describe rising events and trends. This information is useful for marketers, intelligencers, and businesses to stay streamlined on current motifs and acclimatize their strategies consequently.

10. *Influencer Marketing and stoner Profiling*

NLP plays a vital part in relating and assaying influential numbers within social media platforms. By checking stoner-generated content, commentary, and engagement criteria, NLP algorithms can produce detailed stoner biographies. It provides insights that greatly improve the effectiveness of influencer marketing tactics by maximizing the audience's exposure and resonance. This increased awareness is a vital component that supports the impact and efficacy of advertising efforts by guaranteeing the best possible relationship with the target audience (Maas, A. L., et al., 2011). The integration of NLP in social media enhances the stoner experience, enables data-driven decision- timber, and provides precious perceptivity for businesses and associations.

7. CASE STUDIES

In the modern digital era, Natural Language Processing (NLP) has significantly transformed the ways in which companies engage with and analyze extensive volumes of user-generated content. Many platforms have utilized the capabilities of NLP to enhance their services, elevate customer experiences, and extract valuable insights. This discussion delves into how prominent organizations are employing NLP through the following case studies: Twitter's Sentiment Analysis, Facebook's Content Moderation, KLM Royal Dutch Airlines' Customer Service, Hootsuite's Influencer Marketing, and Reddit's Trend Analysis. These examples highlight the substantial impact of NLP on various aspects of the digital environment.

Twitter's Sentiment Analysis

Twitter has leveraged NLP to gain insights into public sentiment about various topics, events, and products. By collecting vast amounts of tweet data, Twitter employs sentiment analysis algorithms to categorize tweets as positive, negative, or neutral. The platform utilizes a mix of machine learning models, including Support Vector Machines (SVM) and deep learning models such as recurrent neural networks (RNNs) and transformers.

This implementation helps businesses track public opinion regarding their brands and products, allows Twitter to provide valuable sentiment analysis data to advertisers and researchers, and aids in identifying trending topics during significant events like elections or natural disasters.

Facebook's Content Moderation

Facebook has implemented NLP to enhance content moderation and ensure a safe online environment. By analyzing text, images, and videos posted on the platform, Facebook uses text classification, entity recognition, and context analysis to detect hate speech, fake news, and other inappropriate content. The platform employs deep learning models, including convolutional neural networks (CNNs) for image analysis and transformers for text analysis. This approach automates the detection and removal of harmful content, reduces the dependence on human moderators, improves user safety, and helps Facebook comply with regulatory standards and community guidelines (Kalchbrenner et al., 2017).

KLM Royal Dutch Airlines' Customer Service

KLM Royal Dutch Airlines has adopted NLP to improve its customer service interactions on social media platforms like Twitter and Facebook. By analyzing customer queries and interactions, KLM uses chatbots and sentiment analysis to respond to customer inquiries promptly and accurately. The airline employs natural language understanding (NLU) models and platforms such as IBM Watson and Dialogflow for chatbot development. This implementation allows KLM to provide 24/7 customer support, reduce wait times, handle a large volume of queries efficiently, and enhance overall customer satisfaction.

Hootsuite's Influencer Marketing

Hootsuite uses NLP to assist brands in identifying and collaborating with social media influencers. By gathering data on social media interactions, follower counts, and engagement rates, Hootsuite uses named entity recognition (NER) and sentiment analysis to identify influential users and assess their impact. The platform employs machine learning models and NLP libraries like SpaCy and NLTK to facilitate this process. As a result, brands can find relevant influencers for their marketing campaigns, measure the effectiveness of influencer marketing efforts through engagement metrics, and gain insights into audience demographics and interests.

Reddit's Trend Analysis

Reddit has implemented NLP to identify emerging trends and topics of interest across its various subreddits. By analyzing posts, comments, and user interactions, Reddit uses topic modeling, sentiment analysis, and clustering algorithms to detect trends and patterns. The platform employs libraries such as Gensim for topic modeling and scikit-learn for clustering. This implementation helps moderators manage and promote trending topics, provides advertisers with insights into popular discussions and user interests, and enhances user engagement by highlighting trending content (J. Li et al., 2022).

8. CONCLUSION AND FUTURE SCOPE

NLP plays a pivotal role at the intersection of computer science and linguistics, facilitating machines in comprehending and generating human language. Its applications in social media data processing, including sentiment analysis, content moderation, and trend analysis, highlight its transformative impact on human-computer interaction. NLP's core aspects, such as language understanding, generation, and machine translation, form the foundation for its diverse applications, ranging from virtual assistants to personalized user experiences.

Despite challenges posed by informal language, abbreviations, and evolving vocabulary in social media, NLP contributes to improved content understanding, efficient content moderation, and personalized user experiences. Ethical considerations underscore the importance of transparency and user consent in sentiment analysis on social media, balancing the extraction of valuable insights with user privacy. The fusion of NLP with image and video processing, coupled with strides in Explainable

AI (XAI), enriches the complexity and clarity of NLP models. Looking forward, the evolution of NLP in analyzing social media data anticipates advancements in contextual comprehension, precision, flexibility, and instantaneous data handling. Ultimately, NLP continues to be a formidable influence, transforming digital communication and fostering innovation across various industries and societal spheres.

NLP stands at the vanguard of a revolutionary era, experiencing unparalleled growth and weaving its intricate applications across a myriad of industries. The escalating capabilities of AI-driven systems underscore the imperative necessity to harness the distinctive problem-solving capacities inherent in the human mind. NLP acts as a pivotal bridge, facilitating seamless communication between humans and machines, empowering machines to interpret inputs and make decisions in a manner closely mirroring human cognition. This not only streamlines interactions between humans and machines but also nurtures a collaborative environment where both entities synergize to produce innovative and impactful outcomes.

Future projections for the trajectory of NLP emphasize its potential infiltration into pivotal sectors, with healthcare exemplifying this trend. Anticipated applications include the streamlined organization of extensive medical reports, ensuring accessibility for efficient decision-making processes. Similarly, in the cybersecurity domain, NLP is poised to play an integral role in managing complex big data concepts to bolster system security and confidentiality, particularly in military applications. The inherent adaptability of NLP positions it as a transformative force across diverse industries, promising heightened efficiency and optimization.

Looking ahead, the evolution of NLP pivots on advancements in critical areas such as speech recognition, automated machine translation, sentiment analysis, and the refinement of sophisticated chatbots. These advancements are set to reshape the landscape of human-machine interactions, fostering more intuitive and responsive interfaces. Furthermore, the seamless integration of NLP with cutting-edge technologies like artificial intelligence (AI), the Internet of Things (IoT), and blockchain holds the promise of creating a secure network of communication between devices and systems. This integration is poised to further automation and optimization across various processes, heralding a new era of technological synergy.

An emerging frontier for NLP lies in the domain of digital marketing, where companies increasingly focus on personalized messaging and establishing deeper connections with consumers in the dynamic realm of online advertising. NLP emerges as a pivotal player in this context, analyzing customer language patterns, sentiments, and preferences to significantly contribute to the optimization of advertising campaigns. This ensures more targeted and effective outreach, ultimately enhancing client engagement and fostering brand loyalty in an increasingly competitive market.

REFERENCES

Acheampong, F., Nunoo-Mensah, H., & Chen, W. (2020). Comparative analyses of BERT, RoBERTa, DistilBERT, and XLNet for text-based emotion recognition.

Cesar, L. B., Manso-Callejo, M.-Á., & Cira, C.-I. (2023). BERT (Bidirectional Encoder Representations from Transformers) for missing data imputation in solar irradiance time series. *Engineering Proceedings, 39*(26). DOI: 10.3390/engproc2023039026

Chiramel, S., Logofătu, D., & Goldenthal, G. (2020). Detection of social media platform insults using Natural language processing and comparative study of machine learning algorithms. In 2020 24th International Conference on System Theory, Control and Computing (ICSTCC), Sinaia, Romania (pp. 98-101). DOI: 10.1109/ICSTCC50638.2020.9259730

Cho, K., van Merrienboer, B., Gulcehre, C., Bougares, F., Schwenk, H., & Bengio, Y. (2014). Learning phrase representations using RNN encoder-decoder for statistical machine translation. *CoRR*, abs/1406.1078.

Clark, E., & Araki, K. (2011). Text normalization in social media: Progress, problems and applications for a pre-processing system of casual English. In **Proceedings of the Pacific Association for Computational Linguistics (PACLING 2011)**. DOI: 10.1016/j.sbspro.2011.10.577

Gelbukh, A. (2005). Natural language processing. In *Proceedings of the Fifth International Conference on Hybrid Intelligent Systems (HIS'05)* (pp. 1). Rio de Janeiro, Brazil: IEEE. DOI: 10.1109/ICHIS.2005.79

Haldar, R., & Mukhopadhyay, D. (2011). Levenshtein distance technique in dictionary lookup methods: An improved approach. *Computing Research Repository (CoRR)*.

Han, B. (2014). *Improving the utility of social media with natural language processing*. The University of Melbourne.

Hutto, C. J., & Gilbert, E. (2014). VADER: A parsimonious rule-based model for sentiment analysis of social media text. **Eighth International AAAI Conference on Weblogs and Social Media**. DOI: 10.1609/icwsm.v8i1.14550

Jiang, K., & Lu, X. (2020). Natural Language Processing and Its Applications in Machine Translation: A Diachronic Review. In 2020 IEEE 3rd International Conference of Safe Production and Informatization (IICSPI), Chongqing City, China (pp. 210-214). IEEE. DOI: 10.1109/IICSPI51290.2020.9332458

Jurafsky, D., & Martin, J. H. (2008). *Speech and language processing: An introduction to natural language processing, computational linguistics, and speech recognition* (2nd ed.). Prentice Hall.

Kalchbrenner, N., Espeholt, L., Simonyan, K., van den Oord, A., Graves, A., & Kavukcuoglu, K. (2017). Neural machine translation in linear time. *arXiv preprint arXiv:1610.10099v2*.

Kanan, T.. (2019). A Review of Natural Language Processing and Machine Learning Tools Used to Analyze Arabic Social Media. In *2019 IEEE Jordan International Joint Conference on Electrical Engineering and Information Technology (JEEIT)* (pp. 622-628). Amman, Jordan: IEEE. DOI: 10.1109/JEEIT.2019.8717369

Khyani, D., Siddhartha, B. S., Niveditha, N. M., & Divya, B. M. (2021). An interpretation of lemmatization and stemming in natural language processing. *. *Shanghai Ligong Daxue Xuebao.*

Le, Q., & Mikolov, T. (2014). Distributed representations of sentences and documents. In **Proceedings of the 31st International Conference on Machine Learning (ICML 2014)**.

Li, J., Sun, A., Han, J., & Li, C. (2022). A survey on deep learning for named entity recognition. *IEEE Transactions on Knowledge and Data Engineering, 34*(1), 50-70. DOI: 10.1109/TKDE.2020.2981314

Maas, A. L., Daly, R. E., Pham, P. T., Huang, D., Ng, A. Y., & Potts, C. (2011). Learning word vectors for sentiment analysis. In **Proceedings of the 49th Annual Meeting of the Association for Computational Linguistics: Human Language Technologies**.

Marrero, M., Sánchez-Cuadrado, S., Morato, J., & Andreadakis, I. (2013). *Named entity recognition: Fallacies, challenges and opportunities. *University Carlos III of Madrid.* Department of Computer Science.

Mikolov, T., Sutskever, I., Chen, K., Corrado, G. S., & Dean, J. (2013). Distributed representations of words and phrases and their compositionality. In *Advances in Neural Information Processing Systems (NeurIPS)*.

Mikolov, T., Yih, W., & Zweig, G. (2013). Linguistic regularities in continuous space word representations. In **Proceedings of the 2013 Conference of the North American Chapter of the Association for Computational Linguistics: Human Language Technologies** (pp. 746-751).

Pennington, J., Socher, R., & Manning, C. (2014). GloVe: Global vectors for word representation. In **Proceedings of the 2014 Conference on Empirical Methods in Natural Language Processing (EMNLP)** (pp. 1532-1543). DOI: 10.3115/v1/D14-1162

Ridzuan, F., & Wan Zainon, W. M. N. (2019). A review on data cleansing methods for big data. *Procedia Computer Science, 161*, 731-738. DOI: 10.1016/j.procs.2019.11.177

Sharma, H. K., & Kshitiz, K., & Shailendra. (2018). NLP and machine learning techniques for detecting insulting comments on social networking platforms. In *2018 International Conference on Advances in Computing and Communication Engineering (ICACCE)* (pp. 265-272). Paris, France: IEEE. DOI: 10.1109/ICACCE.2018.8441728

Shayaa, S., Jaafar, N. I., Bahri, S., Sulaiman, A., Seuk Wai, P., Wai Chung, Y., Piprani, A. Z., & Al-Garadi, M. A. (2018). Sentiment Analysis of Big Data: Methods, Applications, and Open Challenges. *IEEE Access : Practical Innovations, Open Solutions*, *6*, 37807–37827. DOI: 10.1109/ACCESS.2018.2851311

Smith, J. D., & Johnson, K. L. (2023). Enhancing Data Quality in Big Data: A Comprehensive Review. *Journal of Big Data Management, 7*(2), 145-156. https://doi.org/DOI: 10.1016/j.jbdm.2023.07.009

Someswararao, C., Rajanikanth, J., Vasamsetty, C., & Bhadri Raju, M. S. V. S. (2012). Data cleaning: A framework for robust data quality in enterprise data warehouse. *International Journal of Computer Science and Technology*. Retrieved from www.ijcst.com

Surabhi, M. C. (2013). Natural language processing future. In *Proceedings of the 2013 International Conference on Optical Imaging Sensor and Security (ICOSS)* (pp. 1-3). Coimbatore, India: IEEE. DOI: 10.1109/ICOISS.2013.6678407

Wangikar, V. C., & Deshmukh, R. R. (2011). Data cleaning: Current approaches and issues. *Department of Computer Science & IT, Dr. Babasaheb Ambedkar Marathwada University, Aurangabad (MS), India*.

Žukov-Gregorič, A., Bachrach, Y., & Coope, S. (2018). Named entity recognition with parallel recurrent neural networks. In *Proceedings of the 56th Annual Meeting of the Association for Computational Linguistics (Volume 2: Short Papers)* (pp. 69–74). Melbourne, Australia: Association for Computational Linguistics. DOI: 10.18653/v1/P18-2012

Chapter 8
Tongue Image Biometric Using Computational Intelligence

G. Revathy
https://orcid.org/0000-0002-0691-1687
SASTRA University, India

S. Kiruthika
Erode Sengunthar Engineering College, India

M. C. Savithri
https://orcid.org/0009-0009-5068-9743
J.K.K. Munirajah College of Technology, India

N. Nanthini
Cherraan's Arts Science College, India

ABSTRACT

Artificial intelligence development has advanced dramatically over the previous two decades and will increase 100 times more in the coming years. With a variety of uses, artificial intelligence is assisting humanity. Biometric system is an example of such an application. Individual-specific behavioural or physiological characteristics are used by biometric systems

DOI: 10.4018/979-8-3693-2935-1.ch008

to automatically identify a person. Verification and identification are the two operational modes of biometric systems. When a claimed identity is verified, it is either approved or rejected, whereas when a claimed identity is identified, a description of the claimed identity is given. Like fingerprints, each person's tongue print is distinctive. The tongue was chosen for this case study because it is different from other similar organs. The lips provide protection for the tongue. This prevents the capturing of a tongue print via force. It is a special structure that displays data on physiological texture as well as geometric shape, both of which could be helpful in identification verification. With more explanation, the tongue can be utilized as a new method for identifying a person because even identical twins have varied tongue shape, color, and texture. Some people alter their fingerprints, rendering fingerprint identification software useless. The tongue was utilized as a fingerprint in this case study because accidents can alter the face, which makes it difficult for the system to tell apart facial prints. The exposed part of the tongue carries information that can be used to distinguish between individuals and is therefore useful for identification. The database consists of 2405 tongue images and the images are trained with various deep models such as CNN, VGG16, VGG19, MobileNetV2 and RESNET50. Since the deep models predicts the exact details of the patient it would suggest the specific doctor based on the artificial intelligence. The proposed system is planned to set as an GUI for the hospital to book appointments and for the consultation purpose and treatments.

1. INTRODUCTION

Behavioural or physical characteristics can now be used to identify a person thanks to the introduction of biometric identification technologies. In contrast to behavioural biometrics, which include gait, keystrokes, and signatures, physiological biometrics include facial, hand and hand vein, odor, ear, fingerprint, retina, tongue, and DNA. A biometric characteristic can be any attribute related to human behaviour or physiology as long as it meets certain criteria that Universality: The trait ought to be possessed by every person. Individuality: It is important for every two people to be unique. The trait must possess sufficient invariance to be considered permanent. Collectability refers to the feature's ability to be quantified. Because of its many applications, identifying people is one of the most significant processes that has recently piqued the interest of academics. In automated presence recording or person proof schemes, it can be utilized as protection. Researchers developed a number of techniques, but they still require help with challenges related to speed, safety, and cost (Li et al., 2024).

Till biometric-based explanations remained developed, there was a research vacuum in this area. A person's distinct behavioural and physiological traits can be automatically used by biometrics to recognize and confirm that individual's identification. With its defensive casing of the oral crater, the tongue is a vital inner tissue defended from the external environment. The distinctive features of the tongue vary significantly between individuals and identical twins. As with all other organs, it should come as no wonder that the tongue has a grid of blood vessels, muscles, and nerves. The tongue print is unique in that no two tongues are same, and even identical twin tongues differ. Both are present on the tongue. Mechanisms for static and dynamic authentication are available. As a result of utilizing The use of tongue prints as a biometric identification technique is becoming more popular increasing popularity. Biometrics technology, as part of Significant attention has been drawn to technical advancement. In recent years, notably in reference to cutting-edge methods such as machine learning and artificial intelligence Deep intelligence is a modern approach to intelligence. Learning was established as a result of this never-ending pursuit (Kamath et al., 2024). The proposed chapter is designed in the following format, second title is literature survey third one is dataset description and the fourth one is methodology and fifth one is results and discussions followed by conclusion.

2. LITERATURE SURVEY

Tongue print recognition, according to the authors, has lately been a hot study area in biometric applications. The tongue is an important interior tissue that is isolated from the rest of the world by the mouth cavity. Tongue print is both a useful forensic tool and a cutting-edge biometric technology. The goalmouth of this work is to describe a Tongue Pattern Recognition structure that extracts properties from tongue photos using Convolutional Neural Network Models. Our own database was used to legalize the projected method. The outcomes of the experimentations show that the projected VGG16 has an F1 Score of 98.9%. The recommended biometric identification method is secure, durable, and trustworthy, according to the findings (Kannan et al., 2022).

Authors discuss Forensic odontology is an important branch of science that aids in the resolution of many criminal cases as well as in person identification by providing dental knowledge in a court of law so that the proper justice is given. Because it is tightly encased within the mouth cavity, the tongue is an important crucial organ of the human body that is well protected from the outside world. The tongue contains unique traits that differ from person to person, even in identical twins. As a result, tongue prints may now be used in forensic dentistry as a biometric authentication method. Because the tongue is sexually dimorphic, it also aids in identification (Khan et al., 2023).

The authors claim that their tongue print biometric system collects photographs of tongue motifs by means of a Raspberry Pi as the CPU and a Raspberry Pi Camera through an 8-megapixel Sony IMX219 sensor. Before employing the CLAHE for image pre-processing, the system takes a picture of the user's tongue. Before constructing picture descriptors, the ORB method collects attributes from the Region of Interest. The signifiers are then saved in a database together with the user's evidence. Thirty (30) real test subjects were employed to collect data, and twenty (20) tongue prints from real users were acquired to train the original. Following training, the system was gauged five times on each legitimate and imposter user, with an complete accuracy of 90.33% (Caya, Lechoncito, & Deveraturda, 2022).

Authors says that tongue prints can be used to authenticate humans. The structure of the tongue, like finger prints, are unique and vary from person to person. The purpose of this review was to confirm the prevalence of Tongue traits and the extent to which Tongue traits are useful in forensic identification. Tongue has distinct characteristics that allow for personal identification. Tongue printing is evolving into a novel biometric tool as well as a powerful forensic tool (Sangala et al., 2022).

Tongue image data, according to the authors .K-means divides the diabetic population into four categories based on VQ-VAE characteristics (Li et al., 2022; Li et al., 2005). The silhouette scores are 0.391, 673.256, and 0.809.

The authors provide a unique LDA approach Under considerable changes in perspective, the distribution of tongue pictures is well acknowledged to be quite nonlinear (Jiang et al., 2021).

According to the authors, one current research emphasis in TCM modernization is employing tongue image processing techniques for automated ailment detection. Although deep learning beats standard algorithms for automated (Song, Wang, & Xu, 2020).

3. DATASET DESCRIPTION

Tongue photos from various databases were gathered https://dataverse .harvard.edu/dataset.xhtml?persistentId=doi:10.7910/DVN/COJZMQ .https://www.kaggle.com/datasets/shivam17299/oral-cancer-lips-and-tongue-images and an original dataset was obtained from 550 people, with eight photographs taken with a VIVO pro max camera with a tenacity of (9 Megapixels) for each participant.

Figure 1. Sample Tongue images in our database

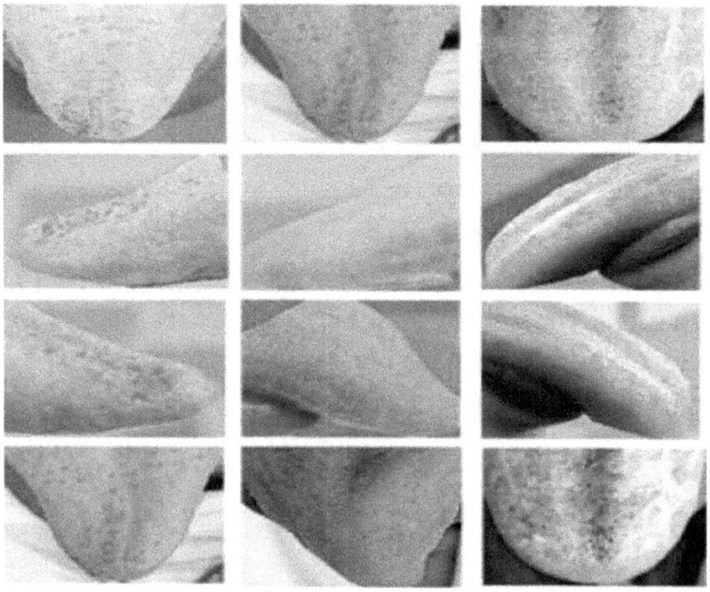

We traditional up an apposite atmosphere for image capture. This habitat may be fashioned with a box of 45.51727.5 cm3 high-density fiber board. Some examples of photos are provided below for your convenience.Figure 1 explains the various tongue images of various age groups. We are deals with various age groups because the biometric is planning about hospital management which deals with various age groups and hence the data is also trained with various age of people. Totally we have around 2405 images.

4. METHODOLOGY

There are 5 models we are used in training the database. They are CNN, VGG16, VGG19, MobileNetV2 and RESNET50. The discussions of each and every model is discussed below.

4.1 CNN

The architectural diagram for CNN is described below in the following figure 2.

Figure 2. CNN architecture

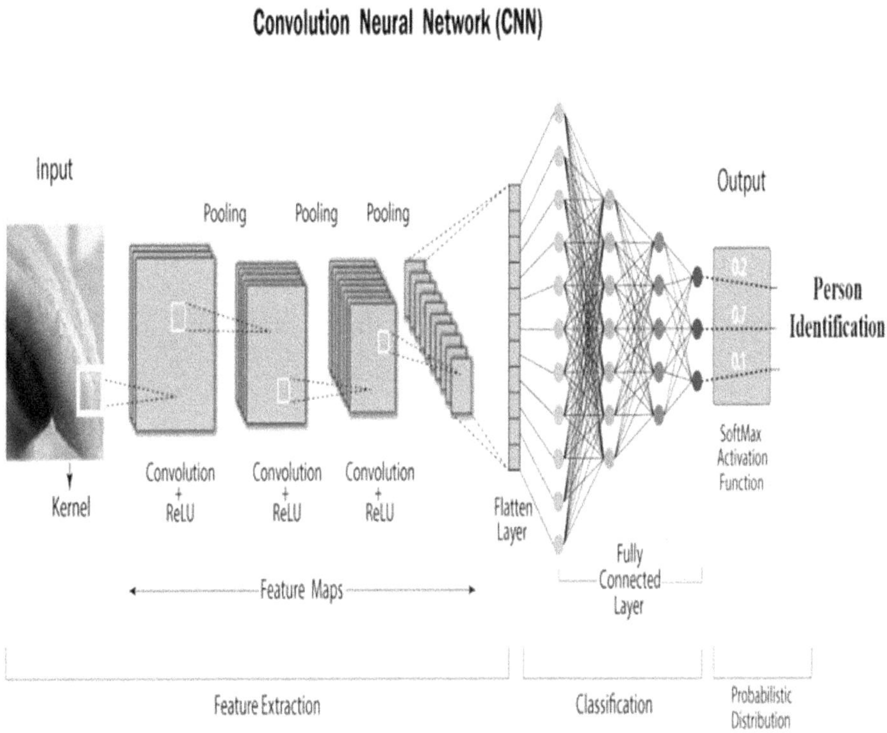

Figure 1 explains the basics of CNN.

*Vectors of Input * Feature Detector* = *Feature Map* Eq 1

Padding permits the kernel to encompass more of the image, increasing image analysis accuracy. Because of padding, information on picture margins is retained in the same way as it is in the center of the image. Figure 3 shows CNN padding.

Figure 3. Padding of CNN

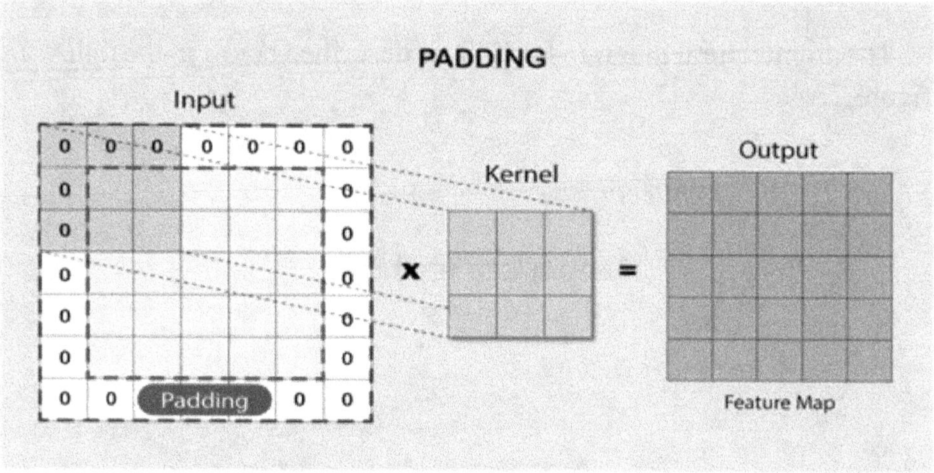

Figure 4 shows that the higher the stride value, the smaller the final result.

Figure 4. Striding in CNN

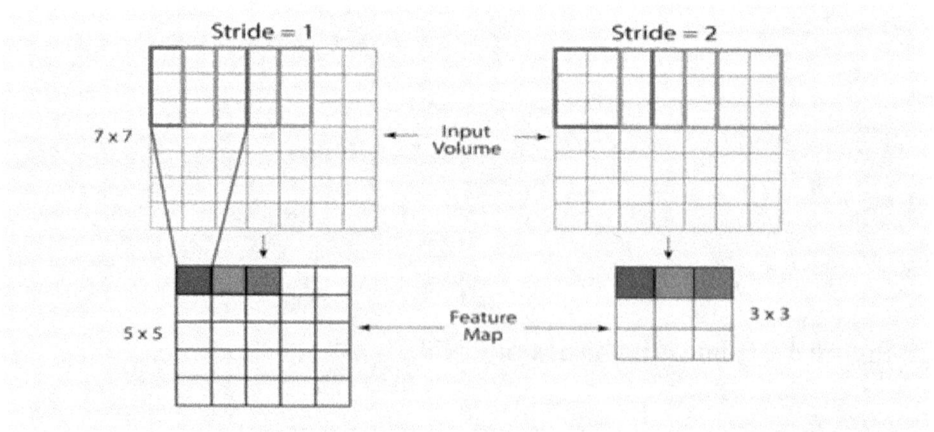

ReLU is calculated afterwards complication. It is the furthermost often employed activation purpose, allowing the neural network to interpretation for nonlinear interactions. In a specified matrix (x), ReLU sets all undesirable ideals to zero while leaving all other ethics unchanged.

$y = MAX(0, X)$ Eq 2

Figure 5 depicts how the pooling layer impacts each feature plot separately. This decreases the resolution of the feature map by lowering the height and breadth of the feature maps while retaining the map's critical categorization elements. This is referred to as downsampling. Pooling can be achieved in several ways, including:

It chooses the most components from the feature map using max-pooling. The ensuing max-pooled layer contains significant portions of the feature map. It is the utmost extensively used method since it produces the best outcomes.

Calculating an middling for individually region of the feature map is part of average pooling.

Figure 5. Pooling in CNN

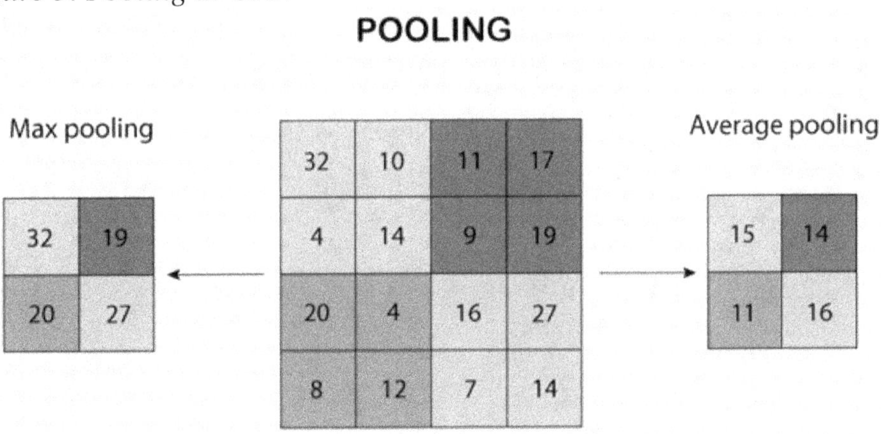

The fully connected layer, which links all neurons and provides the network's last few levels, is analogous to a traditional neural network.

4.2 VGG16

The architectural design of the VGG16 is shown in Figure 6. VGG16 is an abbreviation for sixteen weighted layers. VGG16 has 13 convolutional layers, five Max Pooling layers, and three Dense layers for a total of 21 layers, but only sixteen weight layers, or learnable parameters layers.

Figure 6. VGG – 16 Architecture

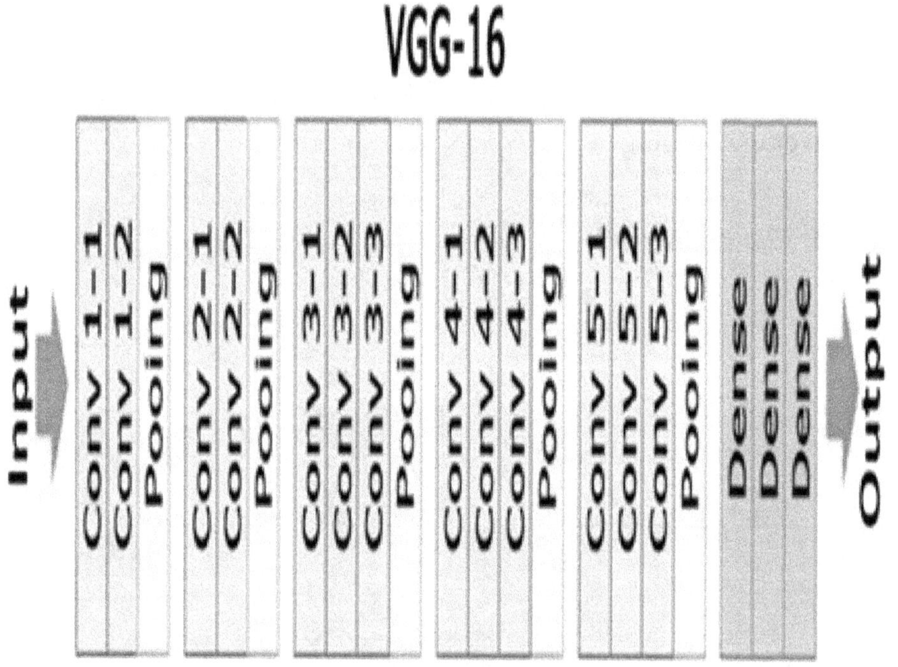

4.3 VGG 19

The VGG19 architecture is seen in Figure 7. The model's input layer receives a tongue image. VGG19 are components for feature extraction. The first block has a convolution layer as well as a ReLU layer. The second block is composed of two convolution layers, two ReLU layers, a batch normalizing layer, a maximum pooling layer, and a dropout layer.

Figure 7. VGG 19 Architecture

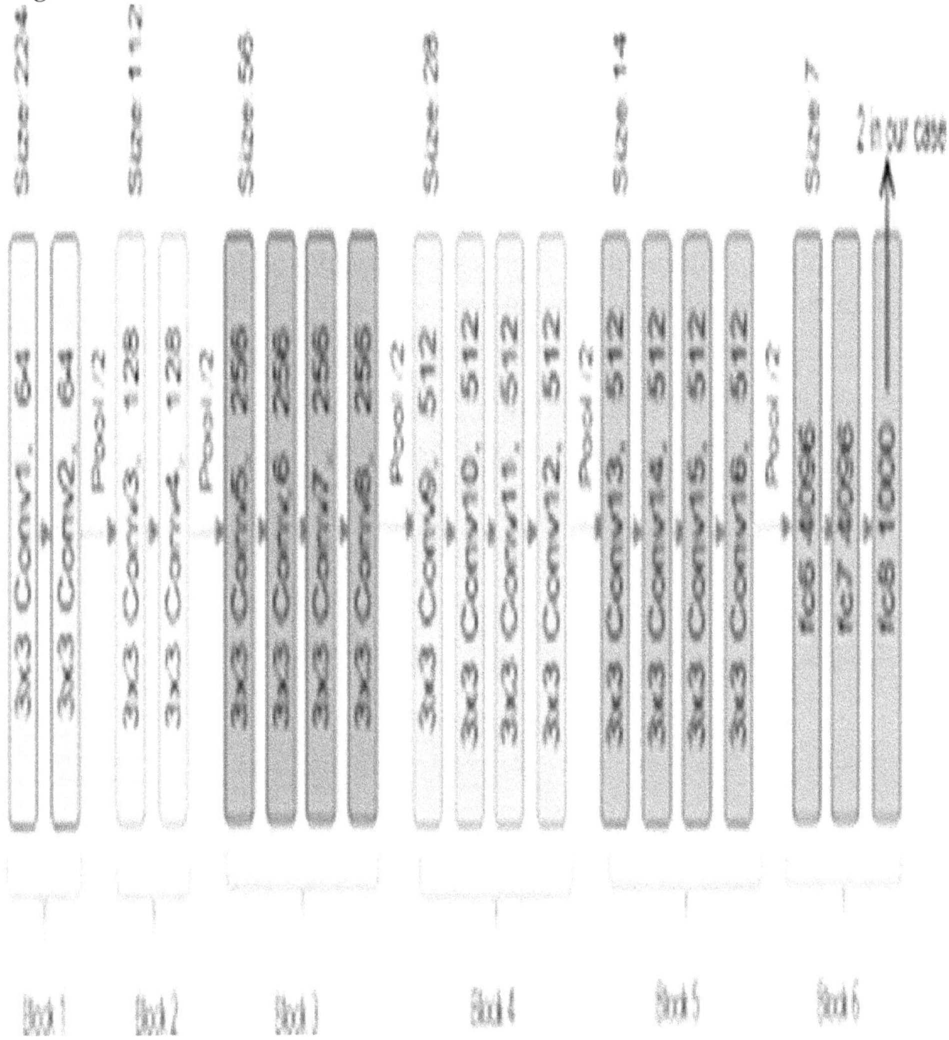

4.2 MOBILENET V2

Figure 8 shows the architecture of MobileNetV2. The classifier is built on the MobileNet V2 architecture, which employs slighter representations with low inexpression and parameterization power. This enhances mobile model accuracy across a variety of activities and benchmarks. It also simplifies things by not needing the deployment of a trained operator to categorize big quantities of images and perform other detecting operations for mobile applications. When paired with the Single Shot Detector Lite, MobileNetV2 recognizes objects 35% faster than the prior version. Because it encodes intermediate inputs and outputs, the Bottleneck is more accurate and uses 30% less parameters.

Figure 8. MobileNetV2 Architecture

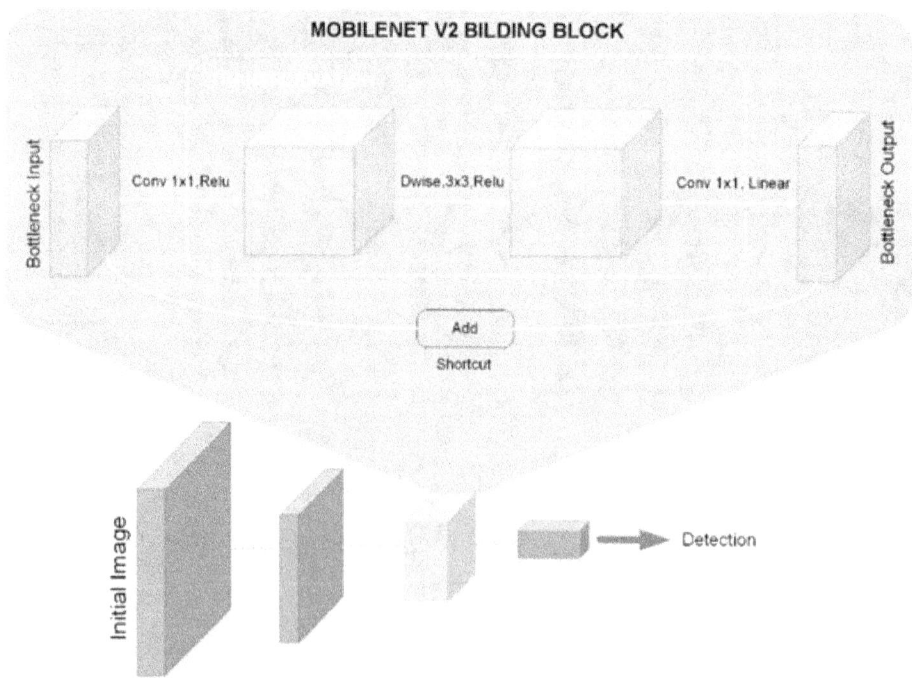

4.3 ResNet 50

Figure 9 depicts the ResNet 50 architecture. ResNet stands for residual network and refers to the residual blocks that comprise the network's architecture. ResNet-50 is built on a deep residual learning architecture, allowing it to train extraordinarily deep networks with hundreds of layers. A surprise observation in deep learning research inspired the ResNet architecture: adding extra layers to a neural network did not necessarily improve the results. This startled me since adding a layer to a network should allow it to learn both what the preceding network had learnt and new information.

The ResNet-50 architecture can be broken down into 6 parts

1. Input Pre-processing
2. Cfg[0] blocks
3. Cfg[1] blocks
4. Cfg[2] blocks
5. Cfg[3] blocks
6. Fully-connected layer

Figure 9. ResNet Architecture

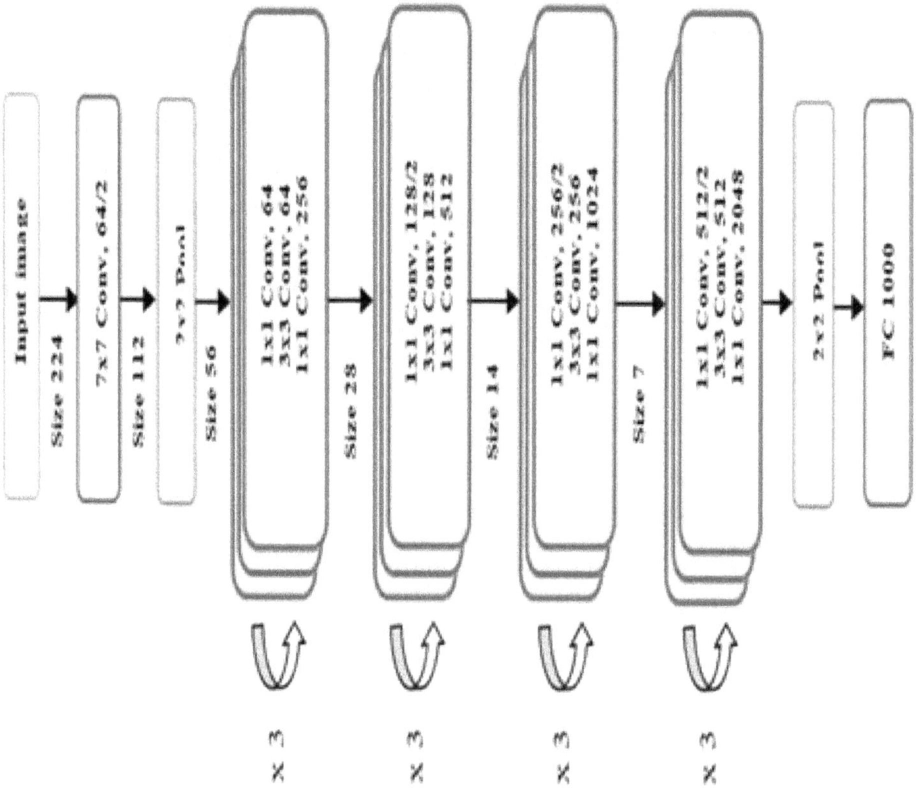

ResNet-50 is made up of 50 layers separated into 5 blocks, each with its own set of residual blocks. The residual blocks assist the network in developing stronger representations of the input data by maintaining information from previous layers. The network's last layer is a fully linked layer that sends the output of the last residual block to the output classes. The quantity of neurons in the totally related layer is identical to the quantity of output lessons. The architectural diagram for the complete workflow is given as

Figure 10. Proposed Model

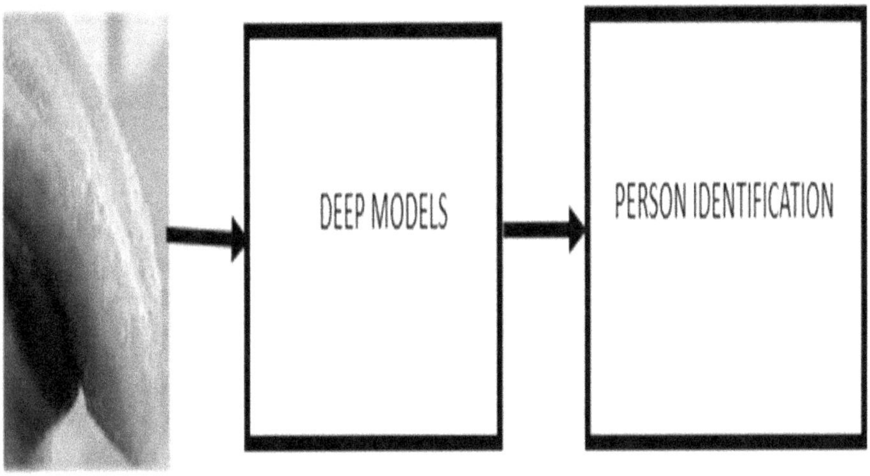

Figure 10 describes the proposed model. Here the deep models are the 5 techniques CNN, VGG16, VGG19, MobileNetV2 and RESNET50. Each model is trained and executed.

5. RESULTS AND DISCUSSIONS

The annotated image dataset consists of 2405 images. The images are divided into training and testing set with a ratio of 60:40, 70:30, 80:20 and 90:10. The results are recorded for each and every model and shown in the below table.

Table 1. Accuracy for various models

MODEL	60:40	70:30	80:20	90:10
CNN	83	84	86.2	89.1
VGG16	84.2	85.33	87.11	90.1
VGG19	85.43	85.93	88.56	92
MOBILENETV2	84.2	84.6	85.1	85.3
RESNET50	91.1	94.2	94.4	94.6

Table 1 gives the results of various training and testing result for all the deep models.

Figure 11. Accuracy Graph

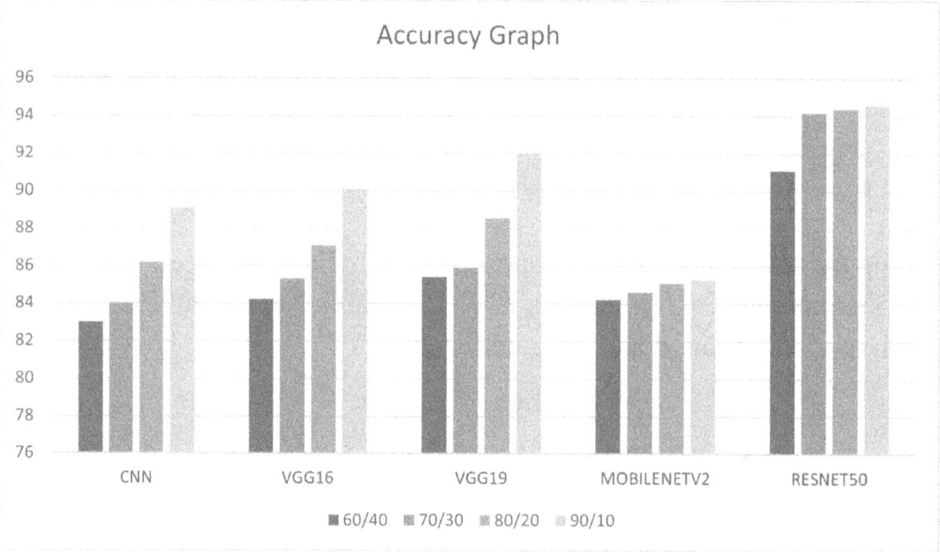

Figure 11 gives the accuracy graph based on the Table 1.

AI BASED BIOMETRIC SYSTEM IN HEALTHCARE

The various deep models are been trained and tested with 2405 tongue images and based on the results we concluded that the RESNET50 chooses best for the tongue image classification. The hospital employee database along with the 8 different annotated images of tongue are stored in the database. The total images are trained well with RESNET and if the employee scans his tongue his attendance is automatically recorded in the database. There is second another database called the patient database where the patient's history all along the 8 variant of tongue images are stored and used and if any patient need he can scan the tongue image in the GUI or mobile app of the hospital management to book an appointment or further medical processing assistance. The case study diagram is given below in the Figure 12.

Figure 12. Case Study Model

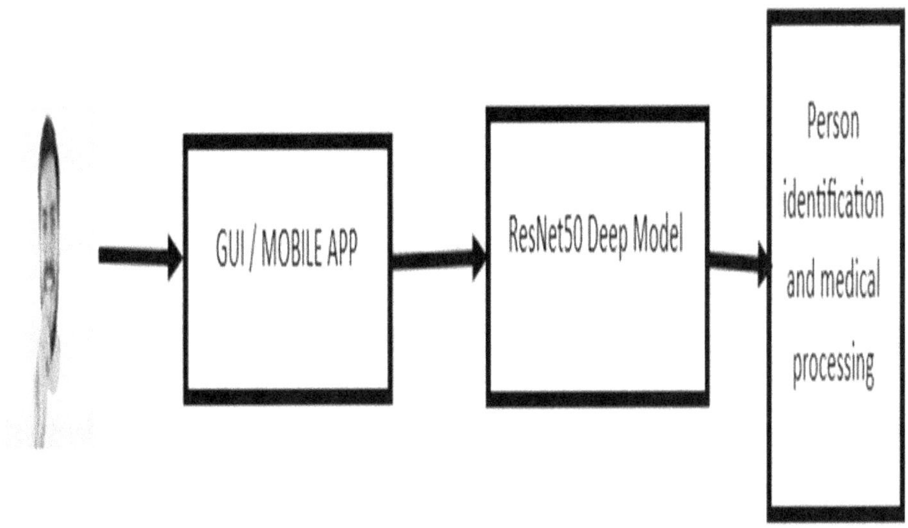

Users can access through mobile application or GUI and using ResNet50 deep models the person are identified and the prescribed medical processing are processed.

CONCLUSION

In todays digital world everyone and everything are to be modern and more equipped and hence if a biometric in tongue image is there to support hospital attendance and for hospital appointments and doctors medical consultation it would help lot of people to save time and energy. The model is trained with 5 different deep models and based on the results the best deep model ResNet50 with 50 Convolutions layers suits good for the proposed tongue image classification. The GUI and mobile application are built further for the hospital management for the biometric as well as doctors appointment.

REFERENCES

Caya, M. V. C., Lechoncito, A. R. D., & Deveraturda, G. Q. (2022, July). Recognition of tongue print biometric using oriented FAST and rotated BRIEF (ORB). In *2022 International Conference on Data Science and Its Applications (ICoDSA)* (pp. 59-64). IEEE. DOI: 10.1109/ICoDSA55874.2022.9862830

Jiang, T., Hu, X. J., Yao, X. H., Tu, L. P., Huang, J. B., Ma, X. X., Cui, J., Wu, Q., & Xu, J. T. (2021). Tongue image quality assessment based on a deep convolutional neural network. *BMC Medical Informatics and Decision Making*, *21*(1), 147. DOI: 10.1186/s12911-021-01508-8 PMID: 33952228

Kamath, P., Kamath, P., Saldanha, S. J., Shetty, T. B., Rodrigues, S. J., Pai, U. Y., & Mukherjee, S. (2024). A BRIEF EXPLORATION OF ARTIFICIAL INTELLIGENCE IN DENTAL HEALTHCARE: A Narrative review. *F1000 Research*, *13*, 37. DOI: 10.12688/f1000research.140481.2

Kannan, S., Vinod, K. D., Murali, G., & Baskar, D. (2022, June). Tongue print image recognition and authentication using convolutional neural networks. In *2022 7th International Conference on Communication and Electronics Systems (ICCES)* (pp. 1301-1305). IEEE. DOI: 10.1109/ICCES54183.2022.9835972

Khan, T., Manna, A., Sapri, A. M. S., Bashir, T., & Ahmad, N. (2023). Tongue prints-Unique as well as potential forensic tool for biometric authentication. *Archives of Dental Research*, *13*(1), 10–14. DOI: 10.18231/j.adr.2023.002

Li, H., Gui, X., Wang, P., Yue, Y., Li, H., Fan, X., Li, X., & Liu, R. (2024). Research on rapid quality identification method of Panax notoginseng powder based on artificial intelligence sensory technology and multi-source information fusion technology. *Food Chemistry*, *440*, 138210. DOI: 10.1016/j.foodchem.2023.138210 PMID: 38118320

Li, J., Huang, J., Jiang, T., Tu, L., Cui, L., Cui, J., Ma, X., Yao, X., Shi, Y., Wang, S., Wang, Y., Liu, J., Li, Y., Zhou, C., Hu, X., & Xu, J. (2022). A multi-step approach for tongue image classification in patients with diabetes. *Computers in Biology and Medicine*, *149*, 105935. DOI: 10.1016/j.compbiomed.2022.105935 PMID: 35986968

Li, W., Xu, J., Zhou, C., & Zhang, Z. (2005, September). A novel method of tongue image recognition. In *The Fifth International Conference on Computer and Information Technology (CIT'05)* (pp. 586-590). IEEE.

Sangala, B. N., Munisekhar, M. S., Ganji, K. K., Salloum, M. G., Kassab, M. F., & Alam, M. K. (2022). Role of Tongue Prints in Forensic Odontology and Biometrics: A Systematic Review. *International Medical Journal*, *29*(5), 262–265.

Song, C., Wang, B., & Xu, J. (2020, June). Classifying tongue images using deep transfer learning. In *2020 5th International conference on computational Intelligence and Applications (ICCIA)* (pp. 103-107). IEEE. DOI: 10.1109/ICCIA49625.2020.00027

Chapter 9
Unveiling the Future: An Introduction to AI-Powered Multimedia Data Processing

Preeti Rathi
https://orcid.org/0000-0002-5958-1685
KR Mangalam University, Gurgaon, India

ABSTRACT

We embark on a journey to decipher the synergies between AI technologies and the intricate world of multimedia, unravelling their combined potential to reshape the way we perceive, analyse, and interact with diverse forms of digital content. This paper commences with a comprehensive overview of fundamental AI concepts, establishing a solid foundation for readers unfamiliar with the field. Delving into practical applications, the narrative illustrates how AI enhances content understanding, manipulation, and generation across various multimedia domains. Throughout the exploration, emphasis is placed on real-world use cases, shedding light on how AI-driven advancements are influencing industries such as entertainment, healthcare, education, and beyond. Considerations for ethical implications and responsible AI practices are woven into the fabric of the discussion, underscoring the importance of mindful deployment in this rapidly evolving landscape. "Unveiling the Future" serves as a gateway for both novices and seasoned professionals to grasp the profound impact of AI on multimedia data processing. By fostering an understanding of these interconnected technologies, this paper aims to inspire curiosity, spark innovation, and

DOI: 10.4018/979-8-3693-2935-1.ch009

pave the way for a future where AI and multimedia seamlessly converge to redefine the boundaries of human-computer interaction.

1. INTRODUCTION

1.1. Background

Over several decades, multimedia processing has undergone significant changes in paradigm and technological advancements. Multimedia processing advances have brought about significant changes in how we create, share, and interact with digital content (Turaga et al., 2010). An outline of the significant turning points in the development of multimedia processing is provided below:

1960s - Early Beginnings

The term "multimedia" started gaining traction in the 1960s, referring to the integration of various forms of media, such as text, images, audio, and video.

Early experiments involved the combination of slide projectors, audio recordings, and filmstrips to create basic multimedia presentations.

1970s - Rise of Computer Graphics

The advent of computer graphics in the 1970s marked a significant milestone. Researchers began exploring ways to digitize and manipulate visual content on computers.

Xerox PARC (Palo Alto Research Centre) played a pivotal role in developing early graphical user interfaces and computer graphics technologies.

1980s - Desktop Publishing and Compact Discs

The 1980s witnessed the rise of desktop publishing, enabling users to combine text and graphics for print.

The introduction of compact discs (CDs) revolutionized audio storage and playback, paving the way for multimedia applications.

1990s - Multimedia on Personal Computers

The proliferation of personal computers in the 1990s brought multimedia capabilities to the masses. Software applications and operating systems incorporated multimedia features (Richardson & Domingos, 2006).

CD-ROMs became a popular medium for distributing multimedia content, including interactive games, educational software, and reference materials.

Late 1990s - Internet and Streaming Media

The late 1990s saw the integration of multimedia with the internet. The rise of broadband connectivity facilitated the streaming of audio and video content.

RealNetworks introduced RealPlayer, enabling users to stream audio and video over the internet.

Early 2000s - Convergence of Technologies

The 2000s witnessed the convergence of various multimedia technologies. Digital cameras, smartphones, and camcorders became ubiquitous, leading to an explosion of user-generated multimedia content (Tenenbaum et al., 2000).

MPEG-4 and other compression standards improved the efficiency of multimedia file storage and transmission.

2010s - Rise of social media and Mobile Multimedia

Social media platforms became dominant channels for sharing multimedia content. The integration of photos, videos, and live streaming became integral to platforms like Facebook, Instagram, and YouTube.

Advances in mobile technology and the widespread adoption of smartphones further democratized multimedia creation and consumption.

Present - AI-Powered Multimedia Processing

The application of artificial intelligence (AI) in multimedia processing is an essential characteristic of the modern era. AI algorithms are used for content recommendation, audio natural language processing, and image and video recognition.

Technologies including augmented reality (AR) and virtual reality (VR) are expanding the possibilities for immersive multimedia experiences..

1.2 Motivation

Intelligent multimedia processing has become increasingly crucial in addressing complex challenges across various industries. The integration of artificial intelligence (AI) with multimedia processing capabilities has opened up new possibilities for solving intricate problems (Krizhevsky et al., 2012). Below are key reasons highlighting the need for intelligent multimedia processing in tackling complex challenges:

Information Overload

The digital age has led to an unprecedented influx of multimedia data, including images, videos, and audio content. Intelligent processing is essential to sift through vast amounts of information and extract meaningful insights.

Complexity of Data

Multimedia data is inherently complex, often containing multiple modalities (text, image, audio, and video). Traditional processing methods struggle to handle the intricacies of such diverse data types, necessitating intelligent algorithms for effective analysis.

Real-Time Decision-Making

Many applications require real-time decision-making based on multimedia data. This is especially critical in areas such as healthcare (diagnosis from medical images), security (video surveillance), and autonomous vehicles (object recognition).

Personalized Experiences

In fields like entertainment and marketing, personalization is key. Intelligent multimedia processing enables the tailoring of content recommendations, advertisements, and user interfaces based on individual preferences and behaviour.

Cross-Modal Understanding

Intelligent processing allows for the integration and understanding of information across different modalities (Pearl, 2000). For instance, a system can analyze both textual and visual content to derive a more comprehensive understanding of a given scenario.

Enhanced Accessibility

Intelligent multimedia processing can contribute to making digital content more accessible. Through technologies like image and speech recognition, it enables individuals with disabilities to interact with and comprehend multimedia content more effectively.

Healthcare Diagnostics

In healthcare, intelligent processing of medical images, videos, and audio can aid in diagnostics. AI algorithms can assist in the early detection of diseases, interpretation of medical scans, and even suggest treatment plans.

Security and Surveillance

Surveillance systems leverage intelligent multimedia processing for threat detection. AI algorithms can analyze video feeds in real-time, identifying anomalies, and alerting security personnel to potential risks.

Education and Training

In education, intelligent multimedia processing can facilitate personalized learning experiences. AI-driven systems can adapt content delivery based on individual student progress, providing targeted support and challenges.

Natural Language Understanding

Processing multimedia data often involves understanding natural language in audio or textual forms. AI-powered natural language processing (NLP) contributes to better comprehension and extraction of information from spoken or written content.

Fraud Detection in Finance

In the financial sector, intelligent multimedia processing aids in fraud detection. By analyzing patterns in audio, video, and textual data, algorithms can identify potentially fraudulent transactions and activities.

Scientific Research

Researchers benefit from intelligent multimedia processing in fields such as astronomy and biology. Image analysis and pattern recognition help process large datasets, contributing to breakthroughs in scientific understanding.

The integration of artificial intelligence (AI) in multimedia has been driven by a myriad of real-world applications across diverse industries. These applications leverage AI to enhance the processing, analysis, and understanding of multimedia data. Here are several real-world scenarios that highlight the integration of AI in multimedia and its transformative impact:

Image and Video Analysis in Healthcare

Application: AI is used to analyze medical images (X-rays, MRIs, CT scans) for diagnostic purposes.

Impact: Faster and more accurate diagnoses, early detection of diseases, and personalized treatment plans.

Facial Recognition in Security and Surveillance

Application: AI-powered facial recognition systems are employed for security and surveillance in public spaces.

Impact: Enhanced security measures, identification of individuals in real-time, and crime prevention.

Speech Recognition in Virtual Assistants

Application: Virtual assistants like Siri and Alexa use AI-driven speech recognition for natural language understanding.

Impact: Improved user interactions, voice-activated commands, and hands-free device control.

Content Recommendation in Entertainment

Application: Streaming services use AI algorithms to analyze user preferences and recommend personalized content.

Impact: Enhanced user experience, increased engagement, and content discovery.

Autonomous Vehicles and Computer Vision

Application: AI-enabled computer vision is crucial for object detection and recognition in autonomous vehicles.

Impact: Improved safety, navigation, and decision-making in self-driving cars.

Generative Art and Content Creation

Application: AI algorithms are used to generate art, music, and other creative content.

Impact: A new paradigm in artistic expression, exploration of creative possibilities, and automation of content creation.

Language Translation and Multilingual Processing

Application: AI-based language translation services enable real-time translation of text, audio, and video content.

Impact: Facilitates cross-cultural communication, breaking down language barriers in various contexts.

Virtual and Augmented Reality (VR/AR)

Application: AI enhances immersive experiences in VR/AR applications by recognizing gestures, tracking movement, and overlaying contextual information.

Impact: Revolutionizes training simulations, gaming, education, and virtual collaboration.

Social Media Content Analysis

Application: AI algorithms analyze multimedia content on social media platforms for content moderation, sentiment analysis, and trend identification.

Impact: Ensures platform safety, provides actionable insights for marketers, and identifies emerging trends.

Medical Image Segmentation for Surgery Planning

Application: AI is utilized to segment and analyze medical images for precise surgery planning.

Impact: Improves surgical outcomes, reduces risks, and enhances the precision of medical procedures.

Emotion Recognition in Customer Service

Application: AI analyses facial expressions and voice tone for emotion recognition in customer interactions.

Impact: Personalized customer experiences, sentiment analysis, and improved service quality.

News and Media Content Analysis

Application: AI algorithms analyze multimedia content for news reporting, fact-checking, and identifying trends.

Impact: Enhances journalism, improves content accuracy, and aids in information dissemination.

These real-world applications demonstrate the tangible benefits of integrating AI into multimedia processing across various sectors. As technology continues to advance, the scope and impact of AI in multimedia are expected to grow, unlocking new possibilities and addressing evolving challenges in the real world.

1.3 Objectives

The fusion of artificial intelligence (AI) and multimedia data processing has catalysed a paradigm shift in how we perceive, analyse, and interact with digital content. This comprehensive overview explores the multifaceted landscape of AI-powered multimedia data processing, delving into its foundations, applications, ethical considerations, and future trends.

AI's integration into multimedia processing extends across diverse domains, from image and video analysis to speech recognition and content generation. Understanding the scope and significance of this integration is paramount for unlocking transformative applications and addressing complex challenges.

The potential impact and future trends in AI-powered multimedia data processing are vast and transformative. From revolutionizing industries to shaping the way we create and consume content, AI's role in multimedia processing is destined to redefine our digital landscape. As we navigate this dynamic field, it is essential to remain vigilant, addressing ethical concerns, and shaping policies that ensure the responsible and beneficial integration of AI into our multimedia-driven world. The demand for explainable AI will become more pronounced, especially in critical applications like healthcare and security (Manyika et al., 2011). The industry will focus on developing AI models that can provide transparent explanations for their decisions, fostering trust and accountability.

2. MACHINE LEARNING AND NEURAL NETWORKS

2.1 Machine Learning

Machine Learning (ML) is a subset of artificial intelligence that enables systems to learn and improve from experience without being explicitly programmed. It focuses on developing algorithms that can analyze and interpret data to make informed decisions.

The primary objectives of machine learning are to enable systems to:

- Learn patterns from data.
- Make predictions or decisions without explicit programming.
- Improve performance over time through experience.

Types of Machine Learning

1. **Supervised Learning:** In supervised learning, the algorithm is trained on a labelled dataset, where each input is associated with the corresponding output. The model learns to map inputs to outputs, making it capable of making predictions on new, unseen data.
2. **Unsupervised Learning:** Unsupervised learning involves training the algorithm on unlabelled data. The model explores the data's inherent structure, identifying patterns and relationships without predefined outputs. Clustering and dimensionality reduction are common tasks in unsupervised learning.
3. **Reinforcement Learning:** Reinforcement learning focuses on training agents to make sequential decisions (Witten et al., 2011). The agent receives feedback in the form of rewards or penalties based on its actions in an environment, allowing it to learn optimal strategies through trial and error.

Machine Learning Workflow

1. **Data Collection:** The first step in a machine learning project involves collecting relevant data. The quality and quantity of data significantly impact the model's performance.

2. **Data Preprocessing:** Data preprocessing involves cleaning, transforming, and organizing the collected data to make it suitable for training a machine learning model. This step includes handling missing values, normalizing data, and encoding categorical variables.
3. **Model Selection:** Choosing the appropriate machine learning model depends on the problem at hand. Common models include linear regression, decision trees, support vector machines, and neural networks.
4. **Model Training:** During the training phase, the selected model is fed with the labeled data. The model adjusts its parameters iteratively to minimize the difference between its predictions and the actual outcomes.
5. **Model Evaluation:** The trained model is evaluated using a separate dataset to assess its performance. Common metrics include accuracy, precision, recall, and F1 score, depending on the nature of the problem.
6. **Model Deployment:** Once satisfied with the model's performance, it can be deployed for making predictions on new, unseen data (LeCun et al., 2010). Deployment involves integrating the model into a system or application.

Key Features of Machine Learning Concepts

1. **Features and Labels:** Features are the input variables that the model uses for making predictions, while labels are the output or the target variable that the model aims to predict.
2. **Training and Testing Data:** Data is typically split into training and testing sets. The model is trained on the training set and evaluated on the testing set to assess its generalization to new data.
3. **Overfitting and Underfitting:** Overfitting occurs when a model learns the training data too well but performs poorly on new data. Underfitting happens when a model is too simple to capture the underlying patterns in the data.
4. **Hyperparameters:** Hyperparameters are settings that are not learned from the data but are set before the training process. Tuning hyperparameters is essential for optimizing a model's performance.

Applications of Machine Learning

1. **Image and Speech Recognition:** Machine learning powers advanced image and speech recognition systems, enabling applications like facial recognition, voice assistants, and automated image categorization.
2. **Natural Language Processing:** In natural language processing (NLP), machine learning algorithms analyze and understand human language. Applications include sentiment analysis, language translation, and chatbots.
3. **Predictive Analytics:** Machine learning is widely used in predictive analytics for tasks such as stock market forecasting, weather prediction, and customer behavior analysis.
4. **Autonomous Vehicles:** Autonomous vehicles rely on machine learning algorithms for tasks like object detection, path planning, and real-time decision-making to navigate the environment safely.

Challenges and Considerations

1. **Bias in Models:** Machine learning models can inherit biases present in the training data. Addressing bias is crucial to ensure fair and ethical decision-making.
2. **Data Privacy:** The use of personal data in machine learning raises concerns about privacy. Implementing robust data protection measures is essential to maintain user trust.
3. **Model Interpretability:** Interpreting complex machine learning models is challenging. Ensuring model transparency is vital, especially in applications where decisions impact individuals' lives.

2.2 Neural networks

Neural networks play a pivotal role in multimedia data processing, contributing to advancements in various tasks such as image recognition, video analysis, and audio processing (Mesink et al., 2012). These artificial intelligence models, inspired by the structure of the human brain, excel at learning complex patterns and representations from large datasets.

The key roles of neural networks play in multimedia data processing:

1. Image Recognition and Classification: Convolutional Neural Networks (CNNs)

Role: CNNs are specifically designed for image-related tasks. They automatically learn hierarchical features from images, allowing them to recognize patterns, objects, and textures.

Application: Image classification, object detection, facial recognition, and image segmentation benefit significantly from CNNs.

2. Video Analysis: Spatiotemporal Learning

Role: Neural networks, especially 3D CNNs and recurrent neural networks (RNNs), excel in capturing spatial and temporal information in videos.

Application: Action recognition, video summarization, and anomaly detection leverage these networks to understand both spatial features and temporal dynamics.

3. Audio and Speech Processing: Recurrent Neural Networks (RNNs) and Long Short-Term Memory (LSTM)

Role: RNNs and LSTMs are effective in processing sequential data, making them suitable for tasks involving audio signals and speech.

Application: Speech recognition, music generation, and audio classification benefit from the sequential learning capabilities of RNNs and LSTMs.

4. Generative Models for Content Creation: Generative Adversarial Networks (GANs)

Role: GANs consist of a generator and a discriminator, trained adversarial. They are proficient at generating realistic multimedia content.

Application: Image synthesis, style transfer, and content creation in areas like art and design leverage the generative capabilities of GANs.

5. Multimodal Fusion: Multimodal Neural Networks

Role: Integrating information from multiple modalities (text, image, audio) is a common challenge. Multimodal neural networks effectively fuse information for comprehensive understanding.

Application: Visual question answering, multimedia retrieval, and sentiment analysis across multiple modalities benefit from these networks.

6. Transfer Learning: Pre-trained Models

Role: Neural networks pre-trained on vast datasets (e.g., ImageNet) serve as feature extractors. These pre-trained features can be transferred to new tasks with limited data.

Application: Fine-tuning pre-trained models for specific tasks in multimedia data processing accelerates training and improves performance.

7. Real-Time Processing and Edge Computing: Lightweight Neural Networks

Role: For applications with constraints on computational resources, lightweight neural networks, such as MobileNet and EfficientNet, enable real-time processing on edge devices.

Application: Real-time image and video analysis on mobile devices, surveillance cameras, and IoT devices.

8. Adaptive Learning and Personalization: Neural Collaborative Filtering

Role: Neural networks can learn user preferences and provide personalized recommendations in multimedia content.

Application: Content recommendation systems in entertainment platforms and personalized user experiences in multimedia applications.

3. CHALLENGES AND CONSIDERATIONS

1. **Explainability and Interpretability:** Challenge: Complex neural networks can be challenging to interpret (Sanchez & Perronnin, 2011). Ensuring transparency and interpretability in multimedia applications is crucial, especially in sensitive domains like healthcare.
2. **Data Bias and Fairness:** Challenge: Neural networks trained on biased datasets may perpetuate biases in multimedia content processing. Ensuring fairness and addressing bias is essential for equitable outcomes.

4. IMAGE ANALYSIS AND RECOGNITION

4.1 Image Classification

AI algorithms for categorizing and labelling images. Applications in image-based search and organization.

4.2 Object Detection and Segmentation

Detecting and delineating objects within images. Use cases in autonomous vehicles, surveillance, and healthcare.

4.3 Image Generation

Generative models and their role in creating realistic images. AI-generated art and its implications.

5. VIDEO PROCESSING AND ANALYSIS

5.1 Action Recognition

Identifying and understanding actions within videos. Applications in security, sports analytics, and entertainment.

5.2 Video Summarization

AI techniques for condensing lengthy videos into concise summaries. Enhancing content accessibility and user experience.

5.3 Deepfake Detection

Addressing the challenges posed by AI-generated synthetic videos. Techniques for identifying manipulated content.

6. SPEECH AND AUDIO PROCESSING

6.1 Speech Recognition

Advancements in automatic speech recognition (ASR) systems. Integration in virtual assistants, transcription services, and more.

6.2 Music Generation

AI's role in composing and generating music. Collaborations between AI and human musicians.

6.3 Emotion Recognition

Analysing emotions through voice and audio signals. Applications in healthcare, customer service, and entertainment.

7. VIRTUAL AND AUGMENTED REALITY

7.1 VR and AR Technologies

Overview of virtual reality (VR) and augmented reality (AR). AI's contribution to enhancing immersive experiences.

7.2 Object Recognition in AR

AI algorithms enabling object recognition in augmented reality applications. Bridging the digital and physical worlds.

8. CHALLENGES AND ETHICAL CONSIDERATIONS

8.1 Bias in AI Algorithms

Addressing and mitigating biases in multimedia data processing. Ensuring fairness and equity in AI applications.

8.2 Privacy Concerns

Balancing the benefits of AI with privacy considerations. Regulations and ethical guidelines in multimedia AI.

9. FUTURE TRENDS

Exploring the trajectory of AI models in multimedia processing. Potential breakthroughs and innovations on the horizon. With privacy concerns on the rise, federated learning is likely to become more prevalent. This approach allows models to be trained across decentralized devices without sharing raw data. It is particularly relevant in applications where data privacy is a paramount concern. Generative models, such as Generative Adversarial Networks (GANs), are likely to become more sophisticated, leading to new applications in creative fields like art, music, and content creation. AI models may play a more active role in generating novel and diverse content.

10. CONCLUSION

Emphasizing the transformative potential of AI in multimedia processing. Commencing with a foundational overview of fundamental AI concepts, we aimed to establish a solid groundwork for readers unfamiliar with the complexities of the field. This comprehensive understanding sets the stage for a deeper dive into the practical applications of AI in multimedia processing. We've navigated through the ways in which AI enhances content understanding, manipulation, and generation across diverse multimedia domains, showcasing the tangible impact of these technologies.

"Unveiling the Future" is not merely a compilation of insights but serves as a gateway—an accessible portal for both novices and seasoned professionals alike. It opens doors for exploration and understanding, offering a profound glimpse into the symbiotic relationship between AI and multimedia data processing. By fostering this comprehension of interconnected technologies, our paper seeks to inspire curiosity and spark innovation.

REFERENCES

Krizhevsky, A., Sutskever, I., & Hinton, G. E. (2012). ImageNet classification with deep convolutional neural networks. In Advances in Neural Information Processing Systems (NeurIPS). DOI: 10.1145/3065386

LeCun, Y., Kavukcuoglu, K., & Farabet, C. (2010). Convolutional networks and applications in vision. In *2010 IEEE International Symposium on Circuits and Systems (ISCAS)* (pp. 253–256). IEEE. DOI: 10.1109/ISCAS.2010.5537907

Manyika, J., Chui, M., Brown, B., Bughin, J., Dobbs, R., Roxburgh, C., & Byers, A. (2011). *Big data: The next frontier for innovation, competition, and productivity* [Technical report]. McKinsey Global Institute.

Mensink, T., Verbeek, J., Perronnin, F., & Csurka, G. (2012, October). Metric learning for large scale image classification: Generalizing to new classes at near-zero cost. In *European Conference on Computer Vision (ECCV)*, Florence, Italy. DOI: 10.1007/978-3-642-33709-3_35

Pearl, J. (2000). *Causality: Models, reasoning, and inference*. Cambridge University Press.

Richardson, M., & Domingos, P. (2006). Markov logic networks. *Machine Learning*, *62*(1-2), 107–136. DOI: 10.1007/s10994-006-5833-1

Sanchez, J., & Perronnin, F. (2011). High-dimensional signature compression for large-scale image classification. In *2011 IEEE Conference on Computer Vision and Pattern Recognition (CVPR)* (pp. 1665–1672). IEEE. DOI: 10.1109/CVPR.2011.5995504

Tenenbaum, J. B., Silva, V., & Langford, J. C. (2000). A global geometric framework for nonlinear dimensionality reduction. *Science*, *290*(5500), 2319–2323. DOI: 10.1126/science.290.5500.2319 PMID: 11125149

Turaga, S. C., Murray, J. F., Jain, V., Roth, F., Helmstaedter, M., Briggman, K., Denk, W., & Seung, H. S. (2010). Convolutional networks can learn to generate affinity graphs for image segmentation. *Neural Computation*, *22*(2), 511–538. DOI: 10.1162/neco.2009.10-08-881 PMID: 19922289

Witten, I. H., Frank, E., & Hall, M. A. (2011). *Data mining: Practical machine learning tools and techniques* (3rd ed.). Morgan Kaufmann.

Compilation of References

Abdat, F., Maaoui, C., & Pruski, A. (2011, November). Human-computer interaction using emotion recognition from facial expression. In 2011 UKSim 5th European Symposium on Computer Modeling and Simulation (pp. 196-201). IEEE. DOI: 10.1109/EMS.2011.20

Acheampong, F., Nunoo-Mensah, H., & Chen, W. (2020). Comparative analyses of BERT, RoBERTa, DistilBERT, and XLNet for text-based emotion recognition.

Adeniyi, A. E., Olagunju, M., Awotunde, J. B., Abiodun, M. K., Awokola, J., & Lawrence, M. O. (2022). Augmented Intelligence Multilingual Conversational Service for Smart Enterprise Management Software. *Computational Science and Its Applications - Iccsa 2022 Workshops, Part V, 13381*, 476-488. https://doi.org/DOI: 10.1007/978-3-031-10548-7_35

Agarwal, N., Ünlü, T., Wani, M. A., & Bours, P. (2021, October). Predatory conversation detection using transfer learning approach. In *International Conference on Machine Learning, Optimization, and Data Science* (pp. 488-499). Cham: Springer International Publishing.

Agarwal, N., Wani, M. A., & Bours, P. (2020). Lex-pos feature-based grammar error detection system for the English language. *Electronics (Basel)*, *9*(10), 1686. DOI: 10.3390/electronics9101686

Agarwal, S., Saxena, V., Singal, V., & Aggarwal, S. (2018, November). LSTM-based music generation with dataset preprocessing and reconstruction techniques. In *2018 IEEE Symposium Series on Computational Intelligence (SSCI)* (pp. 455–462). IEEE. DOI: 10.1109/SSCI.2018.8628712

Ahmad, F., Najam, A., & Ahmed, Z. (2013). Image-based face detection and recognition:" state of the art". arXiv preprint arXiv:1302.6379.

Ahmad, P. N., Liu, Y., Ali, G., Wani, M. A., & ElAffendi, M. (2023). Robust benchmark for propagandist text detection and mining high-quality data. *Mathematics, 11*(12), 2668. DOI: 10.3390/math11122668

Alrihaili, A., Alsaedi, A., Albalawi, K., & Syed, L. (2019, October). Music recommender system for users based on emotion detection through facial features. In 2019 12th International Conference on Developments in eSystems Engineering (DeSE) (pp. 1014-1019). IEEE. DOI: 10.1109/DeSE.2019.00188

Altieri, A., Ceccacci, S., Ciabattoni, L., Generosi, A., Talipu, A., Turri, G., & Mengoni, M. (2019, January). An Adaptive System to Manage Playlists and Lighting Scenarios Based on the User's Emotions. In *2019 IEEE International Conference on Consumer Electronics (ICCE)* (pp. 1-2). IEEE. DOI: 10.1109/ICCE.2019.8662061

Aly, E. S., & van der Haar, D. T. (2020). Slang-Based Text Sentiment Analysis in Instagram. *Fourth International Congress on Information and Communication Technology,* Vol 2, *1027*, 321-329. https://doi.org/DOI: 10.1007/978-981-32-9343-4_25

American Diabetes Association. (2014). Standards of medical care in diabetes—2014. *Diabetes Care, 37*(Supplement_1), S14–S80. DOI: 10.2337/dc14-S014 PMID: 24357209

American Diabetes Association. (2015). Standards of medical care in diabetes—2015 abridged for primary care providers. *Clinical Diabetes : a Publication of the American Diabetes Association, 33*(2), 97–111. DOI: 10.2337/diaclin.33.2.97 PMID: 25897193

Amiot, E. (2016). *Music through Fourier space*. Springer International Publishing. DOI: 10.1007/978-3-319-45581-5

Annadurai, S., Arock, M., & Vadivel, A. (2023). Real and fake emotion detection using enhanced boosted support vector machine algorithm. *Multimedia Tools and Applications*, *82*(1), 1333–1353. DOI: 10.1007/s11042-022-13210-6

Arias-Vergara, T., Klumpp, P., Vasquez-Correa, J. C., Nöth, E., Orozco-Arroyave, J. R., & Schuster, M. (2021). Multi-channel spectrograms for speech processing applications using deep learning methods. *Pattern Analysis & Applications*, *24*(2), 423–431. DOI: 10.1007/s10044-020-00921-5

Arora, S., May, A., Zhang, J., & Ré, C., & Assoc Computat, L. (2020). Contextual Embeddings: When Are They Worth It? *58th Annual Meeting of the Association for Computational Linguistics (Acl 2020)*, 2650-2663. DOI: 10.18653/v1/2020.acl-main.236

Arora, A., Kaul, A., & Mittal, V. (2019, March). Mood based music player. In *2019 International Conference on Signal Processing and Communication (ICSC)* (pp. 333-337). IEEE. DOI: 10.1109/ICSC45622.2019.8938384

Assiri, A., Emam, A., & Al-dossari, H. (2016). Real-Time Sentiment Analysis of Saudi Dialect Tweets Using SPARK. *2016 ieee international conference on big data (big data)*, 3947-3950.

Azzi, S., Gagnon, S., Ramirez, A., & Richards, G. (2020). Healthcare applications of artificial intelligence and analytics: A review and proposed framework. *Applied Sciences (Basel, Switzerland)*, *10*(18), 6553. DOI: 10.3390/app10186553

Babu, T., Gupta, D., Singh, T., Hameed, S., Zakariah, M., & Alotaibi, Y. (2021). Robust magnification independent colon biopsy grading system over multiple data sources. *Computers, Materials & Continua*, *69*(1), 99–128. DOI: 10.32604/cmc.2021.016341

Babu, T., Singh, T., & Gupta, D. (2020). Colon cancer prediction using 2dreca segmentation and hybrid features on histopathology images. *IET Image Processing*, *14*(16), 4144–4157. DOI: 10.1049/iet-ipr.2019.1717

Bah, S. M., & Ming, F. (2020). An improved face recognition algorithm and its application in attendance management system. *Array (New York, N.Y.)*, *5*, 100014. DOI: 10.1016/j.array.2019.100014

Balarajan, Y., Selvaraj, S., & Subramanian, S. V. (2021). Health care and equity in India. *Lancet*, *377*(9764), 505–515. DOI: 10.1016/S0140-6736(10)61894-6 PMID: 21227492

Batalden, M., Batalden, P., Margolis, P., Seid, M., Armstrong, G., Opipari-Arrigan, L., & Hartung, H. (2023). Coproduction of healthcare service. *BMJ Quality & Safety*. PMID: 26376674

Batra, A., Gowda, S. N., Sevilla-Lara, L., & Keller, F. (2022). A closer look at temporal ordering in the segmentation of instructional videos. arXiv. https://doi.org//arXiv.2209.15501DOI: 10.48550

Bergwerk, M., Gonen, T., Lustig, Y., Amit, S., Lipsitch, M., Cohen, C., Mandelboim, M., Levin, E. G., Rubin, C., Indenbaum, V., Tal, I., Zavitan, M., Zuckerman, N., Bar-Chaim, A., Kreiss, Y., & Regev-Yochay, G. (2021). Covid-19 breakthrough infections in vaccinated health care workers. *The New England Journal of Medicine*, *385*(16), 1474–1484. DOI: 10.1056/NEJMoa2109072 PMID: 34320281

Bhargavi, K., Mashankar, P., Sreevarsh, P. V., Bilolikar, R., & Ranganathan, P. (2022). Machine Learning-Based Sentiment Analysis Towards Indian Ministry. *Computational Vision and Bio-Inspired Computing (Iccvbic 2021)*, *1420*, 381-391. https://doi.org/DOI: 10.1007/978-981-16-9573-5_28

Born, J., Beymer, D., Rajan, D., Coy, A., Mukherjee, V. V., Manica, M., Prasanna, P., Ballah, D., Guindy, M., Shaham, D., Shah, P. L., Karteris, E., Robertus, J. L., Gabrani, M., & Rosen-Zvi, M. (2021). On the role of artificial intelligence in medical imaging of covid-19. *Patterns (New York, N.Y.)*, *2*(6), 100269. DOI: 10.1016/j.patter.2021.100269 PMID: 33969323

Bowman, S. (2023). Impact of electronic health record systems on information integrity: Quality and safety implications. *Perspectives in Health Information Management*, *10*(Fall). PMID: 24159271

Brinkmann, P., & Sekretariat, M. A. (2005). MidiKinesis—MIDI controllers for (almost) any purpose. In LAC2005 Proceedings (pp. 9–12).

Briot, J. P., & Pachet, F. (2020). Deep learning for music generation: Challenges and directions. *Neural Computing & Applications, 32*(4), 981–993. DOI: 10.1007/s00521-018-3813-6

Carnovalini, F., & Rodà, A. (2020). Computational creativity and music generation systems: An introduction to the state of the art. *Frontiers in Artificial Intelligence, 3*, 14. DOI: 10.3389/frai.2020.00014 PMID: 33733133

Caya, M. V. C., Lechoncito, A. R. D., & Deveraturda, G. Q. (2022, July). Recognition of tongue print biometric using oriented FAST and rotated BRIEF (ORB). In *2022 International Conference on Data Science and Its Applications (ICoDSA)* (pp. 59-64). IEEE. DOI: 10.1109/ICoDSA55874.2022.9862830

Cesar, L. B., Manso-Callejo, M.-Á., & Cira, C.-I. (2023). BERT (Bidirectional Encoder Representations from Transformers) for missing data imputation in solar irradiance time series. *Engineering Proceedings, 39*(26). DOI: 10.3390/engproc2023039026

Chartier, Y. (Ed.). (2024). *Safe management of wastes from health-care activities*. World Health Organization.

Cheng, J., Liu, S., Tsai, Y.-H., Hung, W.-C., De Mello, S., Gu, J., Kautz, J., Wang, S., & Yang, M.-H. (2017). Learning to segment instances in videos with spatial propagation network. arXiv: Computer Vision and Pattern Recognition. https://arxiv.org/abs/ (DOI/URL incomplete—please verify)

Chiramel, S., Logofătu, D., & Goldenthal, G. (2020). Detection of social media platform insults using Natural language processing and comparative study of machine learning algorithms. In 2020 24th International Conference on System Theory, Control and Computing (ICSTCC), Sinaia, Romania (pp. 98-101). DOI: 10.1109/ICSTCC50638.2020.9259730

Cho, K., van Merrienboer, B., Gulcehre, C., Bougares, F., Schwenk, H., & Bengio, Y. (2014). Learning phrase representations using RNN encoder-decoder for statistical machine translation. *CoRR*, abs/1406.1078.

Cho, K. O., & Jang, H. J. (2020). Comparison of different input modalities and network structures for deep learning-based seizure detection. *Scientific Reports, 10*(1), 1–11. DOI: 10.1038/s41598-019-56958-y PMID: 31924842

Clark, E., & Araki, K. (2011). Text normalization in social media: Progress, problems and applications for a pre-processing system of casual English. In **Proceedings of the Pacific Association for Computational Linguistics (PACLING 2011)**. DOI: 10.1016/j.sbspro.2011.10.577

Cuthbert, M. S., & Ariza, C. (2010). music21: A toolkit for computer-aided musicology and symbolic music data.

Cuthbert, M. S., Ariza, C., & Friedland, L. (2011, October). Feature extraction and machine learning on symbolic music using the music21 toolkit. In ISMIR (pp. 387–392).

Cuthbert, M. S., Ariza, C., Cabal-Ugaz, J., Hadley, B., & Parikh, N. (2011). Hidden beyond MIDI's reach: Feature extraction and machine learning with rich symbolic formats in music21. In *Proceedings of the NIPS 2011 Workshop on Music and Machine Learning*.

Dagar, D., Hudait, A., Tripathy, H. K., & Das, M. N. (2016, May). Automatic emotion detection model from facial expression. In *2016 International Conference on Advanced Communication Control and Computing Technologies (ICACCCT)* (pp. 77-85). IEEE. DOI: 10.1109/ICACCCT.2016.7831605

de Freitas, P. V. A., dos Santos, G. N. P., Busson, A. J. G., Guedes, A. L. V., & Colcher, S., & Assoc Comp, M. (2019). A Baseline for NSFW Video Detection in E-Learning Environments. *Webmedia 2019:Proceedings of the 25th Brazillian Symposium on Multimedia and the Web*, 357-360. https://doi.org/DOI: 10.1145/3323503.3360625

de Mendonca, R. R., de Brito, D. F., Rosa, F. D., dos Reis, J. C., & Bonacin, R. (2020). A Framework for Detecting Intentions of Criminal Acts in Social Media: A Case Study on Twitter. *Information (Basel), 11*(3), 154. Advance online publication. DOI: 10.3390/info11030154

Dhasarathan, C., Hasan, M. K., Islam, S., Abdullah, S., Mokhtar, U. A., Javed, A. R., & Goundar, S. (2023). Covid-19 health data analysis and personal data preserving: A homomorphic privacy enforcement approach. *Computer Communications, 199*, 87–97. DOI: 10.1016/j.comcom.2022.12.004 PMID: 36531214

Divyapushpalakshmi, M., & Ramalakshmi, R. (2021). An efficient sentimental analysis using hybrid deep learning and optimization technique for Twitter using parts of speech (POS) tagging. *International Journal of Speech Technology, 24*(2), 329–339. DOI: 10.1007/s10772-021-09801-7

Dmitrichenkova, S. V., Dolzhich, E. A., & Pozuelo, Y. S. (2020, Apr 24-25). YOUTH SLANG IN SOCIAL NETS (A CASE STUDY OF SPANISH LANGUAGE).*European Proceedings of Social and Behavioural Sciences*. 9th International Research and Practical Conference on Topical Issues of Linguistics and Teaching Methods in Business and Professional Communication (TILTM), Peoples Friendship Univ Russia, RUSSIA.

Elbedwehy, S., Medhat, T., Hamza, T., & Alrahmawy, M. F. (2022). Efficient Image Captioning Based on Vision Transformer Models. *Cmc-Computers Materials & Continua, 73*(1), 1483–1500. DOI: 10.32604/cmc.2022.029313

Fang, H., Eggleston, K., Hanson, K., & Wu, M. (2019). Enhancing financial protection under China's social health insurance to achieve universal health coverage. *bmj, 365.*

Farrokhmanesh, M., & Hamzeh, A. (2016, April). A novel method for malware detection using audio signal processing techniques. In 2016 Artificial Intelligence and Robotics (IRANOPEN) (pp. 85–91). IEEE.

Fernández, A. P., & Sindre, G. (2020). Software Assisted Privacy Impact Assessment in Interactive Ubiquitous Computing Systems. *Digital Transformation for a Sustainable Society in the 21st Century, 573*, 60-71. https://doi.org/DOI: 10.1007/978-3-030-39634-3_6

Flores-Martin, D., Rojo, J., Moguel, E., Berrocal, J., & Murillo, J. M. (2021). Smart Nursing Homes: Self-Management Architecture Based on IoT and Machine Learning for Rural Areas. *Wireless Communications and Mobile Computing*, *2021*(1), 8874988.

Foulkes, S. B., & Booth, D. M. (1997). Improved object segmentation using Markov random fields, artificial neural networks, and parallel processing techniques. DOI: 10.1117/12.280826

Fuse Brown, E. C., & Hall, M. A. (2024). Private Equity and the Corporatization of Health Care. *Stanford Law Review*, •••, 76.

Gandhi, T. K., Kaplan, G. S., Leape, L., Berwick, D. M., Edgman-Levitan, S., Edmondson, A., Meyer, G. S., Michaels, D., Morath, J. M., Vincent, C., & Wachter, R. (2018). Transforming concepts in patient safety: A progress report. *BMJ Quality & Safety*, *27*(12), 1019–1026. DOI: 10.1136/bmjqs-2017-007756 PMID: 30018115

Gan, W. H., Lim, J. W., & Koh, D. (2020). Preventing intra-hospital infection and transmission of coronavirus disease 2019 in health-care workers. *Safety and Health at Work*, *11*(2), 241–243. DOI: 10.1016/j.shaw.2020.03.001 PMID: 32292622

Gelbukh, A. (2005). Natural language processing. In *Proceedings of the Fifth International Conference on Hybrid Intelligent Systems (HIS'05)* (pp. 1). Rio de Janeiro, Brazil: IEEE. DOI: 10.1109/ICHIS.2005.79

Ghosal, S., & Jain, A. (2023). Weighted aspect based sentiment analysis using extended OWA operators and Word2Vec for tourism. *Multimedia Tools and Applications*, *82*(12), 18353–18380. DOI: 10.1007/s11042-022-13800-4

Ghounane, N. (2020). A Thorough Examination of Teens Drug Slang in Algeria. *Arab World English Journal*, *11*(1), 419–431. DOI: 10.24093/awej/vol11no1.28

Gilda, S., Zafar, H., Soni, C., & Waghurdekar, K. (2017, March). Smart music player integrating facial emotion recognition and music mood recommendation. In 2017 international conference on wireless communications, signal processing and networking (wispnet) (pp. 154-158). IEEE.

Godman, B., Haque, M., Islam, S., Iqbal, S., Urmi, U. L., Kamal, Z. M., Shuvo, S. A., Rahman, A., Kamal, M., Haque, M., Jahan, I., Islam, M. Z., Hossain, M. M., Munzur-E-Murshid, , Kumar, S., Charan, J., Bhatt, R., Dutta, S., Abhayanand, J. P., & Sefah, I. (2020). Rapid assessment of price instability and paucity of medicines and protection for COVID-19 across Asia: Findings and public health implications for the future. *Frontiers in Public Health*, *8*, 585832. DOI: 10.3389/fpubh.2020.585832 PMID: 33381485

Guo, J. W., Kimmel, J., & Linder, L. A. (2022). Text Analysis of Suicide Risk in Adolescents and Young Adults. *Journal of the American Psychiatric Nurses Association. Article, 10783903221077292.* Advance online publication. DOI: 10.1177/10783903221077292 PMID: 35130778

Gupta, A., Taneja, S., Malik, G., Vij, S., Tayal, D., & Jain, A. (2019). fSLANGZY: A fuzzy logic-based algorithm for English slang meaning selection [Article]. *Progress in Artificial Intelligence*, *8*(1), 111–121. DOI: 10.1007/s13748-018-0159-3

Gupta, V., & Hewett, R. (2020). Real-Time Tweet Analytics Using Hybrid Hashtags on Twitter Big Data Streams. *Information (Basel)*, *11*(7), 341. Advance online publication. DOI: 10.3390/info11070341

Hadjeres, G., & Nielsen, F. (2020). Anticipation-RNN: Enforcing unary constraints in sequence generation, with application to interactive music generation. *Neural Computing & Applications*, *32*(4), 995–1005. DOI: 10.1007/s00521-018-3868-4

Hagen, S., & de Zeeuw, D. (2023). Based and confused: Tracing the political connotations of a memetic phrase across the web. *Big Data & Society*, *10*(1), 20539517231163175. Advance online publication. DOI: 10.1177/20539517231163175

Haldar, R., & Mukhopadhyay, D. (2011). Levenshtein distance technique in dictionary lookup methods: An improved approach. *Computing Research Repository (CoRR)*.

Hammad, M., Wani, M. A., Shakil, K. A., Shaiba, H., & Abd El-Latif, A. A. (2024). Deep cancelable multibiometric finger vein and fingerprint authentication with non-negative matrix factorization. *IEEE Access : Practical Innovations, Open Solutions*, *12*, 120638–120660. DOI: 10.1109/ACCESS.2024.3450372

Han, B. (2014). *Improving the utility of social media with natural language processing*. The University of Melbourne.

Han, K. X., Chien, W., Chiu, C. C., & Cheng, Y. T. (2020). Application of Support Vector Machine (SVM) in the Sentiment Analysis of Twitter DataSet. *Applied Sciences (Basel, Switzerland)*, *10*(3), 1125. Advance online publication. DOI: 10.3390/app10031125

Hassan, I., Chisty, A., & Bui, T. (2024). Structural and Social Determinants of Health. In *Leading an Academic Medical Practice* (pp. 343–355). Springer International Publishing.

Ho, I. H. J., Goh, H. N., & Tan, Y. F. (2022). Inducing a Malay Lexicon from an Unlabelled Dataset Using Word Embeddings. *Lecture Notes in Computer Science*, *13343*, 382–394. DOI: 10.1007/978-3-031-08530-7_32

Hossain, M. S., Cucchiara, R., Muhammad, G., Tob́on, D. P., and Saddik, A. E. (2022). Special section on ai-empowered multimedia data analytics for smart healthcare.

Humphrey, E. J., Bello, J. P., & LeCun, Y. (2012, October). Moving beyond feature design: Deep architectures and automatic feature learning in music informatics. In ISMIR (pp. 403–408).

Hunter, J. D. (2007). Matplotlib: A 2D graphics environment. *IEEE Annals of the History of Computing*, *9*(03), 90–95.

Hutto, C. J., & Gilbert, E. (2014). VADER: A parsimonious rule-based model for sentiment analysis of social media text. **Eighth International AAAI Conference on Weblogs and Social Media**. DOI: 10.1609/icwsm.v8i1.14550

Ibrahim, M. S., & Saber, S. (2023). Machine learning and predictive analytics: Advancing disease prevention in healthcare. *Journal of Contemporary Healthcare Analytics*, *7*(1), 53–71.

Imran, A. S., Hodnefjeld, H., Kastrati, Z., Fatima, N., Daudpota, S. M., & Wani, M. A. (2023). Classifying european court of human rights cases using transformer-based techniques. *IEEE Access : Practical Innovations, Open Solutions*, *11*, 55664–55676. DOI: 10.1109/ACCESS.2023.3279034

Jiang, K., & Lu, X. (2020). Natural Language Processing and Its Applications in Machine Translation: A Diachronic Review. In 2020 IEEE 3rd International Conference of Safe Production and Informatization (IICSPI), Chongqing City, China (pp. 210-214). IEEE. DOI: 10.1109/IICSPI51290.2020.9332458

Jiang, T., Hu, X. J., Yao, X. H., Tu, L. P., Huang, J. B., Ma, X. X., Cui, J., Wu, Q., & Xu, J. T. (2021). Tongue image quality assessment based on a deep convolutional neural network. *BMC Medical Informatics and Decision Making*, *21*(1), 147. DOI: 10.1186/s12911-021-01508-8 PMID: 33952228

Jurafsky, D., & Martin, J. H. (2008). *Speech and language processing: An introduction to natural language processing, computational linguistics, and speech recognition* (2nd ed.). Prentice Hall.

Kalchbrenner, N., Espeholt, L., Simonyan, K., van den Oord, A., Graves, A., & Kavukcuoglu, K. (2017). Neural machine translation in linear time. *arXiv preprint arXiv:1610.10099v2*.

Kamath, P., Kamath, P., Saldanha, S. J., Shetty, T. B., Rodrigues, S. J., Pai, U. Y., & Mukherjee, S. (2024). A BRIEF EXPLORATION OF ARTIFICIAL INTELLIGENCE IN DENTAL HEALTHCARE: A Narrative review. *F1000 Research*, *13*, 37. DOI: 10.12688/f1000research.140481.2

Kamruzzaman, M. (2020). *Architecture of smart health care system using artificial intelligence. In 2020 IEEE international conference on multimedia & expo workshops (ICMEW).* IEEE.

Kanan, T.. (2019). A Review of Natural Language Processing and Machine Learning Tools Used to Analyze Arabic Social Media. In *2019 IEEE Jordan International Joint Conference on Electrical Engineering and Information Technology (JEEIT)* (pp. 622-628). Amman, Jordan: IEEE. DOI: 10.1109/JEEIT.2019.8717369

Kannan, S., Vinod, K. D., Murali, G., & Baskar, D. (2022, June). Tongue print image recognition and authentication using convolutional neural networks. In *2022 7th International Conference on Communication and Electronics Systems (ICCES)* (pp. 1301-1305). IEEE. DOI: 10.1109/ICCES54183.2022.9835972

Karatsareas, P. (2021). From village talk to slang: The re-enregisterment of a non-standardised variety in an urban diaspora. *Journal of Multilingual and Multicultural Development, 42*(9), 827–839. DOI: 10.1080/01434632.2020.1767115

Karkaeva, M. A. (2018). A socio-cultural phenomenon of youth slang in the cyberspace. *Filologicheskie Nauki-Nauchnye Doklady Vysshei Shkoly-Philological Sciences-Scientific Essays of Higher Education*, (3), 45–49. DOI: 10.20339/PhS.3-18.045

Keidar, D., Opedal, A., Jin, Z., Sachan, M., & Assoc Computat, L. (2022). Slangvolution: A Causal Analysis of Semantic Change and Frequency Dynamics in Slang. *Proceedings of the 60th Annual Meeting of the Association for Computational Linguistics (Acl 2022), Vol 1: (Long Papers)*, 1422-1442.

Khan, M., Shiwlani, A., Qayyum, M. U., Sherani, A. M. K., & Hussain, H. K. (2024). AI-powered healthcare revolution: An extensive examination of innovative methods in cancer treatment. *BULLET: Jurnal Multidisiplin Ilmu, 3*(1), 87–98.

Khan, T., Manna, A., Sapri, A. M. S., Bashir, T., & Ahmad, N. (2023). Tongue prints-Unique as well as potential forensic tool for biometric authentication. *Archives of Dental Research, 13*(1), 10–14. DOI: 10.18231/j.adr.2023.002

Khyani, D., Siddhartha, B. S., Niveditha, N. M., & Divya, B. M. (2021). An interpretation of lemmatization and stemming in natural language processing. *. *Shanghai Ligong Daxue Xuebao.*

Kishore, S., Nair, R. R., Mehra, V., & Babu, T. (2023). A generalized framework for brain tumor and pneumonia detection using streamlite application. In 2023 4th International Conference for Emerging Technology (INCET) (pp. 1-6). IEEE.

Knagg, R., Dorey, J., Evans, R., & Hitchman, J. (2024). Sustainability in healthcare: Patient and public perspectives. *Anaesthesia, 79*(3), 278–283. DOI: 10.1111/anae.16159 PMID: 38205532

Kolajo, T., Daramola, O., Adebiyi, A., & Seth, A. (2020). A framework for pre-processing of social media feeds based on integrated local knowledge base. *Information Processing & Management, 57*(6), 102348. Advance online publication. DOI: 10.1016/j.ipm.2020.102348

Kongyoung, S., Trakultaweekoon, K., & Rugchatjaroen, A. (2021). Thai Language Tweet Emotion Prediction based on Use of Emojis. *16th International Joint Symposium on Artificial Intelligence and Natural Language Processing (Isai-Nlp 2021).* https://doi.org/DOI: 10.1109/iSAI-NLP54397.2021.9678160

Krishnan, G., Singh, S., Pathania, M., Gosavi, S., Abhishek, S., Parchani, A., & Dhar, M. (2023). Artificial intelligence in clinical medicine: Catalyzing a sustainable global healthcare paradigm. *Frontiers in Artificial Intelligence, 6*, 6. DOI: 10.3389/frai.2023.1227091 PMID: 37705603

Krizhevsky, A., Sutskever, I., & Hinton, G. E. (2012). ImageNet classification with deep convolutional neural networks. In Advances in Neural Information Processing Systems (NeurIPS). DOI: 10.1145/3065386

Kurera, W. S. A., Rajapaksha, R. K., Rupasinghe, H. A. P., Liyanage, K., Kasthuriarachchi, S., & Rajapakshe, S. & Ieee. (2022, Nov 30-Dec 01). Building NLP Tools to Process Sinhala Text Data Written using English Letters.*International Conference on Advances in ICT for Emerging Regions*, Univ Colombo Sch Comp, Colombo, SRI LANKA.

Kwan, A. C., Salto, G., Cheng, S., & Ouyang, D. (2021). Artificial intelligence in computer vision: Cardiac MRI and multimodality imaging segmentation. *Current Cardiovascular Risk Reports*, *15*(9), 18. Advance online publication. DOI: 10.1007/s12170-021-00678-4 PMID: 35693045

Lal, M., Kumar, K., Arain, R. H., Maitlo, A., Ruk, S. A., & Shaikh, H. (2018). Study of face recognition techniques: A survey. *International Journal of Advanced Computer Science and Applications*, *9*(6). Advance online publication. DOI: 10.14569/IJACSA.2018.090606

LeCun, Y., Kavukcuoglu, K., & Farabet, C. (2010). Convolutional networks and applications in vision. In *2010 IEEE International Symposium on Circuits and Systems (ISCAS)* (pp. 253–256). IEEE. DOI: 10.1109/ISCAS.2010.5537907

Le, Q., & Mikolov, T. (2014). Distributed representations of sentences and documents. In **Proceedings of the 31st International Conference on Machine Learning (ICML 2014)**.

Li, D., Rzepka, R., Ptaszynski, M., & Araki, K. (2019). *A Novel Machine Learning-based Sentiment Analysis Method for Chinese Social Media Considering Chinese Slang Lexicon and Emoticons.*

Li, J., Sun, A., Han, J., & Li, C. (2022). A survey on deep learning for named entity recognition. *IEEE Transactions on Knowledge and Data Engineering, 34*(1), 50-70. DOI: 10.1109/TKDE.2020.2981314

Li, H., Gui, X., Wang, P., Yue, Y., Li, H., Fan, X., Li, X., & Liu, R. (2024). Research on rapid quality identification method of Panax notoginseng powder based on artificial intelligence sensory technology and multi-source information fusion technology. *Food Chemistry*, *440*, 138210. DOI: 10.1016/j.foodchem.2023.138210 PMID: 38118320

Li, J., Huang, J., Jiang, T., Tu, L., Cui, L., Cui, J., Ma, X., Yao, X., Shi, Y., Wang, S., Wang, Y., Liu, J., Li, Y., Zhou, C., Hu, X., & Xu, J. (2022). A multi-step approach for tongue image classification in patients with diabetes. *Computers in Biology and Medicine*, *149*, 105935. DOI: 10.1016/j.compbiomed.2022.105935 PMID: 35986968

Li, K., Jin, Y., Akram, M. W., Han, R., & Chen, J. (2020). Facial expression recognition with convolutional neural networks via a new face cropping and rotation strategy. *The Visual Computer*, *36*(2), 391–404. DOI: 10.1007/s00371-019-01627-4

Lin, M. F., & Wu, D. D. (2022). Rapport building by Chinese celebrities on Weibo and Facebook. *Chinese Language and Discourse*, *13*(1), 7–27. DOI: 10.1075/cld.21031.lin

Liu, J. X., Cheng, J. R., Wang, Z. Y., Lou, C. Q., Shen, C. L., & Sheng, V. S. (2022). A Survey of Deep Learning for Named Entity Recognition in Chinese Social Media. *Artificial Intelligence and Security. Lecture Notes in Computer Science*, *13338*(Pt I), 573–582. DOI: 10.1007/978-3-031-06794-5_46

Liu, Q., & Xia, Z. (2019, 21-22 Sept. 2019). Multi-layer LSTM Network Statement Generation Based on Mixed Input. *2019 Seventh International Conference on Advanced Cloud and Big Data (CBD)* DOI: 10.1109/CBD.2019.00048

Liu, S., Gui, D.-Y., Zuo, Y., & Dai, Y. (2019). Good Slang or Bad Slang? Embedding Internet Slang in Persuasive Advertising. *Frontiers in Psychology*, *10*, 1251. DOI: 10.3389/fpsyg.2019.01251 PMID: 31231278

Liu, W., Wu, Y., & Gong, W. (2022). Measuring Internet Slang Style in the Marketing Context: Scale Development and Validation. *Frontiers in Psychology*, *12*, 751806. Advance online publication. DOI: 10.3389/fpsyg.2021.751806 PMID: 35115982

Li, W., Xu, J., Zhou, C., & Zhang, Z. (2005, September). A novel method of tongue image recognition. In *The Fifth International Conference on Computer and Information Technology (CIT'05)* (pp. 586-590). IEEE.

Li, Y., Wang, H., Jin, X. R., Li, X., Pender, M., Song, C. P., Tang, S.-L., Cao, J., Wu, H., & Wang, Y. G. (2018). Experiences and challenges in the health protection of medical teams in the Chinese Ebola treatment center, Liberia: A qualitative study. *Infectious Diseases of Poverty*, *7*(1), 1–12. DOI: 10.1186/s40249-018-0468-6 PMID: 30134982

Lu, W. T., & Su, L. (2018, November). Deep learning models for melody perception: An investigation on symbolic music data. In 2018 Asia-Pacific Signal and Information Processing Association Annual Summit and Conference (APSIPA ASC) (pp. 1620–1625). IEEE.

Maag, K., Rottmann, M., Varghese, S., Hüger, F., Schlicht, P., & Gottschalk, H. (2021). Improving video instance segmentation by light-weight temporal uncertainty estimates. DOI: 10.1109/IJCNN52387.2021.9534407

Maas, A. L., Daly, R. E., Pham, P. T., Huang, D., Ng, A. Y., & Potts, C. (2011). Learning word vectors for sentiment analysis. In **Proceedings of the 49th Annual Meeting of the Association for Computational Linguistics: Human Language Technologies**.

MacMillan, K., Droettboom, M., & Fujinaga, I. (2002). Gamera: Optical music recognition in a new shell. In ICMC.

Manjushree, R., Bhoomika, D., Nair, R. R., & Babu, T. (2022). Automated detection of diabetic retinopathy using deep learning in retinal fundus images: Analysis. In 2022 3rd International Conference on Communication, Computing and Industry 4.0 (C2I4), pages 1–6. IEEE.

Manyika, J., Chui, M., Brown, B., Bughin, J., Dobbs, R., Roxburgh, C., & Byers, A. (2011). *Big data: The next frontier for innovation, competition, and productivity* [Technical report]. McKinsey Global Institute.

Marrero, M., Sánchez-Cuadrado, S., Morato, J., & Andreadakis, I. (2013). *Named entity recognition: Fallacies, challenges and opportunities. *University Carlos III of Madrid.* Department of Computer Science.

McFee, B., Raffel, C., Liang, D., Ellis, D. P., McVicar, M., Battenberg, E., & Nieto, O. (2015, July). Librosa: Audio and music signal analysis in Python. In *Proceedings of the 14th Python in Science Conference* (Vol. 8, pp. 18–25). DOI: 10.25080/Majora-7b98e3ed-003

McKinney, S. M., Sieniek, M., Godbole, V., Godwin, J., Antropova, N., Ashrafian, H., Back, T., Chesus, M., Corrado, G. S., Darzi, A., Etemadi, M., Garcia-Vicente, F., Gilbert, F. J., Halling-Brown, M., Hassabis, D., Jansen, S., Karthikesalingam, A., Kelly, C. J., King, D., & Shetty, S. (2020). International evaluation of an ai system for breast cancer screening. *Nature*, *577*(7788), 89–94. DOI: 10.1038/s41586-019-1799-6 PMID: 31894144

Mensink, T., Verbeek, J., Perronnin, F., & Csurka, G. (2012, October). Metric learning for large scale image classification: Generalizing to new classes at near-zero cost. In *European Conference on Computer Vision (ECCV)*, Florence, Italy. DOI: 10.1007/978-3-642-33709-3_35

Mikolov, T., Sutskever, I., Chen, K., Corrado, G. S., & Dean, J. (2013). Distributed representations of words and phrases and their compositionality. In *Advances in Neural Information Processing Systems (NeurIPS)*.

Mikolov, T., Yih, W., & Zweig, G. (2013). Linguistic regularities in continuous space word representations. In **Proceedings of the 2013 Conference of the North American Chapter of the Association for Computational Linguistics: Human Language Technologies** (pp. 746-751).

Music, T. (2022). Protecting patients, protecting healthcare workers: A review of the role of influenza vaccination. *International Nursing Review*, *59*(2), 161–167. DOI: 10.1111/j.1466-7657.2011.00961.x PMID: 22591085

Nair, R. R., Babu, T., & Kishore, S. (2023a). Recent and emerging technologies in industrial iot. Opportunities and Challenges of Industrial IoT in 5G and 6G Networks, pages 50–72. DOI: 10.4018/978-1-7998-9266-3.ch003

Nair, R. R., Babu, T., & Singh, T. (2023b). Multiresolution approach on medical image fusion by modified local energy. *Signal, Image and Video Processing*, *17*(8), 1–8. DOI: 10.1007/s11760-023-02636-6

Nair, R. R., & Singh, T. (2022). Optimal wavelet-based multi-modal medical image fusion with quantitative analysis for colour images using different colour models. *International Journal of Biomedical Engineering and Technology*, *40*(3), 262–288. DOI: 10.1504/IJBET.2022.126496

Nair, R. R., Singh, T., Basavapattana, A., & Pawar, M. M. (2022). Multi-layer, multi-modal medical image intelligent fusion. *Multimedia Tools and Applications*, *81*(29), 42821–42847. DOI: 10.1007/s11042-022-13482-y

Nair, R. R., Singh, T., Sankar, R., & Gunndu, K. (2021). Multi-modal medical image fusion using lmf-gan-a maximum parameter infusion technique. *Journal of Intelligent & Fuzzy Systems*, *41*(5), 5375–5386. DOI: 10.3233/JIFS-189860

Nasr, M., Islam, M. M., Shehata, S., Karray, F., & Quintana, Y. (2021). Smart healthcare in the age of ai: Recent advances, challenges, and future prospects. *IEEE Access : Practical Innovations, Open Solutions*, *9*, 145248–145270. DOI: 10.1109/ACCESS.2021.3118960

Neskovic, P., & Cooper, L. N. (2001). Object segmentation using an array of interconnected neural networks with local receptive fields. DOI: 10.1109/IJCNN.2001.938468

Nguyen, B. T., Trinh, M. H., Phan, T. V., & Nguyen, H. D. (2017, April). An efficient real-time emotion detection using camera and facial landmarks. In 2017 seventh international conference on information science and technology (ICIST) (pp. 251-255). IEEE. DOI: 10.1109/ICIST.2017.7926765

Ogugua, J. O., Anyanwu, E. C., Olorunsogo, T., Maduka, C. P., & Ayo-Farai, O. (2024). Ethics and strategy in vaccination: A review of public health policies and practices. *International Journal of Science and Research Archive*, *11*(1), 883–895. DOI: 10.30574/ijsra.2024.11.1.0141

Patel, P., Babu, T., & Nair, R. (2023). *Breast cancer detection framework using evolutionary search and svm classifier*. DOI: 10.1109/ICoAC59537.2023.10249874

Pearl, J. (2000). *Causality: Models, reasoning, and inference*. Cambridge University Press.

Pennington, J., Socher, R., & Manning, C. (2014). GloVe: Global vectors for word representation. In **Proceedings of the 2014 Conference on Empirical Methods in Natural Language Processing (EMNLP)** (pp. 1532-1543). DOI: 10.3115/v1/D14-1162

Petrova, B. (2023). *Predictive Analytics in healthcare. Ponnusamy, V., Vasuki, A., Clement, J. C., and Eswaran, P. (2022). Ai-driven information and communication technologies, services, and applications for next-generation healthcare system*. Smart Systems for Industrial Applications.

Phon-Amnuaisuk, S. (2019, July). Exploring Music21 and Gensim for music data analysis and visualization. In *International Conference on Data Mining and Big Data* (pp. 3–12). Springer, Singapore. DOI: 10.1007/978-981-32-9563-6_1

Pool, J., Akhlaghpour, S., Fatehi, F., & Burton-Jones, A. (2024). A systematic analysis of failures in protecting personal health data: A scoping review. *International Journal of Information Management*, *74*, 102719. DOI: 10.1016/j.ijinfomgt.2023.102719

Rakesh, S., Jeyageetha, K., Nishant, S., Nageswari, D., Prakash, R. B. R., & Mary, S. S. C. (2023, June). Machine learning and internet of things-based driver safety and support system. In 2023 8th International Conference on Communication and Electronics Systems (ICCES) (pp. 955-960). IEEE.

Ramadevi, Y., Sridevi, T., Poornima, B., & Kalyani, B. (2010). Segmentation and object recognition using edge detection techniques. International Journal of Computer Science and Information Technology, 2(6), [page range not provided]. DOI: 10.5121/ijcsit.2010.2614

Ramanathan, R., Kumaran, R., Rohan, R. R., Gupta, R., & Prabhu, V. (2017, December). An intelligent music player based on emotion recognition. In 2017 2nd International Conference on Computational Systems and Information Technology for Sustainable Solution (CSITSS) (pp. 1-5). IEEE. DOI: 10.1109/CSITSS.2017.8447743

Rawat, A., Wani, M. A., ElAffendi, M., Imran, A. S., Kastrati, Z., & Daudpota, S. M. (2022). Drug adverse event detection using text-based convolutional neural networks (TextCNN) technique. *Electronics (Basel), 11*(20), 3336. DOI: 10.3390/electronics11203336

Reddy, V. (2019). Natural Language Processing in healthcare.

Richardson, M., & Domingos, P. (2006). Markov logic networks. *Machine Learning, 62*(1-2), 107–136. DOI: 10.1007/s10994-006-5833-1

Ridzuan, F., & Wan Zainon, W. M. N. (2019). A review on data cleansing methods for big data. *Procedia Computer Science, 161*, 731-738. DOI: 10.1016/j.procs.2019.11.177

Ringeval, F., Schuller, B., Valstar, M., Cummins, N., Cowie, R., Tavabi, L., Schmitt, M., Alisamir, S., Amiriparian, S., Messner, E. M., & Song, S. (2019, October). AVEC 2019 workshop and challenge: State-of-mind, detecting depression with AI, and cross-cultural affect recognition. In Proceedings of the 9th International on Audio/Visual Emotion Challenge and Workshop (pp. 3–12).

Rodriguez, C. R., Angeles, D., Chafloque, R., Kaseng, F., & Pandey, B. (2020, September). Deep learning audio spectrograms processing to the early COVID-19 detection. In 2020 12th International Conference on Computational Intelligence and Communication Networks (CICN) (pp. 429–434). IEEE.

Rohmetra, H., Raghunath, N., Narang, P., Chamola, V., Guizani, M., & Lakkaniga, N. R. (2023). AI-enabled remote monitoring of vital signs for COVID-19: Methods, prospects and challenges. *Computing*, •••, 1–27.

Runciman, B., Merry, A., & Walton, M. (2017). *Safety and ethics in healthcare: a guide to getting it right*. CRC Press.

Saba, T., Rehman, A., Al-Dhelaan, A., & Al-Rodhaan, M. (2014). Evaluation of current documents image denoising techniques: A comparative study. *Applied Artificial Intelligence, 28*(9), 879–887. DOI: 10.1080/08839514.2014.954344

Sanchez, J., & Perronnin, F. (2011). High-dimensional signature compression for large-scale image classification. In *2011 IEEE Conference on Computer Vision and Pattern Recognition (CVPR)* (pp. 1665–1672). IEEE. DOI: 10.1109/CVPR.2011.5995504

Sangala, B. N., Munisekhar, M. S., Ganji, K. K., Salloum, M. G., Kassab, M. F., & Alam, M. K. (2022). Role of Tongue Prints in Forensic Odontology and Biometrics: A Systematic Review. *International Medical Journal, 29*(5), 262–265.

Sedik, A., El-Latif, A. A. A., Wani, M. A., El-Samie, F. E. A., Bauomy, N. A. S., & Hashad, F. G. (2023). Efficient multi-biometric secure-storage scheme based on deep learning and crypto-mapping techniques. *Mathematics, 11*(3), 703. DOI: 10.3390/math11030703

Seibold, C., Künzel, J., Hilsmann, A., & Eisert, P. (2022). From explanations to segmentation: Using explainable AI for image segmentation. DOI: 10.5220/0010893600003124

Shaik, T., Tao, X., Higgins, N., Li, L., Gururajan, R., Zhou, X., & Acharya, U. R. (2023). Remote patient monitoring using artificial intelligence: Current state, applications, and challenges. *Wiley Interdisciplinary Reviews. Data Mining and Knowledge Discovery, 13*(2), e1485. DOI: 10.1002/widm.1485

Shakil, K. A., Tabassum, K., Alqahtani, F. S., & Wani, M. A. (2021). Analyzing user digital emotions from a holy versus non-pilgrimage city in Saudi Arabia on Twitter Platform. *Applied Sciences (Basel, Switzerland), 11*(15), 6846. DOI: 10.3390/app11156846

Sharma, H. K., & Kshitiz, K., & Shailendra. (2018). NLP and machine learning techniques for detecting insulting comments on social networking platforms. In *2018 International Conference on Advances in Computing and Communication Engineering (ICACCE)* (pp. 265-272). Paris, France: IEEE. DOI: 10.1109/ICACCE.2018.8441728

Sharma, M., Savage, C., Nair, M., Larsson, I., Svedberg, P., & Nygren, J. M. (2022). Artificial intelligence applications in health care practice: Scoping review. *Journal of Medical Internet Research, 24*(10), e40238. DOI: 10.2196/40238 PMID: 36197712

Shastry, K. A., & Shastry, A. (2023). An integrated deep learning and natural language processing approach for continuous remote monitoring in digital health. *Decision Analytics Journal, 8*, 100301. DOI: 10.1016/j.dajour.2023.100301

Shayaa, S., Jaafar, N. I., Bahri, S., Sulaiman, A., Seuk Wai, P., Wai Chung, Y., Piprani, A. Z., & Al-Garadi, M. A. (2018). Sentiment Analysis of Big Data: Methods, Applications, and Open Challenges. *IEEE Access : Practical Innovations, Open Solutions, 6*, 37807–37827. DOI: 10.1109/ACCESS.2018.2851311

Sikka, R., Morath, J. M., & Leape, L. (2020). The quadruple aim: Care, health, cost and meaning in work. *BMJ Quality & Safety, 24*(10), 608–610. DOI: 10.1136/bmjqs-2015-004160 PMID: 26038586

Singh, B., & Kaunert, C. (2025). Cloud Computing and IoMT in Disease Screening and Diagnosis: AI Approaches in Transmuting Healthier Homes. In B. S & S. Kadry (Eds.), *Revolutionizing Healthcare Systems Through Cloud Computing and IoT* (pp. 99-120). IGI Global. DOI: 10.4018/979-8-3693-7225-8.ch005

Singh, B., & Kaunert, C. (2025). Leveraging IoT for Patient Monitoring and Smart Healthcare: Connected Healthcare System. In B. S & S. Kadry (Eds.), *Revolutionizing Healthcare Systems Through Cloud Computing and IoT* (pp. 27-46). IGI Global. https://doi.org/DOI: 10.4018/979-8-3693-7225-8.ch002

Singh, B., & Kaunert, C. (2024). Adventure in High Altitude of Mountainous Topographies and Health Impacts: Lensing Tourism Sustainability via Reducing Ecological and Sociocultural Footprint and Health Emergency and Medical Assistance Management. In Meraj, G., Hashimoto, S., & Kumar, P. (Eds.), *Navigating Natural Hazards in Mountainous Topographies. Disaster Risk Reduction*. Springer., DOI: 10.1007/978-3-031-65862-4_15

Singh, B., & Kaunert, C. (2025). Featuring Healthcare, Environment, and Human Rights: Applications of Artificial Intelligence in the Health Domain. In Chakraborty, S., & Satapathy, S. (Eds.), *Gender, Environment, and Human Rights: An Intersectional Exploration* (pp. 45–74). IGI Global., DOI: 10.4018/979-8-3693-6069-9.ch004

Singh, B., Kaunert, C., & Singh, G. (2025). Scaling Legal Framework for Plastic Pollution and Advancing Cutting Edge Water Governance: Reducing and Eliminating Marine Pollution in Alignment With SDG 14 (Life Below Water). In Gaur, N., Sharma, E., Nguyen, T., Bilal, M., & Melkania, N. (Eds.), *Societal and Environmental Ramifications of Plastic Pollution* (pp. 197–222). IGI Global., DOI: 10.4018/979-8-3693-9163-1.ch010

Smith, J. D., & Johnson, K. L. (2023). Enhancing Data Quality in Big Data: A Comprehensive Review. *Journal of Big Data Management, 7*(2), 145-156. https://doi.org/DOI: 10.1016/j.jbdm.2023.07.009

Someswararao, C., Rajanikanth, J., Vasamsetty, C., & Bhadri Raju, M. S. V. S. (2012). Data cleaning: A framework for robust data quality in enterprise data warehouse. *International Journal of Computer Science and Technology*. Retrieved from www.ijcst.com

Song, C., Wang, B., & Xu, J. (2020, June). Classifying tongue images using deep transfer learning. In *2020 5th International conference on computational Intelligence and Applications (ICCIA)* (pp. 103-107). IEEE. DOI: 10.1109/ICCIA49625.2020.00027

Sood, A., & Sharma, S. (2016). Image segmentation and object recognition using machine learning. In Proceedings of Advances in Intelligent Systems and Computing (pp. [page range not provided]). DOI: 10.1007/978-981-10-3433-6_25

Suh, I., McKinney, T., & Siu, K.-C. (2023). Current perspective of metaverse application in medical education, research and patient care. In *Virtual Worlds* (Vol. 2, pp. 115–128). MDPI.

Surabhi, M. C. (2013). Natural language processing future. In *Proceedings of the 2013 International Conference on Optical Imaging Sensor and Security (ICOSS)* (pp. 1-3). Coimbatore, India: IEEE. DOI: 10.1109/ICOISS.2013.6678407

Tang, X. (2019). The role of artificial intelligence in medical imaging research. *BJR Open*, *2*(1), 20190031. DOI: 10.1259/bjro.20190031 PMID: 33178962

Tenenbaum, J. B., Silva, V., & Langford, J. C. (2000). A global geometric framework for nonlinear dimensionality reduction. *Science*, *290*(5500), 2319–2323. DOI: 10.1126/science.290.5500.2319 PMID: 11125149

Tomas, M. E., Kundrapu, S., Thota, P., Sunkesula, V. C., Cadnum, J. L., Mana, T. S. C., Jencson, A., O'Donnell, M., Zabarsky, T. F., Hecker, M. T., Ray, A. J., Wilson, B. M., & Donskey, C. J. (2023). Contamination of health care personnel during removal of personal protective equipment. *JAMA Internal Medicine*, *175*(12), 1904–1910. DOI: 10.1001/jamainternmed.2015.4535 PMID: 26457544

Turaga, S. C., Murray, J. F., Jain, V., Roth, F., Helmstaedter, M., Briggman, K., Denk, W., & Seung, H. S. (2010). Convolutional networks can learn to generate affinity graphs for image segmentation. *Neural Computation*, *22*(2), 511–538. DOI: 10.1162/neco.2009.10-08-881 PMID: 19922289

Wangikar, V. C., & Deshmukh, R. R. (2011). Data cleaning: Current approaches and issues. *Department of Computer Science & IT, Dr. Babasaheb Ambedkar Marathwada University, Aurangabad (MS), India*.

Wani, M. A., Bours, P., Agarwal, N., & Jabin, S. (2019). Emotion-based mining for gender prediction in online social networks. In *Proceedings of the ACM, International Conference on Machine Learning and Data Science*.

Wani, M. A., ELAffendi, M., Bours, P., Imran, A. S., Hussain, A., & Abd El-Latif, A. A. (2024). Codes: A deep learning framework for identifying covid-caused depression symptoms. *Cognitive Computation*, *16*(1), 305–325. DOI: 10.1007/s12559-023-10190-z

Watts, N., Adger, W. N., Agnolucci, P., Blackstock, J., Byass, P., Cai, W., Chaytor, S., Colbourn, T., Collins, M., Cooper, A., Cox, P. M., Depledge, J., Drummond, P., Ekins, P., Galaz, V., Grace, D., Graham, H., Grubb, M., Haines, A., & Costello, A. (2023). Health and climate change: Policy responses to protect public health. *Lancet*, *386*(10006), 1861–1914. DOI: 10.1016/S0140-6736(15)60854-6 PMID: 26111439

Witten, I. H., Frank, E., & Hall, M. A. (2011). *Data mining: Practical machine learning tools and techniques* (3rd ed.). Morgan Kaufmann.

Yang, L. C., Chou, S. Y., & Yang, Y. H. (2017). MidiNet: A convolutional generative adversarial network for symbolic-domain music generation. arXiv preprint arXiv:1703.10847.

Yang, B., Cao, J. M., Jiang, D. P., & Lv, J. D. (2017). Facial expression recognition based on dual-feature fusion and improved random forest classifier. *Multimedia Tools and Applications*, *9*, 20477–20499.

Yin, J., Ngiam, K. Y., & Teo, H. H. (2021). Role of artificial intelligence applications in real-life clinical practice: Systematic review. *Journal of Medical Internet Research*, *23*(4), e25759. DOI: 10.2196/25759 PMID: 33885365

Yust, J. (2017). Review of Emmanuel Amiot, Music through Fourier Space: Discrete Fourier Transform in Music Theory (Springer, 2016). Music Theory Online, 23(3).

Yu, Y., Srivastava, A., & Canales, S. (2021). Conditional LSTM-GAN for melody generation from lyrics. [TOMM]. *ACM Transactions on Multimedia Computing Communications and Applications*, *17*(1), 1–20. DOI: 10.1145/3424116

Zhang, J., Gao, Y., Feng, S., Yuan, Y., & Lee, C.-H. (2016). Automatic image region annotation through segmentation based visual semantic analysis and discriminative classification. DOI: 10.1109/ICASSP.2016.7472018

Zhang, X. (2022). Application of artificial intelligence recognition technology in digital image processing. *Wireless Communications and Mobile Computing, 2022*, 1–10. Advance online publication. DOI: 10.1155/2022/7442639

Zhu, X., Xia, W., Bao, Z., Zhong, Y., Fang, Y., Yang, F., Gu, X., Ye, J., & Huang, W. (2021). Artificial intelligence segmented dynamic video images for continuity analysis in the detection of severe cardiovascular disease. *Frontiers in Neuroscience, 14*, 618481. Advance online publication. DOI: 10.3389/fnins.2020.618481 PMID: 33642970

Žukov-Gregorič, A., Bachrach, Y., & Coope, S. (2018). Named entity recognition with parallel recurrent neural networks. In *Proceedings of the 56th Annual Meeting of the Association for Computational Linguistics (Volume 2: Short Papers)* (pp. 69–74). Melbourne, Australia: Association for Computational Linguistics. DOI: 10.18653/v1/P18-2012

About the Contributors

Ahmed A. Abd El-Latif received the B.Sc. degree with honor rank in Mathematics and Computer Science in 2005 and M.Sc. degree in Computer Science in 2010, all from Menoufia University, Egypt. He received his Ph. D. degree in Computer Science & Technology at Harbin Institute of Technology (H.I.T), Harbin, P. R. China in 2013. He is an associate professor of Computer Science at Menoufia University, Egypt. He is author and co-author of more than 130 papers in reputal journal and conferences. He received many awards, State Encouragement Award in Engineering Sciences 2016, Arab Republic of Egypt; the best Ph.D student award from Harbin Institute of Technology, China 2013; Young scientific award, Menoufia University, Egypt 2014. He is a fellow at Academy of Scientific Research and Technology, Egypt. His areas of interests are multimedia content encryption, secure wireless communication, IoT, applied cryptanalysis, perceptual cryptography, secret media sharing, information hiding, biometrics, forensic analysis in digital images, and quantum information processing. Dr. Abd El-Latif is an associate editor of Journal of Cyber Security and Mobility, and Mathematical Problems in Engineering.

Mudasir Ahmad Wani is currently working as a Researcher in Natural Language Processing (NLP) at Prince Sultan University, KSA. He has served as a Lecturer and Researcher at the Department of Information Security and Communication Technology (IIK) at the Norwegian University of Science and Technology (NTNU), Norway. He pursued his postdoctoral research at the Norwegian Biometrics Laboratory, NTNU,

Norway and He is the recipient of the Alain Bensoussan Fellowship award under the European Research Consortium for Informatics and Mathematics (ERCIM), Sophia Antipolis Cedex, France. He obtained his Ph.D. from Jamia Millia Islamia (A Central University), New Delhi, India in 2019 in Computer Science. He holds a Master's in Computer Applications (MCA) and an M.Phil. (Data Mining) from the University of Kashmir (UoK) in 2012 and 2014 respectively. His research focuses on the extraction and analysis of social data, and the application of different statistical, machine/ deep learning, and NLP techniques in developing prediction models.

Mohamed Hammad received his Ph.D. degree in 2019, at the School of Computer Science and Technology, Harbin Institute of Technology, Harbin, China. He is an associate professor in the Faculty of Computers and Information, Menoufia University, Egypt. He is currently a researcher in the EIAS Data Science Lab, College of Computer and Information Sciences, Prince Sultan University. He is an ACM Professional Member. His research interests include Biomedical Imaging, Bioinformatics, Cyber Security, IoT, Computer Vision, Machine Learning, Deep Learning, Pattern Recognition, and Biometrics. He has published more than 50 papers in international SCI-IF journals and edited five books. Furthermore, he has served as an Editor Board member in BMC Bioinformatics journal, Editor-in-Chief of Journal of Computational Optimization and Reasoning, an Associate Editor in IJISP, a Topics Board editor in Forensic Sciences (MPDI) journal, a guest editor in many international journals such as IJDCF, World Journal of Methodology, Sensors (MDPI) and Information (MDPI). Reviewer of more than 500 papers for many prestigious journals and listed in the top 2% of scientists worldwide (According to the recently released list by Stanford University USA in 2022, 2023 and 2024).

***

Sreeja Balachandran Nair Premakumari is an Assistant Professor in the Department of Information Technology at Karpagam College of Engineering, Coimbatore, Tamil Nadu, India. She holds a Bachelor of Technology degree in Information Technology, Master of Technology in Computational Engineering and Networks and a PhD in Information and Communication Engineering. Her research interests include wireless sensor network, network security and machine learning

Tina Babu is an accomplished engineering educator and researcher specializing in computer science with over a decade of experience in academia. She currently serves as an Assistant Professor in the Department of Computer Science and Engineering at Alliance University in Bengaluru, where she teaches courses including Data Structures, Database Management Systems, Artificial Intelligence, Mobile Computing, Machine Learning, and Cloud Computing. Dr. Babu earned her Ph.D. from Amrita Vishwa Vidyapeetham, focusing on automated colon cancer screening and grading using advanced techniques in biomedical image processing, pattern recognition, and machine learning. Her research has led to numerous publications in esteemed journals and conferences, particularly in areas like medical image fusion, cancer detection, and insect classification. Dr. Babu's work is widely recognized, as reflected in her h-index and i10-index of 8, underscoring the impact and relevance of her contributions to the field. She holds a Master's degree in Computer Science and Information Systems from MG University and a Bachelor's degree in Information Technology from Rajagiri School of Engineering and Technology. In addition to her academic pursuits, Dr. Babu is skilled in various programming languages and tools, including C++, Java, Python, MATLAB, and Weka, further enhancing her capability to lead cutting-edge research and guide her students in innovative projects.

Kiran Bellam holds a Ph.D. in Computer Science from Auburn University and has served as a faculty member at Prairie View A&M University, where she currently holds the position of Associate Dean for the College of Engineering. Dr. Bellam's research has significantly contributed to fields like cloud computing, energy-efficient storage disks, and Engineering education. She secured substantial research grants to support her research. Her work has been widely published and recognized.

Saurabh Chandra is an accomplished legal scholar and currently serves as an Associate Professor & Assistant Dean at the School of Law, Bennett University, India. With a robust academic foundation, he earned his Bachelor of Arts and Bachelor of Laws (B.A. LL.B.) from the prestigious Aligarh Muslim University (A.M.U.). He further specialized in Business Laws, completing his Master of Laws (LL.M.) at the renowned National Law School of India University (NLSIU), Bangalore. Dr. Chandra's academic journey culminated in a Doctorate in Law (Ph.D.) from the esteemed National Law University (NLU) Delhi.Dr. Saurabh Chandra also holds a master's degree in Management with specialization in Human Resources in Management and another in Journalism and Mass Communication. With 16 years of teaching experience, he has established himself as an expert in Business Laws, with numerous publications to his credit. Dr. Saurabh Chandra is an expert in Business Laws, with a profound understanding of the intricate legal frameworks that govern the business world.Dr. Chandra brings a wealth of experience in Academic Administration, having successfully held various key administrative positions.

G.Saranya Assistant Professor, Department of Networking and communications, School of Computing, SRM Institute of Science and Technology, Chennai, India. She received the B.Tech degree in Information technology from Sri Venkateswara College of Engineering, Chennai, India in 2009, M.Tech degree in Information technology from Vel Tech Multi Tech Dr.Rangarajan Dr.Sakunthala Engineering College, Chennai, India in 2011 and Ph.D degree in Computer Science and Engineering from Sathyabama Institute of Science and Technology, Chennai, India in 2023. She has 10 years of teaching experience and 2 years of Industry Experience. She has published more than 20 research papers and articles in various journals and conferences. Her principal interests are computational intelligence, machine learning and deep learning.

Amartya Mukherjee, is the Head of the department of the Department of CSE(AIML), CSBS, Institute of Engineering & Management, Kolkata, India. He is also a research consultant at IEMA Research & Development private limited, India and convenor of center of excellence for cloud and IoT, IEM Salt lake, Kolkata, India. He is currently doing his PhD research at the Maulana Abul Kalam Azad University of Technology, West Bengal, India. He holds a master's degree in Computer Science and Engineering from the NIT, Durgapur, West Bengal, India. His research interest includes IoT, Internet of Drones, 5G and 6G networks, Wireless communication, Sensor networks, Machine learning, He has written many research articles and books in the domain of IoT, Machine learning, Bio medical systems, Sensor networks in very renowned press such as IEEE, Elsevier, Springer, Taylor & Francis. His book “Embedded systems and robotics with opensource tools” is one of the best-selling books globally.

Rekha R. Nair presently holds the position of Assistant Professor within the Department of Computer Science & Engineering. She earned her doctoral degree in Computer Science from the Amrita School of Engineering, Amrita Vishwa Vidyapeetham, Bengaluru. Her doctoral research was centered on the domain of Medical Image Fusion. Dr. Rekha's scholarly pursuits encompass a wide spectrum, ranging from Machine Learning, Image Processing, Biomedical Image Processing, to Data Science. Her impactful intellectual contributions are vividly demonstrated through her participation in numerous prestigious journal publications and conference papers. These achievements underscore her unwavering dedication to advancing knowledge and conducting research within her areas of expertise. computer vision, and soft computing

Kishore S is currently serving as an Assistant Professor at Nitte University and is pursuing his doctoral studies in Computer Science at NMAMIT, Nitte. His academic interests cover a wide range of areas including Machine Learning, Image Processing, Biomedical Image Processing, and the Internet of Things (IoT). He has contributed to several reputed journals and conferences through his research work.

Bhupinder Singh working as Professor at Sharda University, India. Also, Honorary Professor in University of South Wales UK and Santo Tomas University Tunja, Colombia. His areas of publications as Smart Healthcare, Medicines, fuzzy logics, artificial intelligence, robotics, machine learning, deep learning, federated learning, IoT, PV Glasses, metaverse and many more. He has 3 books, 139 paper publications, 163 paper presentations in international/national conferences and seminars, participated in more than 40 workshops/FDP's/QIP's, 25 courses from international universities of repute, organized more than 59 events with international and national academicians and industry people's, editor-in-chief and co-editor in journals, developed new courses. He has given talks at international universities, resource person in international conferences such as in Nanyang Technological University Singapore, Tashkent State University of Law Uzbekistan; KIMEP University Kazakhstan, All'ah meh Tabatabi University Iran, the Iranian Association of International Criminal law, Iran and Hague Center for International Law and Investment, The Netherlands, Northumbria University Newcastle UK,

Priyanga Subbiah. received the B.Tech degree in Information Technology from New Prince Shri Bhavani College of Engineering and Technology, Chennai, India, in 2015 and the M.E. degree in Computer Science and Engineering from Thiagarajar College of Engineering, Madurai, in 2020. She is currently pursuing the Ph.D. degree in Computer Science and Engineering at SRM Institute of Science and Technology, Chengalpattu, Tamil Nadu, India. From 2022, she was a Research Scholar with the Computer Science and Engineering. His research interest includes the processing of images and detection of disease in the plant using Artificial Intelligence.

Kannimuthu Subramanian is a Professor in the Department of Computer Science and Engineering at Karpagam College of Engineering, Coimbatore, Tamil Nadu, India. He also serves as the Coordinator of the Centre of Excellence in Algorithms and is an IBM-certified Cybersecurity Analyst. With over 18 years of combined teaching and industrial experience, he brings a wealth of practical and academic knowledge to the field. He holds a Bachelor of Technology degree in Information Technology, Master of Engineering degree in Computer Science and Engineering and a PhD in Computer Science and Engineering from Anna University, Chennai. His research interests include artificial intelligence, data structures and algorithms, machine learning, computer vision, big data analytics, blockchain, and virtual reality.

Aishwarya Sundaram is an ISTQB certified Software Test Manager with approximately 12 years of experience in functional, automation, and performance testing. She holds a Bachelor of Technology degree in information technology from Karpagam College of Engineering and a Master of software engineering (software technology) degree from Universiti Malaya. She earned her PhD in Computing from Universiti

Malaya, where her research focused on anxiety prediction through social media analytics. Her research interests include advanced positive computing, social media analytics, sentiment analysis, AI for mental health (AI4MH), and advanced software testing methodologies.

Index

A

B

C

D

F

H

I

L

T

U

V

W

www.ingramcontent.com/pod-product-compliance
Lightning Source LLC
LaVergne TN
LVHW061542290926
849162LV00004B/878